I0805050

"Pidge," Texas Ranger

"PIDGE,"
Texas Ranger

CHUCK PARSONS

TEXAS A&M UNIVERSITY PRESS

College Station

Copyright © 2013 by Chuck Parsons
Manufactured in the United States of America
All rights reserved
First edition

This paper meets the requirements of
ANSI/NISO Z39.48-1992 (Permanence of Paper).
Binding materials have been chosen for durability. ♾

Library of Congress Cataloging-in-Publication Data
Parsons, Chuck.
"Pidge," Texas Ranger / Chuck Parsons. — 1st ed.
p. cm.
Includes bibliographical references and index.
ISBN-13: 978-1-60344-974-8 (cloth : alk. paper)
ISBN-10: 1-60344-974-4 (cloth : alk. paper)
ISBN-13: 978-1-60344-997-7 (e-book)
ISBN-10: 1-60344-997-3 (e-book)
1. Robinson, T. C., 1846?–1876. 2. Robinson, T. C., 1846?–1876—Correspondence. 3. Texas Rangers—Biography. 4. Peace officers—Texas—Biography. 5. Frontier and pioneer life—Texas—Biography. 6. Texas—Biography. I. Title.
F391.R65P373 2013
363.2092—dc23
[B]
2012037537

FRONTISPIECE
Two of McNelly's Rangers. Although neither is identified, the man on the left conveys the same kind of air and personality as Pidge's letters—smoothly composed, relaxed, and detached. Perhaps a photographer captured him after all. Courtesy Walter Prescott Webb Collection, Briscoe Center for American History, Austin.

Contents

Acknowledgments

I am very appreciative of the many individuals who were more than willing to help me in this endeavor to learn about "Pidge," his life, and especially his experiences as a Texas Ranger. Naming them, I hope, provides at least a token recognition of the debt I owe to U. G. Bailey, Alison Beck, Mrs. Bennett G. Branon, Donaly E. Brice, Jean Carefoot, Joyce L. Chandler, Paul I. Chesnut, Mary Jo Cooper, Michael J. Dabrishus, Georgette M. Dorn, Mark Dugan, Dorothy Eagle, C. W. Ellington, Roy I. Flukinger, Eric Frank, J. B. Fraser, Betty Hartman, Frank L. Hege Jr., Sallie Harrison, Alton Hughes, Dave Johnson, Nola Y. Jones, Jerry L. Kearns, Chester V. Kielman, Gaines Kincaid, William H. Leary, Charles B. McNelly, Louis H. Manarin, Jeanne D. Mead, George P. Parros, D. L. Prentice, Marcia Revis, William H. Richter, Lois A. Riddle, Gladys Perrow Scrogham, William F. Sherman, Robert Shook, Faye Simkin, C. L. Sonnichsen, Robert W. Stephens, and Carl R. Wrotenbery.

A very special thanks to Mary Lenn Dixon, editor-in-chief at Texas A&M University Press, for her enthusiasm and patience in providing another opportunity for my research to be published in this revised edition of the life and letters of T. C. Robinson, the Texas Ranger from Virginia known as "Pidge."

"Pidge," Texas Ranger

Introduction In Search of "Pidge"

I first became acquainted with the newspaper correspondent-ranger "Pidge" while reading C. L. Sonnichsen's *I'll Die before I'll Run: The Story of the Great Feuds of Texas.* In his chapter devoted to the Sutton-Taylor Feud—Texas' most famous and longest blood feud, in which Pidge acted as one of the peace makers—Sonnichsen wrote this about the young man who was a charter member of Capt. Leander H. McNelly's Ranger company:

> There was a young man along with McNelly's troop whom it would have been a pleasure to know. He was strictly an amateur at the ranging business and seems to have gone along primarily to get material for a newspaper column, for he made many jokes about his inexperience, fear of firearms, and general timidity. . . . Signing himself "Pidge," this reporter wrote half a dozen long and humorous letters to his paper from the seat of conflict, thereby throwing much light on the manners and customs of feudists in DeWitt County when times were really rocky.[1]

No further identification was given to this young reporter-ranger. In addition to the letters written for Austin's *Daily Democratic Statesman* while a ranger, Pidge had written about the same number of letters dealing with his early experiences in the capital city prior to joining McNelly's force. Finally, he was again with McNelly when the Rangers were fighting horse and cattle thieves of that master marauder Juan Cortina on the Rio Grande frontier. By this time he was no longer writing for the *Statesman;* now his letters were being published in the *Statesman*'s competition, the *Austin State Gazette.*

In total twenty-three of his writings were published in the two Austin newspapers: letters, original poems, and poems paraphrased from others. These writings were all signed simply "Pidge," so no one reading the newspaper alone would know the real name of this contributor. Searching through the files of the two newspapers from early 1874 to mid-1876 one finds that the closest either came to providing an identification of Pidge was that given when he enlisted in McNelly's newly formed force. The *Statesman* simply listed the names of eight recruits from Austin, followed by the name "T. Chanders." After Chanders's name, in parenthesis, is "Pidge."

Historians can be grateful that the Ranger records preserved in the Texas State Archives in Austin are fairly complete, at least those concerning McNelly and his Rangers, properly termed the Washington County Volunteer Militia Company A. The muster and pay rolls were examined, and among them "T. Chanders" is listed, first as a sergeant and then as a lieutenant. What is revealing is that the name is later crossed out, and the name "T. C. Robinson" is written in, thus providing us with the real identity of "T. Chanders," alias "Pidge": T. C. Robinson.[2]

Once a proper name was determined for this reporter-ranger, the task of learning more about his background and earlier life remained. Secondary sources that provide information on McNelly's force are surprisingly plentiful—in comparison with other segments of the Frontier Battalion. Several members of the force wrote their memoirs, which are most helpful. Possibly the earliest secondary source mentioning Lt. T. C. Robinson appeared in Dudley G. Wooten's two-volume *A Comprehensive History of Texas, 1865 to 1897*.

Adj. Gen. Wilburn H. King authored one chapter of this work, titled "The Texas Ranger Service and History of the Rangers with Observations on Their Value as a Police Protection." King briefly mentioned the six ranger companies organized in mid-1874 and identified collectively as the Frontier Battalion. King's statements concerning McNelly and his company are appropriate here:

> [T]he necessity for more men in certain sections of the State became so urgent and powerful that in July, 1874, one company of volunteer militia from Washington County was mustered in for active service, in DeWitt and other counties in Southwest Texas, and latterly on the Rio Grande River. This company was commanded by Captain L. H. McNelly, with T. C. Robinson first and J. W. Guyon second lieutenants; and, though it was in service but two years, in that time McNelly and his officers and men proved so active, vigilant, daring, and successful, in dealing with lawless characters and with hostile Mexicans, as to secure a permanent good name for themselves and beneficial results to the border, by their gallant and zealous performance of duty.[3]

A number of later secondary sources have made reference to T. C. Robinson's service as a ranger. Sonnichsen brought before the public the name

"Pidge"—but so far as known no one has established in print that Lt. T. C. Robinson and correspondent "Pidge" were one and the same man. Nine years after the Wooten history of Texas a somewhat fictionalized history of the McNelly force was published: *A Texas Ranger* by N. A. Jennings. This work has occasionally been criticized over the years, with justification, as Jennings telescoped certain events for dramatic effect and placed himself in others in which he did not participate. But whatever his faults as an amateur historian, Jennings was a member of the McNelly company for eight months, and although he never knew Robinson personally, he did become acquainted with rangers who had served with Robinson. Thus he was in a position to learn much about Ranger Pidge Robinson. Jennings wrote this brief account of Robinson's death, which he no doubt learned from fellow rangers. "Lieutenant Robinson was killed in a duel in Virginia, his home. He resigned his commission for the sole purpose of fighting that duel. He killed his man and was killed at the same instant. The duel was occasioned by an insult to Robinson's sister in Virginia."[4] Although there are a number of errors in that passage, it does provide leads for further research.

Rangers William C. Callicott and George P. Durham were two others who did serve along with Pidge and who later recorded their memoirs. Callicott's were written with great difficulty, due to his failing eyesight, for Walter Prescott Webb's 1977 study *The Texas Rangers, A Century of Frontier Defense*.[5] Durham dictated his memoirs to newspaper reporter Clyde Wantland, and they were published as *Taming the Nueces Strip: The Story of McNelly's Rangers,* but one cannot determine how much is actually from Durham and how much the artistic license of Wantland.[6] The memoirs of these two rangers were written decades after their experiences; although they made no mention of Robinson being Pidge, important material was preserved by their reminiscences. Curiously, neither Callicott nor Durham made mention of Robinson being a reporter for any newspaper.

Since the 1985 edition of Pidge's letters, others have authored important general works on the Texas Rangers, replacing Webb's *The Texas Rangers*. Frederick Wilkins's *The Law Comes to Texas: The Texas Rangers 1870–1901* discussed Lieutenant Robinson briefly but did not mention Pidge.[7] Robert M. Utley authored a two-volume history, *Lone Star Justice,* the first volume of which appeared in 2002. He devoted a chapter to McNelly and his successor J. L. Hall and mentions Pidge in an endnote.[8] Mike Cox also authored a two-volume history, *The Texas Rangers,*

1821–1900: Wearing the Cinco Peso (2008) and *Time of the Rangers: From 1920 to the Present* (2009). No new information had surfaced about T. C. Robinson in these recent writings. Fortunately, a recent research trip to Pidge's home state of Virginia uncovered substantial information about the man who left home to find adventure in Texas and who then returned to exact personal vengeance.

Robinson occasionally alluded to his home state in his published letters but said nothing more specific than Virginia. It was learned from the muster roll of McNelly's company that he had died on April 4, 1876, while absent with leave in Campbell County, Virginia. This was written on the roll of April 30, 1876. Some confusion existed in the newspaper accounts describing his death, where he was identified as both Truxton and Thaxton. The initials T. T. were also used.

The Campbell County census reveals the Robinson family in 1850, 1860, and 1870. The 1850 census record shows Thomas Robinson, fifty, as head of household; his wife Harriett, forty, and two children: Thomas T., four years old, and daughter Mary E., two years of age.[9] The 1860 census shows the same family members, but their ages do not reflect ten years of growth.[10] Mrs. Robinson died during the next decade, as the census of 1870 shows only head of household Thomas, seventy-two; son Thomas T., twenty-three; and daughter Mary E., twenty. The census, in spite of errors in ages, does reveal that all were born in Virginia.[11]

Prior to the Civil War the Robinson family was well off, as Thomas Robinson's real estate was valued at $1,800 and personal estate at $3,675. In 1870 he claimed real estate in the value of $4,000 and personal estate in the value of $500, a substantial difference in his personal estate. He was listed as a farmer, with his son working with him on the farm. Daughter Mary E. had no occupation. This was the census as enumerated by Assistant Marshal J. M. Wood, dated September 1, 1870.[12]

Important information can be learned from the family headstones, and fortunately those of three members of the Robinson family have been preserved. Capt. Thomas Robinson died on July 15, 1879, at the age of eighty-four years. His wife Harriett, née Brown, died at the age of sixty-three on October 22, 1869. No stone in the family plot exists for daughter Mary Elizabeth, as she married and moved elsewhere. The stone for the son shows he was born on November 27, 1847. Curiously the stone identifies him as "Pidge" and informs the viewer that at his death he was "Lieut. Co. A. Texas Rangers." We can only speculate as to whether some family member or his ranger friends determined what appeared on his headstone.

The legal records of Campbell County are incomplete as files of law cases between 1867 and 1870 are missing—crucial years. However, the Order Books that are available reveal that on at least one occasion, Pidge Robinson was summoned to the courthouse to answer to the law. Order Book no. 29 shows that on December 11, 1867, Robinson appeared as a defendant, charged with assaulting James W. Wright. He pleaded not guilty to the charge.[13] Robinson appeared again in March and August of 1868, but both times the case was continued. On December 15 of that year Robinson again appeared, apparently this time ready for his trial. Now the attorney for the Commonwealth motioned for the prosecution to be continued due to the absence of James W. Wright himself as well as three others: Richard Wright, Paschal Smith, and Booker Smith. As this quartet had been "duly summoned to this term" they were now summoned to the next term "to show Cause if they can, why they should not be fined according to law, for their said contempt." That same day, December 15, 1868, Judge John F. Perrow set aside an order for continuance. A jury of eleven men listened to arguments and returned the verdict of not guilty.[14] For an unstated reason the regular scheduled judge, James C. Walton, was absent.

What is curious is that a later newspaper report accused Robinson of "cowhiding," or whipping, James C. Walton before going to Texas. Although no date is given, it is suspected that the reason Walton absented himself from the bench was due to recognizing a conflict of interest in this cause because of the treatment he had received from defendant Robinson. He had been on the bench earlier that same day. If indeed Robinson did cowhide Walton, then Walton would have had cause to remember it and exact his own type of revenge later, in 1876.

Ranger Jennings wrote in his memoirs that Lieutenant Robinson had resigned his commission to return home to fight a duel. The details of this "duel" and the feud that culminated in the duel are discussed in the final chapter. Suffice it to say here that the probable cause for Robinson leaving Virginia was that Jesse E. Mitchell, a neighbor, somehow forced him to leave, possibly in actual flight. It is not surprising that he chose to go to Texas. In the postwar years as well as the early 1870s Texas was a favorite place to go if a man wanted to leave his past behind him.

Jesse E. Mitchell was the man who caused Robinson to leave his homeland. Mitchell was older, thirty-one years of age in 1870. He was the son of James S. and Lockett Mitchell and their land adjoined the Robinson land; thus they were "next door" neighbors. Jesse had one sister, Mary Elizabeth R. Mitchell being her given name, but she was affectionately known as "Pidgie," probably a term of endearment given her by her father. Apparently she was better known by this nickname than by her given name, as when Samuel P. Holt visited the household to enumerate the family for the 1870 census he identified her as Pidgie E. Mitchell, seventeen years of age and without occupation.[15]

At one time the two families were on friendly terms, much as any other two families whose lands adjoined were. Sometime in late 1873 Jesse Mitchell was at work near the residence of the Robinsons and injured his leg severely with a saw. Seeking medical assistance, he went to the Robinson home, where his neighbors gave him the best attention they could. The Robinsons were not doctors, but Mitchell received at their hands "the utmost kindness and attention, so much so that in time he recovered from his injuries, though he afterwards suffered from a certain lameness." Of course the Robinson family and Mitchell became well acquainted during his recovery, in particular Mitchell and the young Robinson daughter Lizzie May, described as "an amiable and attractive young lady." Between Mitchell and young Lizzie May, "who had been specially kind to him during his illness, very intimate relations ensued, as was natural on the strength of their association and the sympathy which was manifested for his sufferings."[16] But in spite of the once warm neighborly relationship, something happened. The contemporary press termed it an "estrangement," as Thomas Robinson forbade Mitchell from entering his house again. At the same time Mitchell quarreled with Lizzie May's brother—T. C. Robinson. What brought about the quarrel is unknown, but possibly the feelings of the Robinson son were merely a normal reflection of the father's feelings against Jesse E. Mitchell, as he had somehow offended the honor of the Robinson household. The Mitchell-Robinson feud had begun.

Young T. C. Robinson about this time "became involved in a scandal about a young woman of the county, and was arrested with a view to his criminal prosecution." No details of the "scandal" are known; even the name of the young woman is lost to history, but possibly it was no more criminal than young T. C. Robinson having strong feelings for the sister of Jesse E. Mitchell, the young teen everyone knew as Pidgie. Older brother Jesse resented the attention given to his sister and in retaliation claimed that if he could not see Lizzie May, then T. C. Robinson could not see Pidgie E. Mitchell, a tit-for-tat maneuver.[17]

Thus the Mitchell and Robinson families were feuding in late 1873, although as yet no lives had been lost; no shots had been fired. T. C. Robinson loved Pidgie E. Mitchell but was forbidden by her brother Jesse to carry on the relationship openly. Jesse Mitchell in turn was forbidden to darken the door of the Robinson home. To add to the family difficulties T. C. Robinson was again called to court, although the charge in this instance is unknown. In an act of sisterly devotion Lizzie May helped her brother escape from the clutches of the law, but just how this was done is not recorded. On New Year's Day of 1874 young T. C. Robinson left Virginia, his father and sister, his beloved Pidgie and his friends, and his personal problems. Not for a simple or single reason did T. C. Robinson choose to leave Campbell County, Virginia, and head for Texas.[18]

To travel to Texas from Virginia in the 1870s, unless riding a good horse, the most convenient way was to take the Blue Mountain Route. The daily *Virginian* of Lynchburg, the largest community in the area, only a few miles north of the Robinson hometown of Rustburg, regularly carried this advertisement: "Blue Mountain Route via Selma, Rome & Dalton Railroad." Besides stops at Montgomery, Mobile, and New Orleans, the ad stressed in boldface type "And All Points of Texas." There were two daily connections to New Orleans, and it was only five hours' travel between there and Lynchburg. The Blue Mountain Route was advertised as being "the popular and most expeditious migrant Route to Texas and Northern Louisiana." Thus the logical manner to leave Virginia was by rail to New Orleans. From there Robinson could have taken a steamer to Galveston, Texas, where he could board a train to go to any of several exciting cities in Texas. It is most likely that he chose a steamer to continue his journey, as a number of naval images in his writings suggest that he had recently spent some time on the waters.

However he chose to leave his home and family and beloved Pidgie, T. C. Robinson would be like thousands of others at that time to choose Texas in which to lose himself and start a new life. In January, 1874, he left Virginia; later that month he was in Austin, the capital city of Texas, no longer known as Robinson but now as T. Chanders, soon to become known as "Pidge." The origin of or reason for the alias of T. Chanders is unknown. Besides his family, friends, and Pidgie, Robinson had also left behind whatever library he had accumulated. His writings reveal his above average education in the classics, a smattering of several foreign languages, and familiarity with modes of expression that enabled him to become a popular recorder of daily events for Texas newspapers. No other Texas Ranger compares with Pidge in terms of literary knowledge and manner of expression. His writings present an incongruous image in the reader's mind: this highly educated young Virginian tackled frontier life quoting Shakespeare, paraphrasing with ease such poets as Coleridge, Burns, and Byron, and armed with a command of the language to create images and metaphors to satirize or ridicule others without being insulting. At times one wonders whether Pidge filled his saddlebags with books rather than extra bullets for his revolvers or his saddle gun.

Robinson first concerned himself with finding employment. His early writings discuss the difficulties of finding work to enable him to keep hunger away. Initially he became a cowboy, probably because that was among the most common ways for a young man to earn a livelihood. The first letter to appear in print is a humorous description of his painful experience with an uncooperative cow pony. Apparently he had signed on as a drover with a herd of cattle destined for a Kansas market, possibly Wichita. He remained a cowboy only a few days. He next found employment with the leading Texas newspaper of the day, the *Daily Democratic Statesman* of Austin. The *Statesman* was started in 1871 by a stock company of printers with John Cardwell as editor. By the time Robinson arrived Cardwell controlled the *Statesman*, and with the possible exception of the *Galveston Daily News*, it was the most widely read newspaper of the state.

The first Pidge publication is "Driving Texas Cattle," a long excerpt from a letter written ostensibly to a friend back in Virginia—or at least this was the explanation editor Cardwell provided in his note introducing the new correspondent to his readers. I suspect, however, that the piece was specifically prepared with the "letter to a friend" styling as a means of presenting the new writer to the reading public.

The Austin Letters

The letters T. C. Robinson wrote in Austin, prior to joining up with the Texas Rangers, reveal his sense of humor, dry wit, and self-effacement as well as his extensive knowledge of language and literature. There are more poems among the pieces written for the *Daily Democratic Statesman* while in Austin, some original and some paraphrased, than in his later work. No doubt the Austin atmosphere was more conducive to this type of writing than were the dangerous settings he later encountered in DeWitt County, with its feuding Taylor and Sutton forces, or on the risky Rio Grande frontier. Each item is presented as it appeared in the *Statesman* with the date of publication as well as date of composition, where provided.

Daily Democratic Statesman, April 26, 1874

DRIVING TEXAS CATTLE

The following is an extract from a letter by a young man formerly employed in the STATESMAN *office to a friend in Virginia:*[1]

By nightfall we arrived at the ranch of Mr. D—, near which was the camp, and far out on the verge of the prairie I saw my first herd of cattle, and nearer by, around the fire, were grouped the herders; not a man in the party knew, or wished to know, the name of "any other man," but each one had a *nom de fantasie* which answered every purpose; besides every State in the Union, there was "Lying John," "Shanks," "Cigarette Jim," and others. "Supper's ready," said "Fort Concho," as he placed a tin basin as large as a wash tub full of blistered biscuits on the grass, together with a hay-stack of fried bacon and two huge pots of black and bitter coffee. "Can I eat now," I asked meekly. "You can or not; just as you dern please. Fork me a biscuit, you d—d kioty (to Concho). "Will you take sugar and cream in your coffee?" "If you please," I replied. "I'd admire to see you take either," was the reply. "We're jest ut, but we've sent up to the sto for some, and if their sugar's as sweet as their whiskey's mean, nine ounces will last you to Cheyenne. Shanks throw that stopper out there where

The first job Pidge took was as a cowboy: "Far out on the verge of the prairie I saw my first herd of cattle, and nearer by, around the fire, were grouped the herders; not a man in the party knew, or wished to know, the name of 'any other man,' but each had a *nom de fantasie*." Drawing by Frenzeny and Tavernier, *Supplement, Harper's Weekly*, May 2, 1874.

that dog can smell it; there's too many stray dogs around here for luck." "We've fixed four with it," he added to me, "they jest take one whiff and double over without a kick." By this time the herd was passing to the *corral*. None of the mooleys and Devons, but wild-eyed, devilish looking brutes, with curved horns as long as lightning rods and fronting skywards.[2] Occasionally one would break from the herd and strike on an excursion to the country. A *vaquero*, with jingling spurs and red leather calzoueros [*sic*] would gallop after him, and taking his tail in his grasp, give it a dexterous twist around the horn of his saddle, apply his spurs, and the next moment Mr. Boss would be "busted."[3] Should he persist in going on, then this exciting *tail* was "continued in our next" until he joined the herd, a sadder and wiser beast. The next one came down upon me like the wolf on the fold, and I only saved myself by tumbling into a gulch which was fortunately convenient.[4] I was not afraid of him, but I considered that ravine a good opening for a nice young man. This fellow was lassoed; the curling rope was swung out and embraced both horns in its noose, and the next instant the points of that steer's compass were mixed up, and he was steering on another tack.

The next morning I was awakened by a rough shake. The sun was up and the herd was *en route* for the prairie. "Young man, do you calculate that you can sleep this way on the trail?" I replied that I had no doubt of

Pidge described the branding chute: "The long, narrow gangway, called a shoot, was crowded full; in a large fire near by were five or six strange looking long-handled irons, which I, who had never seen a brand, imagined were instruments of torture belonging to the Spanish Inquisition." Drawing by Frenzeny and Tavernier, *Supplement, Harper's Weekly*, May 2, 1874.

it, if I was not disturbed. "Well, you'll be right apt to be disturbed, if you go with me," rejoined the "boss." In vain I assured him that I could not sleep on as fast a schedule as the rest, and would be compelled to have more time. He was inexorable, and ordered me to rise and help brand a lot brought in that morning. The long, narrow gangway, called a shoot, was crowded full; in a large fire near by were five or six strange looking, long-handled irons, which I, who had never seen a brand, imagined were instruments of torture belonging to the Spanish Inquisition. One of these desperate beasts objected to being crowded. I placed myself before his eyes to turn him, but he turned me; with a tremendous leap he went over me, and his sharp hoofs striking on my head, led me to suppose that he was the identical bovine into which Jupiter transformed himself when he wooed Europa, and that his thunderbolts were confined in his hind legs; in that brief period I regretted ever having left the peanut business.[5] The first words I heard when I recovered consciousness were from the "boss": "You ought to have gotten out of his way," said he. I had never agreed with this gentleman in anything before, but now my opinion was very similar to his own. As soon as I was able I took a seat on the high fence; I did not wish to be in the way of the men who were driving in the cattle; after they were wedged in, the iron was applied to each in succession, the one who floored me was last, when I beheld his sufferings, I could not refrain from shedding tears—I was so sorry I did not have hold of the iron so that I could lift it from his poor back and apply a hotter one; there was a small calf in the shoot which was branded all over, literally covered up with brands—in fact, to use a westernism, *more* than branded, for the burnt hide had peeled off and was hanging round him like a fringe and rattled as he walked; after a long examination a keen-eyed chap who must have been with Livingstone, discovered a small space behind his left ear was clear, a large "K B" was applied—which I suppose meant "keep branding." I was now told to mount one of the ponies and help to drive these to the herd. I had not, as you well know, ridden a horse for a long time. I mounted, somewhat fearful that this pony would go a-ripping and a-tearing around and do himself some bodily injury perhaps in his vain efforts to get me off. But no; he walked off like a lamb for a short distance—a very short distance. Then I felt his back commence arching upwards like a rainbow. "Good, gentle horse," said I, "he is preparing to stretch himself." I soon found out that it was the *rider* he was preparing to stretch, and I then dismounted—I did not alight exactly on my feet, but that was on account of his illtimed officiousness in assisting me. If these ponies were better trained, they might help one to get off in the popular mode, but as it is, they are decided failures. They do not make the necessary allowances for time and distance to the ground. I led this horse down to the camp, and told the boss that circumstances over which I had no control, compelled my immediate return to the city; the wagon was going in on that day. I made me a couch of my blankets and valise and waited for a little breath to fill my lungs before I bid adieu to the sweet spot where I had passed such a brief, but lovely time; the wretched cause of my trouble stood at my head quietly nibbling grass. I called "California" to my side; I knew nothing on earth could ever break him from swearing, and I murmured to him feebly the glowing words of England's laureate:

Prophet cuss me the pitching "rip"
And cuss me the Texas devil I rode;
I know not whether he goes on the Wyoming trip,
But I'm certain he never, no never, will carry his load.
Cuss him now; he is standing here at my head
Not beautiful now, not even kind,
You may take him now, for one never knows his mind,
And that is the reason his rider is nearly dead.[6]

Daily Democratic Statesman, May 17, 1874
[For the Democratic Statesman]

DREAMS

Dedicated to My Sister[7]

Tender and true, so darkly tried,
I joy me, when the night doth fall,
Which gives me visions sweet, of all
Our happier hours, by day denied.
I gladden when the dark descends;
Then fancy bears me home again,
Ceases the heavy toil and pain
The heartsick, weary exile ends.

I see thee at thy household cares
I hear thee cheer our aged sire:
O sister! nobler, purer, higher,
Thy fate-defying love appears
Than if my madness had not been;
Self exiled I, far from thy sight,
I know thy love hath reached a height
Which earthly eye hath seldom seen.

I picture that sweet time to come;
I take thy hand, I kiss thy cheek,
I hear thy gentle voice speak
Sweet words of "welcome brother home!"
Our mother from the happier shore

Smiles sweetly on us; from the skies
She seems to say "their miseries
Hath only made them love the more."
"PIDGE"

Daily Democratic Statesman, June 7, 1874
[For the Democratic Statesman]

THE DULL SEASON

Austin, June 4, 1874

My Dear W.—"Go West, young man," until you get to Austin, but be sure not to arrive there during the dull season; if you do, and meet with the unprecedented success which has attended my efforts, you will be apt to walk home, unless you can beat nine conductors and the clerk of a steamer out of a ride. Do not come here in the summer, for I have often been told that it is the dull season; I have no doubt of the truth, for I have been told so many times. Austin is, by far, the prettiest and healthiest town in the State, and it is actually a pleasure to breathe the pure and invigorating air of this loveliest of lands; the only drawback is "the dull season." I have listened to that phrase until it is indelibly impressed upon my memory; I have heard those words until they seem to be written on my brain in characters of living fire; that tiresome expression has been dinned in my ears till it seems like "passing away" to be "written on the sky." Never in all my life have I heard the same words used so often by such a number of people; when I converse with a citizen of Austin now, I await the utterance of these words with trembling anxiety; I am in a speechless agony until they are spoken, for I am certain that not a single individual in the town has ever held them in and lived; after they are uttered a calm serenity takes possession of my mind again, for only a few have ever inflicted them on me twice, and even these assured me that it was through inadvertance [*sic*] and forgetfulness. When I came back here from the country trip in the blistering Texas sun, I followed the reddest nose up and down Congress Avenue that had ever been seen there, I suppose. This and "the dull season" kept me out of a situation for a long time. I went to every house on one of the principal business streets of the city. "Nobody wanted; the dull sea—." When they got thus far I would make a rush for the door, for I wished to have my spasm in the open air. On several occasions I was pursued, the proprietor thinking me a grab thief, but I would finally succeed in convincing him that I was only trying to escape from "the dull season." Finally I went to a sample room which I had patronized extensively in more prosperous days: the bar-tender appeared to be overjoyed to see me; I asked him to employ me as an assistant: that I had discovered a peculiar method of making the meanest kind of benzine [*sic*] till it could not be told from the nectar of the gods; "young man," said he, "are you aware that the dull season has commenced?" I told him I had only heard so about forty-five thousand times and did not know whether to believe it or not. "Yes, it has commenced, and if you had not returned I would be left desolate indeed. I sincerely hope you may get a good situation conveniently near, but for me to take you would be the most absurd thing I could possibly do. If I keep you outside I may, perhaps, worry through the dull season." I tried to get employment from the sexton of the cemetery, "couldn't afford it as the dull season has set in and nobody was dying." I strolled into a barber's shop; while being scraped, I heard an assistant ask the gentleman in the next chair if he would have his hair trimmed. "No," he replied, "the dull season has—" "Gag him with your strap; daub suds in his mouth; cut his throat with the razor; don't let him say it till I get out of here," I shouted wildly to the barber. When he finished getting off what little skin the sun had left, I handed him a quarter. To my great surprise he gave me back a dime. "How is this," I inquired; "you have reduced your rates." "Yes, sir: it is on account of the dull—" I caught up his largest razor. "Say it, if you dare," I shrieked in agony, "and, by Heaven, I'll be the death of you. I know it has commenced: it began with that implement of torture which you have just used, and has spread like the whiskey crusade. Tell me of a place where the *lively season* has commenced, and I will spare your worthless life." He whispered in my ear the word "frontier." I went immediately to the captain of a frontier company who happened to be in town.[8] I fell upon his neck. "Let me," I implored, "join your command and lend my feeble assistance towards keeping back the copper-colored fiends from the sacred soil of this, my adopted State"; (forty dollars a month), "Let me add my mite to help save our frontier citizens from the horrors of the scalping-knife"; (and rations). "Allow me to devote my services towards saving our women and children from a fate worse than death"; (arms and equipment furnished). "Let me strike a stroke under the Lone Star flag, for I am literally full and running over with martial ardor"; (pay to be drawn quarterly). His company was full he told me and left me in despair. I looked after him and yearned a yearn, for I envied this "rangier" with an envy surpassing that of women; happy soul! thrice blessed scalp-hunter! *he* at least was going where there was no dull season.

At last I got a situation in a printing office; here will I make my fortune thought I; after years of toil, I may get to be local editor and if I puff as well as some will have lots of money, cigars and things showered upon me without money and without price, get invitations to balls, free tickets to theaters, dead-head the railroads and enjoy life to the fullest extent. The first step towards this shining goal was cleaning up a huge cylinder press, with more machinery about it than is contained in the hull of the Great Eastern.[9] After a man reclines on his back, reaches upwards and scours a printing machine for four hours with a rag saturated with kerosene oil, he does not sport quite as delightful an odor about his person as if he had bathed in nightblooming cereus. I had to be soaked in the tank for four hours before the compositors would allow me to come up stairs.

Then I was given some cards to print; I did them quickly, and stood proudly before the job compositor to hear the words of commendation fall from his lips, but I did not hear them, nor have I heard them yet. "Did you do this job?" "Yes, sir," I promptly responded. "Well, take them down and put them in the furnace and bring up the form; there may be one or two of the type not mashed out of all shape." I finished this, my first lesson, by washing the form with soap and a rag, and the job compositor was in despair. A few days afterwards I overheard him tell his assistant that I reminded him strongly of the King of Terrors, for sooner or later, I got my *grippe*r on every *form;* he assured me that as a "job presser" I would never attain any very great pre-eminence, but thought from the happy faculty I had for mashing things, that I would succeed as a cotton presser beyond my most sanguine anticipation.[10]

One day I found a local, the end of a sleeping car had been smashed in a collision. Here was a chance for me to immortalize myself, so I headed it as sensational as possible:

> Dreadful Accident on the Central Railroad—The Sleeping Car Collides with the Train—A Brakesman is Thrown over four Coaches and falls, head-foremost Into the Smoke Stack—The Locomotive turns bottom upwards, and ploughs its way across the Prairie, leaving a path of ruin and desolation Behind it ten Miles in extent—The Engineer Still at his post—"Farewell Vain World"—Report of the concussion heard forty miles—Incident of the Accident—Awful doings, etc., etc.[11]

I carried this to the local man in order to hear his opinion of it; he assured me it would never do as a local, but might be sent as correspondence to the Waco *Examiner*, a paper which never was known to give credit for an article, and, of course, nobody would ever discover the author.[12] A local, he said, was expected to stick to the facts as near as he could, unless it was something not generally known, in which case he might embelish [*sic*] a very little. He told me to try again. After much mental effort I produced the following:

> "Yesterday some time during the day we suppose, or the night before that the sleeping car on the Central Railroad became detached from the rest of the train and ringing the bell caused the engineer to stop going on with the cars which he had and this car having been going faster than those which were not moving so swiftly overtook them of course and just made things squat waking every man on board except one who had been reading H—s last circular breaking open two trunks which had been overlooked by the baggage master and badly bruising the rear end of the car and one old gentleman."

The editor had the unparalleled effrontery to tell me to my face that the above was not written in style, nor punctuated right, and that the last line was ambiguous, and the whole "lay out" unintelligible.[13] I got mad, and concluded to punish this ignoramus by telling him to write his own items in the future—I would not cast my pearls before such swine as him any more.

At last pay day came, and I went up to draw my salary—it all came to six dollars, just for that one week alone. My feelings were too much for me; I was torn to pieces with conflicting emotions; it was such happiness for me to know that, though in a strange land, far away from home and friends, slowly but surely I was laying the foundation of a fortune, which, in future years, would swell to proportions—in a horn. The clerk saw that I was moved, and guessed the cause. "It is too much for his sensitive nature," he observed. "No!" said I, "it is not enough by some dollars!" "We would give you more, but the dull sea—." I placed my fingers in my ears and left. Employing a policeman to guard me home with my treasure, I reached my boarding house in safety, and sat up all night trying every way I knew to make seven go into six, (I was paying seven for my board.) I figured it every way I knew, but there always lacked one of being any remainder. I tried it by algebra; it wouldn't work no way. It may have been because I only used half of an "x" to represent the given quantity; but I considered

John Cardwell, editor of Austin's *Daily Democratic Statesman*, provided employment for Pidge prior to his joining Capt. L. H. McNelly's company of Texas Rangers. Photograph by H. R. Marks of Austin. Courtesy the Austin–Travis County Collection.

it the height of extravagance and prodigality for a man in my present circumstances to waste a whole full grown x on such a salary as that.

I shall start again to-morrow to hunt another situation, and to hear some more about the dull season.

Bye, bye; yours, etc.,
"PIDGE"

Daily Democratic Statesman, June 21, 1874

A "POME"

By Shortfellow[14]

The shades of evening were falling fast,
As through a Texan city passed
A youth who bore, not over nice,
A banner with the strange device,
"Dull season."
His nose was peeled red, his eye was dim,
And things seemed mighty hard for him,
The while on every side there rung
The echoes of that same old song,
"Dull season."
"Try not the stores," the old man said.
"You'll never gain your daily bread."
Old man, you've got a levelhead,
I've tried until I'm nearly dead,
"Dull season."
"Oh, stay!" the maiden cried, "My sweet,
Oh, stay, and rest your weary feet!"
Her father's voice from down the street
Replied, "Not much he wont—'dead beat.'"
"Dull season."
Policemen on their evening round
A gibbering, mocking maniac found,
Stretched out upon the dusty street,
His lips still muttering the sound,
"Dull season."
There, in the evening moon's pale ray,
Considerably played out, he lay,
While through the twilight gray, and thick,
A voice fell like a rocket stick—
"Dull season."
"PIDGE"

Daily Democratic Statesman, June 24, 1874

TO MISS F. W., OF VIRGINIA[15]

Within a flowery vale
She stands, and I upon a barren shore;
Between us rolls the tide forevermore;
No hope that bridge or sail,
Shall place me at her side,
Once more before I die—a little space—
Only to hear her voice—see her face—
Alas, the waters wide!
Yet fancy spans the stream;
I cross and kneel once more before her feet,
I hold her little hand in mine; my sweet!
My darling! do I dream?
Ah me! those golden hours,
'Ere I lost that which I can ne'er regain;
'Ere the dark river swept me to the main,
From that sweet land of flowers,
Which I shall never see
No more, no more; her lovers woo her there.
And I am dead—nay worse—for dead, some care
Were given my memory.
"PIDGE"

Daily Democratic Statesman, June 27, 1874

DRONING

"'Tis easy to sit in the office quite neat,
And, in soft slippered feet, look down on the street
And the clod-knockers too, who pass in review;
To have nothing to do; don't you wish it was you?"
You may wager, "Short Stop," that I do, *every pop;*[16]
I know its tip top to be taking your sop
At a first-class hotel, and a bar room as well,
And to strut and to swell; now, ain't it, "ole fel?"[17]
And then give a squall for a game of base ball,

When *ennuied* with all in the parlor and hall;[18]
Neither toil nor spin, but guzzle H—'s gin,
Which the same it's a sin—the way it's poured in.
You've got a soft thing, is what makes you sing,
And level your fling, when not in the ring;
You attack without cause—stop short, make a pause,
When I go "thwart your hawse," *then* touch up Shakes' raws.
Give me Hamlet's "wise saws."[19]
"PIDGE"

Daily Democratic Statesman, July 11, 1874

"PIDGE" IN THE LUNATIC ASYLUM

Austin, July 10, 1874

Editors Democratic Statesman.—Having nothing to do and a wealth of time in which to accomplish it, I took a stroll to the Lunatic Asylum yesterday.[20] Leaving the main road, I followed a course of my own through a thick grove of mesquit[e] in order to escape the rays of the sun, and was soon completely bewildered, when I fortunately stumbled upon two young men loading wood to be brought to the city. From these two youths I inquired the distance I might probably be from the Asylum, and told them I had been wandering around for two hours. "Escaped, by thunder," I heard one say in a lone tone to his companion; "let's carry him back, Jim, and maybe Dr. Wallace will pay us something for catching him; appears to be harmless, and don't look like he would try to get away."[21] "I'm sorter *jubus* of these luners," says Jim.[22] I thought it was getting time for me to have *my* say, and assured these young barbarians that I was merely going on a visit. "And do you mean to tell us you could not find the way there in a straight, plain road?" "But I did not follow the road." "Well, it can be seen for ten miles; you ought to go to the Blind Asylum." At length he gave me full instructions, and as a piece of parting advice told me to induce the authorities to allow me to remain, if I ever got there.

I had passed through the outer gate and was some distance down the avenue, when a boy who does duty as porter came running and bawling after me. "Do you want work?" said he; "cause if yer do yer can't go no further; they bother Mr. Wilson nearly to death wanting to work." I looked at this once promising child in speechless astonishment; the ther-

The Lunatic Asylum as it appeared in the early 1870s, from an engraving by J. Montin. Pidge visited this institution on July 9, 1874. Courtesy the Austin–Travis County Collection.

mometer was then at 100 degrees in the shade, and he wished to know if I wanted to work! I had started out to see crazy people and behold the most hopeless case in the State was found a quarter of a mile from bolts and bars, without a keeper. I gave this unfortunate creature a look of pity, which was all the small change I had to give any one, and passed on through a lovely park to the inner grounds. These are very tastefully laid off, with walks and carriage drives, and are covered with a profusion of rare exotics, beautiful flowers, and semitropical plants of every variety known to this climate; they have all the attention which an efficiant [*sic*] and industrious floriculturist can bestow, and one can see are well cared for. I passed within the main building, the style of which, dimensions, etc., I will not bore the readers of the STATESMAN by attempting to describe. In company with Mr. Hadley Roberts, Sr., a polite and gentlemanly *attache* of the asylum, I passed through the different wards, and was forcibly struck with the splendid order, the almost immaculate cleanliness, and the perfect taste and comfortable appearance of the different rooms; the beds were models for a good housekeeper, and the linen as neat as it could possibly be; the table ware plain, as it ought to be, and scrupulously clean.

The first ward is devoted to the accommodation of the male patients, seventy-six in number; some of these, however, are confined in a separate establishment built expressly for the dangerously insane. While passing through, my escort opened a door and showed me three or four hopeless idiots. I advanced and took their proffered hands; a blissful sense of being once again in my own elements came over me, and it was with difficulty that I tore myself away. In the corridor one patient was acting the swell, and, with his hat cocked on one side of his head, strutted backwards and forwards, and seemed to be supremely happy when he drew the attention of any one. He was no strange sight to me, for I had observed his prototypes on Congress Avenue time and again.

Good bath rooms are found in all the wards, and the patients, with a few exceptions, present a most creditable appearance. Midway of each corridor is a room with padded walls, in which obstreperous patients are placed to prevent them from injuring themselves.

The female department contains fifty-three patients, twenty-six being domiciled in the second, and twenty-seven in the third ward. The most refractory are placed in the third, which is in the upper story of the building. Some of these unfortunate women wear upon their faces a pleasing expression of peaceful resignation angelic to behold. One young girl—she could not have been more than fourteen—with her arms confined in a straight jacket, sat rocking herself to and fro with such a look of unspeakable misery upon her face that the spectator involuntarily shuddered. Further on an old German lady muttered feebly the words of a ballad of Fatherland. A few sat at the windows, and gazed as if they waited always, and would ever wait, the wished for appearance of some one

Dr. David Richard Wallace was superintendent of the Lunatic Asylum when Pidge visited. Courtesy the Austin–Travis County Collection.

whose coming would wreathe the sorrowful face in smiles of gladness. From here we visited the strong room, which stands about three hundred feet from the main building; in this are confined the most refractory patients, this has heavy lattice work on the outside and in it are twelve or fifteen raving maniacs; a once prominent editor who entranced hundreds with the force and beauty of his writings is here, hopelessly insane; what a warning to those editors who have minds, to be particular with them. On the way we were stopped by "Queen Elizabeth" a colored lady of forty-five. "Who are you and what do you want here?" I told her. "Well" said she, "if I were as great a fool as you are, I would go and hide myself in a hole in the ground and never come out again as long as I lived." My escort assured me that she had many lucid intervals. I hardly knew what to think of this, but passed it over as a joke. "Poor woman! uses those words to everybody I suppose?" "On the contrary never heard her say this to any one but yourself." In this building are strong cribs with open work for the admission of air, which are used as a *dernier resort* [*sic*]; when a man is placed in one of these and the top put on and battened down, he is as helpless as Moody was in Wall street.[23] While I was looking at one of these extinguishers, a man crazy on the subject of religion came up and introduced himself. “Brother” said he, “have you ever found a peace which passeth all understanding?”[24] I told him I had not, but that the readers of tomorrow’s STATESMAN would, provided I could prevail on the editor to publish this “day’s doings.”

A large stone building is in process of erection near the strong house and when finished will be a source of pride to the people of Texas and furnish accommodations for many who at present are denied entrance for want of room. I was told there had been two hundred and fifty applications for the admission of patients, some of whom could be received. The small appropriation made by the last legislature, is, with the strictest economy, barely sufficient for the expenses of the institution. Every one speaks in the highest terms of Dr. Wallace and the other officers of the Asylum, as invariably kind and humane towards these unfortunates; attendants are prohibited from using force except in extreme cases, and one striking a patient under circumstances not actually necessary gets his or her immediate discharge.

The play grounds were visited last; there are two of these enclosures beautifully shaded with post-oaks and surrounded by a strong and lofty fence; to these, patients are brought daily while the rooms, beddings, etc., are aired and placed in order; escapes from here are rare, but I am assured that the females are much more ingenious in devising plans for liberating themselves than the men; in the yard the most dangerous maniac in the asylum was pointed out to me; he had been mowing, and *mopping* too, I suppose, and held a long sythe [*sic*] in his hand; I gave this gentleman the very widest kind of berth and bade my escort a more hasty adieu than was consistent with courtesy. The man with the sythe was the cause of it, and I take this opportunity to express my thanks for the uniform politeness with which I was treated by all the officials and attendants with whom I was brought in contact. The appearance of all things, both within the building and upon the grounds, reflects great credit upon those in charge, and I came away very favorably impressed, and with the opinion that Drs. Wallace and Bibb, Mr. Wilson, the steward, and their assistants, are doing all in their power to make this asylum a credit to the State of Texas.[25]

“PIDGE”

Pidge and the DeWitt County Feud

Young T. C. Robinson, known as "T. Chanders" to most if not all of his acquaintances in Austin, quickly became dissatisfied with his situation in the capital city. No doubt he considered joining a company of Texas Rangers as it would provide regular pay and an outlet for his adventurous spirit. And if he were allowed to continue his newspaper correspondence, his creative powers could be exercised as well. He was aware too that becoming a ranger would not be free of danger. He knew of the troubled situation in DeWitt County and the lawless conditions elsewhere in the state from reading the *Statesman*. The following brief statement appeared in the issue of July 14, 1874:

> AUXILIARY COMPANY—We learn that a company is forming in Washington county, under State authority, to assist the civil officers of DeWitt county in enforcing quiet and obedience to law in that desperado ridden section. This is a move in the right direction.

On July 16 appeared this item, which may have been submitted by Pidge himself: "CAPTAIN MCNELLY will command the men to be raised in Washington county by order of the Governor. They will go to DeWitt to assist in restoring order."

We know from the letter published on August 8 that he had met Captain McNelly in Austin on July 17 and had enlisted. Unfortunately we have no details of the initial interview between T. Chanders and the captain. It is known that for some time McNelly knew his recruit by his alias, as the muster and pay rolls initially show that name. It is not known how or when he revealed to McNelly his writing efforts or if an agreement was made between the two then and there that his literary contributions could continue. McNelly may have been a regular reader of the *Statesman*. It seems likely that the contributions could continue only with the consent of the captain. Chanders certainly impressed the captain, as he first held the rank of sergeant but would soon attain the rank of lieutenant.

McNelly had had an extremely adventuresome career prior to taking

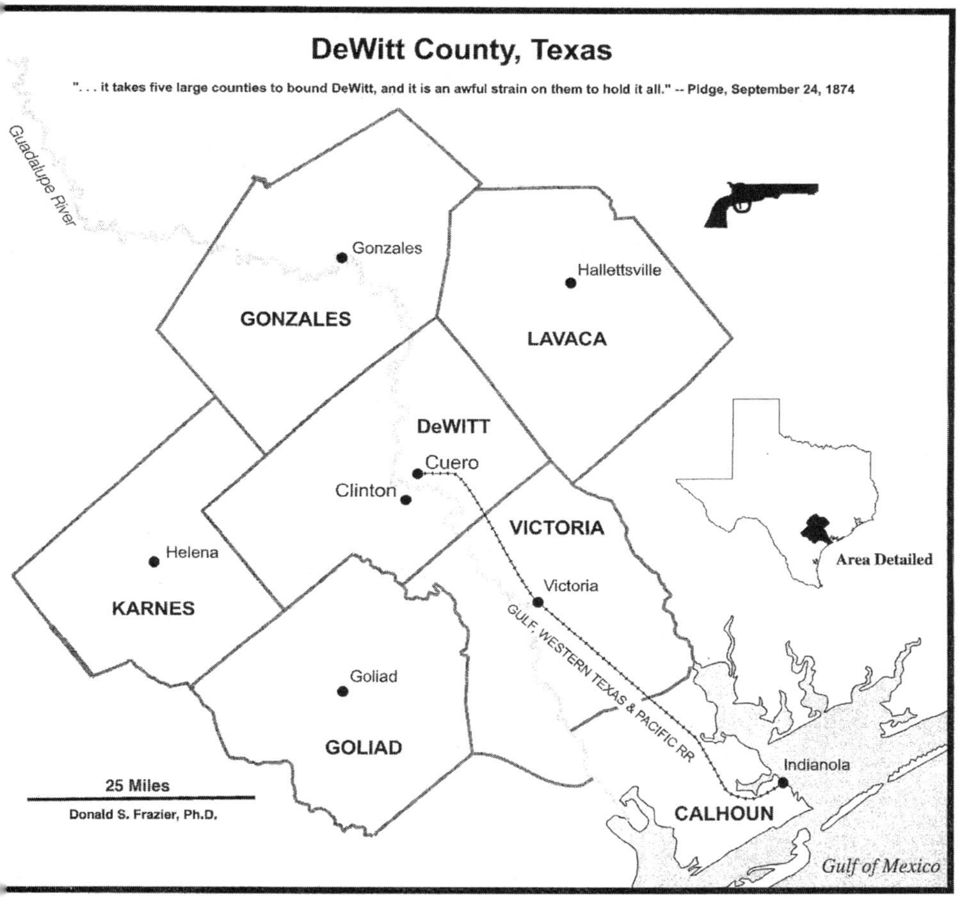

Feuding in the DeWitt County area was so intense that Governor Richard Coke ordered Captain McNelly there to establish peace. Map by Donald S. Frazier.

charge of the Ranger company. In 1861, at the age of seventeen, he had enlisted in Thomas Green's regiment of the H. H. Sibley brigade and had served with distinction throughout the Civil War. In 1864 he was engaged in a skirmish with Federal troops led by Gen. Edmund J. Davis, who would later become governor during the Reconstruction period in Texas. Ironically McNelly served under Governor Davis as a member of the State Police force. After the war's end McNelly farmed near Burton in Washington County. A contemporary newspaper account from the *Statesman* of February 9, 1876, described McNelly's background:

> On one occasion, being sent by [General] Walker with seventeen men to feel the enemy entrenched, seven hundred strong, behind his breastworks, he managed, by continually marching his little band in a circle, to create the impression on the Federal commander that he had four or five thousand men. The Federals surrendered and he immediately procured reinforcements to guard his prisoners. After the war he married Miss Carrie Clark [*sic*, Cheek], of Long Point. He served by appointment of Governor Davis in the State militia, but maintained his popularity. His recent achievements on the Rio Grande have gained national notoriety.

The Texas State Police force had been organized on July 1, 1870, and McNelly was named one of the first four captains. The force itself proved to be quite an unpopular organization. Ironically, Jack Helm, the only other captain to achieve any kind of notoriety, would later be a leading figure in the Sutton-Taylor feud of DeWitt County prior to the arrival of McNelly and his Ranger company. McNelly served in this police organization until its dissolution on April 22, 1873.

A year later, on April 10, 1874, the Texas Legislature created a force of fighting men that was known as the Frontier Battalion, composed of six companies. It soon became apparent that additional men were needed in certain areas, and in July a special company of volunteer militia was created, known officially as the Washington County Volunteer Militia Company A, with McNelly as its captain. The reason for raising a special company was the increased lawlessness in the DeWitt County area. Adj. Gen. William Steele spent some time there in early July, interviewing many citizens to learn the true nature of the difficulties. He returned to Austin on July 10, reporting "unfavorably on the position of affairs in DeWitt county. The Taylor faction is hiding in the brush, but may gather head and avenge themselves on the Sutton party." This item was among the news articles that gave the DeWitt County feudists statewide notoriety because of being printed not only in the Austin newspaper but also elsewhere, in this case in the *San Antonio Daily Express* of July 15.

Apparently T. Chanders was to enlist additional men for the company in Austin prior to reporting to Burton, Captain McNelly's home. It has been suggested that this was a characteristic of McNelly: in some cases he allowed others to recruit for him. Therefore we should consider as accurate the statement in Pidge's letter of August 4 from Clinton that he was to "recruit a few good men." McNelly left Austin for Burton shortly after

Capt. Leander H. McNelly, one of two images by James Inglis of Montreal, Canada, in early 1873. McNelly at the time was in pursuit of absconding Adj. Gen. James Davidson, who eventually found asylum in New Zealand. Courtesy San Jacinto Museum of History Association.

enlisting Chanders as a sergeant. This may have been his first order—to increase the size of the company with reliable men. Further orders were soon to come.

However, in contradiction to Pidge's statement, it was reported at the time of McNelly's death in 1877 that he did his own recruiting. A lengthy article appeared in the *San Antonio Daily Express* of September 6, 1877, claiming that McNelly selected his Rangers from among his own acquaintances. Reportedly he took only those "whose reputation for honesty, sobriety, bravery and gentlemanly conduct, had won for them the respect of the communities in which they resided." The article further stated that because McNelly was an excellent judge of human nature he was able to gather a "band of men whose superiors in point of police efficiency it would be very difficult to find in any part of the world." Possibly McNelly did at times allow others to recruit for him, as the muster and pay rolls show that frequently a man was dishonorably discharged because of drunkenness, disorderly conduct, refusal to obey orders, or conduct unbecoming to an officer and a gentleman.

On July 19 the *Statesman* printed an article that had originally appeared in the *San Antonio Herald* and urged the captain to get to the DeWitt County area quickly to put down the disturbances. Chanders doubtless read this editorial.

> We learn from a gentleman just arrived from Cuero that unless prompt action is taken very soon there will be bloody scenes in DeWitt county, as both parties, each being about one hundred and fifty strong, were about to begin skirmishing. Our informant was stopped and interviewed by three boys on horseback, one of whom was adorned with three revolvers, and a sixteen times shooting gun across the saddle. The young man remarked it would be painful for anybody to capture his party as they were "derned well heeled."

The *Statesman* commented on this:

> Captain McNally [*sic*] ought to hurry up his company if he has not already gone, and take position in DeWitt county with the sheriff, so as to be ready to turn the tide of battle in favor of law and order. Some effectual disposition ought to be made of the factions who now keep the good people of that country in constant dread, and retard the suppression of crime and the enforcement of the laws. Can it be possible that there are not enough good men in that section to put

them down and restore order? We sincerely hope that the present state of affairs may not long continue, and that before long we can announce that both parties have made a final end of the matter.

On July 22 the following notice appeared, conceivably submitted by Sergeant Chanders himself: "FOR THE SEAT OF WAR.—The members of Captain McNally's [*sic*] company now in the city intend leaving for DeWitt county immediately upon the receipt of orders from the Captain, which are expected daily; any one wishing to join can apply today at Dei's stable or at Cook's building, corner Congress Avenue and Pecan street."

Two days later, on July 24, the sergeant and eight others departed for Burton, McNelly's home in Washington County, prior to their leaving for "the seat of war." The *Statesman* of July 25 offered this farewell: "GOOD-BYE. We bid a confectionary good-bye to the young rangers who belong to Capt. McNally's [*sic*] company, and who took their departure last evening on the train for Burton where the company is to rendezvous, preparing to take up the line of march for DeWitt county. We trust that the boys may return home in due time to gladden the hearts of the girls who shed tears as the boys 'lit out' for the war in DeWitt county." The nine young Rangers for whom tears were shed were identified as C. B. Cook, C. C. Carrington, H. G. Rector, Horace Mabin, J. W. Thompson, O. G. Balemun, A. C. Tumey, and E. A. Northington. The final name in the list was T. Chanders, with "Pidge" in parenthesis. This was the first time the *Statesman* gave an identity, albeit an alias, to its popular correspondent.

The *Statesman* reported that on July 24 the nine Rangers left Austin on the train, but Pidge wrote that they rode horseback to Burton. After their arrival they drew their rifles and left for Clinton, then the county seat of DeWitt County. On August 1 the captain with Robinson and others, numbering forty, properly termed the Washington County Volunteer Militia Company A but generally referred to simply as "Rangers" or "State troops," arrived in Clinton, the seat of war. In a manner Pidge would have appreciated, Victor M. Rose wrote: "In conformity to the provisions of the law, Captain McNally [*sic*], formerly a policeman under the [Governor E. J.] Davis regime, organized a company of soldiers, and repaired to the distracted kingdom of De Witt, where the houses of York and Lancaster were struggling for the supremacy."[1] Pidge, the young Ranger from Virginia, entered the town that was the setting of jail deliveries, midnight lynchings, and "ambuscades" on country roads—in short, all the violence that has come to be known as the Sutton-Taylor Feud.

It was from Clinton, a town no longer in existence, that Pidge wrote seven letters dealing with the troubled DeWitt County situation. Clinton had been laid out in 1846 on the west bank of the Guadalupe River, on land belonging to Richard Chisholm. In 1850 it was made the county seat and became a prosperous village with good schools, Presbyterian and Methodist churches, and the county's earliest Masonic Lodge.

The Clinton letters all deal with the feud and social conditions of the county, with one exception, that being the poem with the French title "Les Trois Etoiles" (The Three Stars). It is not absolutely certain that this poem was by Pidge as the *Statesman* provided no name indicating its author. It was dated, however, as being written from DeWitt County on November 8, 1874, when Pidge was there. It is similar in tone to two of Pidge's previously published poems—"Dreams" and "To Miss F. W., of Virginia." Hence it is almost certainly an unsigned poem by Pidge.

The Sutton-Taylor feud is the best known of the many great feuds in Texas during the nineteenth century. A contemporary of Pidge, known to us only as "R," wrote a letter to the *Galveston Daily News,* published on September 24, 1874, stating that the feud had originated in Alabama as far back as the middle 1850s. The two families then moved to Texas and unknowingly settled in the same neighborhood. The Texas era of the feud began when William Sutton, at the head of a posse, shot and killed Charles Taylor and James Sharp, both suspected of horse theft. From this incident the feud began anew.

The principals of the Sutton forces were William E. Sutton; old Indian fighter "Captain Joe" Tumlinson, former state policeman Jack Helm, James W. Cox, and Cuero City Marshal Reuben H. Brown. Those considered leaders of the Taylor forces after the killing of old Pitkin Taylor, were first cousins Jim and Bill Taylor, George Culver Tennille, Mannen Clements, and the notorious gunfighter John Wesley Hardin. These men were all related to one another by blood or marriage or solid friendship.

In more recent months the citizenry of the DeWitt County area had appealed for help. One instrument, dated April 7, 1874, from Indianola, was addressed to and published in the *Galveston Daily News* (reprinted in San Antonio's *Daily Express* of April 12). It reveals clearly the frustration of honest citizens trying to cope in a violent situation in which the officers of the law were inadequate:

> The condition of affairs at Cuero and vicinity induces me to trouble you with this communication. The county is infested with a band of

> very bad people; they are so extensive as to render life and property insecure. Legitimate business is almost suspended entirely, even in this city, on account of it. These outlaws do not hesitate to take the life of any citizen who favors law and order, when an opportunity to assassinate presents itself.
>
> Business men do not like to take an active part against these fellows; for if they do, they know not at what moment they may be burned out or assassinated. A continuance of the present state of affairs is disgraceful to the State, as well as ruinous to business.
>
> The remedy for this evil is to station a company of United States troops at Cuero without delay, to aid the sheriff in the execution of the laws, and to preserve order. We come to the Galveston *News* as the most powerful advocate we can get, and ask your aid, by giving us a hearing through your columns. By doing so, you will do a kindness to MANY CITIZENS.

The *Express* eagerly commented that this lawless situation existing in DeWitt County was due to the dissolution of the State Police force created by Governor Davis. The *Express* was very much against Davis's successor, Governor Richard Coke, and continually equated lawlessness and crime with his administration.

The lawlessness into which Captain McNelly and company entered was frequently described in military terms. The *Cuero Star* of June 11 spoke of "War in Our County," a phrase eagerly repeated by the *San Antonio Express* of June 14. According to the *Star*, during the preceding week groups of armed men had been "swarming through the county in pursuit of each other." Rumors of skirmishes were rife and "a fatal collision" was expected hourly. The *Star* blamed "old family feuds" as being the cause of the situation and claimed that good men had enlisted on both sides "for deadly combat." A meeting of citizens had been called at Clinton for Sunday, June 15, "to devise measures for the suppression of lawlessness and crime." A direct appeal to the governor was the result of this meeting, and on July 2 Adj. Gen. William Steele himself arrived in Cuero to investigate. The purpose of his visit, as the *Express* of July 7 reported, was "to investigate thoroughly the unhappy conditions of things existing in this county." Steele interviewed many citizens of Cuero as well as of Clinton, Victoria in Victoria County, and Indianola in Calhoun County. From this visit it was assumed, as reported by the *Star*, that state troops would soon be stationed in DeWitt County. The *Star* also reported that Steele had made a favorable impression and anticipated his pursuing a "judicious and effectual course in the premises," but warned that not all would welcome him, as in many instances the "contrary, injudicious and injurious councils" would attempt to work against him.

On July 10 William Steele arrived back in Austin. He reported "unfavorably on the position of affairs in DeWitt County." Within days a company was being raised to go to DeWitt County to preserve order. McNelly was a natural to be chosen to raise the company, as he had earned a positive reputation as a captain in the State Police force. This force had been passionately hated in DeWitt, Gonzales, and other counties, but McNelly himself had not lost respect. The *Express* noted in its issue of August 2: "Capt. McNelly, with one company of Gov. Coke's State Police, have moved from Washington to DeWitt county. The Captain was an excellent State Police officer under Gov. Davis, and we hope will do as well under Gov. Coke."

McNelly and his company arrived in Clinton, encamped, and reported to Sheriff William Weisiger on August 1. McNelly was very conscious of the importance of good conduct on the part of his men and stated in his report to Adjutant General Steele on August 3: "The citizens seem to be very pleased with our presence & I will see that they are satisfied with our conduct while here."[2]

Within the week the company saw action. On the evening of August 6 McNelly detailed Sgt. C. M. Middleton and Pts. J. T. Irvin, J. F. Turner, and John W. Chalk to escort John Taylor from his home near Yorktown back to camp at Clinton. Taylor was to be an important witness in an impending murder trial. On the return trip some eight miles from camp, fifteen to twenty-five men commanded by "Old Joe" Tumlinson challenged the Ranger party. In the resulting exchange of gunfire Private Chalk was wounded, as were three of the Ranger horses. Witness Taylor ran off at the first sign of danger but was recaptured the next morning. Victor Rose quoted a *Victoria Advocate* dispatch (date not provided): "McNally's [*sic*] men have already had an engagement with the *Chevaliers d' Encinal,* in which it appears that the soldiers came out second best. Call up the reserve!"[3]

Although history has termed these troubles the Sutton-Taylor Feud, only one Sutton was involved: William E. Sutton. He was killed on March 11, 1874, along with companion Gabriel Webster Slaughter, shortly before the entrance of McNelly's company. James Creed "Jim" Taylor and his cousin William Taylor had finally avenged the death of several Taylors by killing their deadly enemy William E. Sutton. To McNelly the most troublesome figure was Joe Tumlinson, who ironically was related to the Taylor family through marriage. McNelly wrote of Tumlinson to General Steele as follows:

> [He was seen] at the head of seventy five well armed men, and men who have no interest but in obeying his orders; he is a man who has always righted his own wrongs and he tells me that the only way for this county to have peace is to allow him to kill off the Taylor party. He has never been made to feel that the civil law could and should be the supreme arbiter between man and man and I am satisfied that when the sheriff calls upon me to aid him in serving papers on Tumlinson that he will resist or at least refuse to go into Court without his arms and men as he has done heretofore. These men go with the sheriff anywhere so long as he does not attempt to disarm them. . . . I feel entirely able to whip Tumlinson with the men I have if it must be a fight but will need more men, fifty men cannot overawe these people; they have been in the habit of overriding the officers of the law so long that it will require more force than I have, to "bluff' them. We cannot expect help from the citizens; they had rather pay out half of all they own than obey the summons of the sheriff. The firing on my men the other night was done for the purpose of killing a witness whose evidence would convict them of cold-blooded murders, "Joe Tumlinson" included. At the first fire the witness fled and on their approaching my men their first words were, "By God boys, he is gone. 'twas he who ran off through the field." His death would relieve them of many fears.[4]

When the Rangers arrived, the Sutton party, McNelly estimated, numbered about one hundred men "and were defiant and triumphant." He estimated that the Taylor party numbered about the same. McNelly was frustrated by the apparent unwillingness of the authorities to deal meaningfully with the opposing factions. No effort was made by the district judge or state attorney to disarm or disperse the Tumlinson organization, McNelly believed. The Rangers were required to protect the witnesses as well as the prisoners in jail, to prevent their release by their friends or their killing by their enemies while prisoners. A system of espionage was kept upon those considered leaders of the two groups, and scouting parties continually on the move prevented groups from gathering for unlawful purposes.

McNelly's reports to General Steele provide valuable insight into the problem of being a commander in that troublesome situation. In his report of September 2 he expressed confidence in being able to capture John Wesley Hardin and Jim Taylor, who were expected within the next few days. Wrote McNelly: "The capture of Hardin and Taylor would go a long way to quiet things in this County and I feel quite sanguine of success in my contemplated effort." If they came McNelly swore he would capture them even if doing so cost him all his horses. At the same time McNelly felt that the sheriff who was supposedly cooperating with him was in reality in sympathy with known desperadoes.[5]

At least for a period of time the Taylor and Sutton forces were armed in a manner superior to the Rangers themselves. Earlier, according to the report of August 1, McNelly had complained to General Steele that his troops had no pistol ammunition. In addition there is evidence that McNelly did not have permission to act as strongly as he may have liked. William L. Rudd, who served under him, later stated that Governor Coke had instructed McNelly to go down to DeWitt County not so much to fight and kill as to "make friends and help make friends."[6] William Callicott expressed essentially the same idea in his recollections written in 1921: "He had no orders to kill out one side or the other. If a Taylor man killed a Sutton man he would go and arrest him and turn him over to the civil authorities. They never did resist arrest. He stayed in DeWitt County nearly a year and never had to kill a Taylor man nor a Sutton man. So he saw he could not do much good there so he came back to his old home in Burton in Washington County and disbanded his rangers."[7] On the Mexican border two years later McNelly was in full command with virtually no restraints. Callicott wrote that McNelly's orders on the Rio Grande were to deal with the Mexicans the same way Maj. John B. Jones had dealt with the Indians; that is, to kill and to take no prisoners. Had the Mexican cattle thieves been of the same race as the DeWitt County feudists, McNelly's treatment of them would likely have been less severe.

A trace of frustration is apparent in his report of August 7: "You may rely on my not doing anything but what you will endorse or my orders permit. I need Winchester rifles [as] these people are all armed with them and Tumlinson has from 40 to 75 armed men in town (Clinton) every day and if I am compelled to fight I don't want to get whipped."[8]

Although McNelly generally received excellent press reports in his time, occasionally the reverse was true. On August 23 the *San Antonio Express* printed this editorial:

The Sutton-Taylor war in DeWitt county continues with unabatted [*sic*] fury. We have just learned that Capt. McNelly, with his small company of Coke's State Police, finds himself powerless to quell the insurrection, or to give any relief to the county. His company consisted, at first, of forty men, but five of these have deserted him, others are still leaving, and he is unable to cope with the difficulties of the situation. He has called upon Gov. Coke to reinforce him with a hundred men. The Taylor party, we learn, have come into Capt. McNelly's camp, and remain there. We suppose that, finding themselves in danger of being overpowered by the Sutton party, they have sought McNelly's camp, more for protection than anything else. Of course, however, they can be made prisoners, and be turned over to the civil authorities whenever Capt. McNelly chooses, or whenever he is able to assure their protection while in the hands of the civil officers. The Sutton party are still defiant and triumphant. They are banded together to the number of forty men, well armed and mounted, and led by old man Tumlinson, an experienced and daring leader, who is well acquainted with the country. They doubtless have a reserve force at their homes which, in an emergency, could be mustered, and greatly increase the strength of their party.

Is it not passing strange, incomprehensible strange, that the Governor of a great State like Texas should allow a handful of desperadoes to hold a whole county in terror, to take helpless prisoners out of jail and hang them, and to hold possession of a county seat, and disperse the courts at their pleasure, for a period of several months together? What infatuation has seized Gov. Coke? The reputation of the State abroad is being ruined. His reputation is being ruined with his own party at home, and is already ruined with his own party abroad. And yet he is inert, helpless. He has a company of State Police between Corpus Christi and Brownsville that is doing only mischief among innocent Mexican citizens, and another company on the Rio Grande, that is equally useless. Why have they not long ago been sent to DeWitt county? And since the United States expedition against the Indians, both from Texas and from Kansas, have begun to move, there is no use for Maj. Jones' frontier battalion in that direction. Why does not Coke send his State Police where they are needed? If a few negroes or Mexicans were even reported in arms, the cohorts of "Cokery" would be down on them at once. But Democratic desperadoes are to be treated very gently.

The problems involving McNelly's recruits were well founded to a degree. On August 6 Pvt. C. C. Carrington was dishonorably discharged after only twelve days of service. Four days later Pvt. J. H. Chilton was also discharged. On August 14 Pvt. Ohania [?] Meza was discharged, having enlisted but two weeks previously. On August 16 Pvt. J. W. Thompson was discharged. Ten days later Pvt. C. B. Cook was discharged at his own request. Two days later two more were discharged, Pvts. William A. Elliott and Pablo Cario. On September 7 Pvt. O. G. Balemun was discharged for drunkenness and disobedience. On September 1 he had refused to obey the orders of Cpl. Roe P. Orrell. Again on the evening of September 6 he became drunk and troublesome. This was his third offense. On September 10 J. T. Irvin was discharged. On October 4 McNelly had to deliver Pvt. J. F. Turner to the sheriff of Bastrop County on an order signed by General Steele. On October 19 Private Chalk requested to be discharged. The reason was not given, but McNelly wrote that Chalk had provided "unusual good conduct." Thus, in less than three months, half of the eight men identified in the *Statesman* as having enlisted with T. Chanders were no longer in the service. Carrington, Thompson, Cook, and Balemun were out; Rector, Mabin, Northington, and Tumey remained.

The Austin correspondent was Pidge only when writing to the *Statesman*. He was no longer T. Chanders but was known to all by his correct name. Over the months he had impressed McNelly favorably, and he was soon recommended for promotion to the position of lieutenant. McNelly's request to General Steele was written on October 20:

> I find it difficult to get along without the assistance of a commissioned officer and after due time feel Satisfied that my Second Sargt. T. C. Robinson would fill the position with credit to himself & honor to the State & I would respectfully recommend that he be appointed 1st Lieut. of this company & that his commission date from October the first. I think that this would be but a just reward of merit. Very Respectfully L. H. McNelly Capt. Co. A. Vol. Mil.

The communication was not mailed immediately, for in a postscript McNelly added: "I find that the above was not mailed when written I just found it in my coat pocket, hope for an early reply respectfully L.H.M."[9]

By the end of November Captain McNelly could see improvement in the lawless conditions of DeWitt County. In his long report of August 31 he wrote:

> On arrival here about the 1st of Augt, a perfect reign of terror existed in this and adjoining counties; armed bands of men were making predatory excursions throughout the country, overawing the law abiding citizens, while the civil authorities were unable, or unwilling to enforce the law framed for their protection. The lives of peaceful citizens who had given no cause of offence to either party were in jeopardy, as neutrals were considered obnoxious to both factions. From the facility with which treaties of peace had been broken, confidence in each others respective promises was a thing unknown. In a country of such strong prejudices much has been accomplished by the good conduct of the state troops which has been most exemplary. No sympathy with, or favoritism to, either party has been shown by the men of this command, and our presence here is looked on by all peaceful citizens and is considered by them to be an absolute necessity for their protection and for the welfare of the country. Many men whose lives have hitherto been insecure, have been enabled to attend to their usual avocations in peace, although boasts have been made that our withdrawal will be the signal for a renewal of hostilities.

The various episodes of the Sutton-Taylor feud that call for more particular attention because Pidge alluded to them are more fully explained in the endnotes. The first letter is dated August 4 and appeared in the *Statesman* on August 8. As a reminder to his readers, editor Cardwell preluded the letter with this notice:

> "PIDGE" has favored us with a communication, which, like all of his articles, is full of sparkling humor and fun. Write again, "Pidge," and give us the "scenes," and all local news. The friends of the "boys" will be glad to read your letter.

Daily Democratic Statesman, August 8, 1874
Clinton, August 4, 1874

Editors Democratic Statesman—On the seventeenth of July I called on Capt. McNelly, who at that time was organizing a company to go to this county, and was overjoyed to find that I could get in business at last, with a splendid prospect for a permanent place after reaching my destination. The captain having left Austin, I was placed in charge of the men, with instructions to recruit a few good men; then business was lively for a while; one patriotic youth, who brought the city directory for recommendations, had only arrived the previous evening. I had no idea there were so many A No. 1 men in Texas. I was worn out with importunities to join on any terms and with inquiries as to what was furnished by the State. I was so tormented with this ceaseless question, that I appointed a day upon which I might enlighten them to the best of my ability. "We met, we gazed, I saw and sighed."[10] For I well knew from the appearance of some of them, that whiskey was a necessary of life, and the captain had ordered me to inform them that no drinking would be allowed; a large majority left at once.[11] "Is this a blasted temperance society, or a love feast?" said one. "From what I have gleaned from the San Antonio *Herald*, it will probably turn out a buzzard feast," replied another.[12] "We wish to know what the State furnishes?" "Gentlemen," said I, "you are required to furnish your own horses, saddles, bridles, ropes, clothing, *shoething* and six-shooters." "But what does the State furnish?" "Targets, gentlemen, targets for the desperadoes of DeWitt is all I am aware of, and good, lively targets are commanding a dollar a day in scrip, and dirt cheap at that; after they practice on a target for awhile he will not be worth anything; then the State will furnish new ones." Another large majority left. Those who remained, thanked me for my information and said they would go if it was only to see the country. R., of Austin, assured them they would see it in all its loveliness, and perhaps get a bird's eye view from an elevated situation—on the branch of a tree.[13]

Then J. B. deserted us: "*plain* J. B., tough and devilish sly."[14] "nobody will ever see me in DeWitt," said J.B. "No," observed Rector, "and nobody will ever see de wit in you, should you live to be as old as Methuselah's great grandmother." At last the party was made up, and we awaited orders with much impatience, for it was down to brass tacks with most of us. Cigarette Jim, who had returned from his cattle trip, suggested that we have a flag with the letters D. H. in the middle, surrounded by a wreath of skulls, rampant regardant, he thought that with this standard the people of DeWitt and every where else would avoid us as they would the pestilence.[15] At last orders were received to report at Burton, on the Central road, and we started. I was magnificently mounted on a pony, who walked as if he had on hobbles. I named him Bucephalus, after the celebrated quadruped who "pitched" with Alexander the Great.[16] Two days out from Austin I changed his name to Buck, e-fail-us. The last was much more appropriate, and when the scab came off his back it was hard to decide, from a business point of view, whether to save the scab or the horse, as one was equally as large as the other. Mr. Thompson, from San Antonio, was equally as well mounted as your correspondent. We were left in the rear, but I told Thompson to consider himself the rear guard, and I would act as his officer, and we would avoid being "guyed" by the boys.[17] I overtook my rear guard in the scrub oaks between McDade and Giddings, gazing with admiration on my appearance, for he said he never expected to see me again. "I can go no further," said he, "but you are in charge of the men, and your duty lies before you; go, and when you overtake them, tell them I died at my post-oak, valiantly spurring to the last. You will not see them for many years at your present rate of speed, but you must remember my last words. I told Thompson that I would stay with him as long as life lasted; that I scorned the thought of deserting one of my men in the hour of his greatest need. "You can't," said he, "if you wished to ever so much." "Don't you think the infantry presents greater inducements for us, just at this time, than any other arm of the service?" "With the exception of the engineer corps, (on the Central), I think it does, Thompson."[18] What on earth is to become of us?" said he; "we are at least twenty miles from anywhere on earth, without water or provisions, and afoot; worse than afoot, for I have used my limbs spurring till I am unable to walk a step; we are God-forgotten, man-forsaken, even devil-deserted. You lead, and I will drive, and we may get to Giddings, where we will exchange our horses for a couple of tickets to Burton. Let us take a nap, for we have much before us." After mingling our tears together, we sank into a gentle slumber, from which I was aroused by a cry of horror from Thompson. My wretched horse had gotten his hind foot in the neck rope, in attempting to scratch his ear, I suppose, and was standing on his head between two trees, presenting a most horrible appearance. The sight of him had nearly frightened Thompson out of his senses. We cut the rope and got him loose, but from that hour he lost what little self-respect he had originally possessed, and was as much depressed in spirits as he was in flesh. We started, I leading and Thompson driving. "I do not know your pedigree," said Thompson, as he whanged his beast over the hips with a rail, "but I can certify to your being well dammed." Before we had gotten far, we began to be "well heeled." Finally we reached Giddings and stopped in the suburbs, in order to allow our steeds to recuperate enough to bear us through town. "I am sorry it is Sunday, for the people will have nothing to do but look at us, and I do not wish to be looked at just this particular time." "Nonsense, Thompson," said I, "what do we care for the people of Giddings?" "Nothing. And what do the people of Giddings care for us? Less than nothing." Late in the night, or soon in the morning, we reached the camp of the boys, who shouted with joy when they beheld us. Next morning we were again left as the rear guard, and after passing through one of the finest farming countries in the world, reached Burton, where Capt. McNally [*sic*] was awaiting us with the rest of the company. Washington county contains some of the finest farms in the world, but I would advise all the lightning-rod men to try some other field; such a crop of them, I never saw before; a great many of the citizens have them on the cistern and farming implements, and a few have had them placed on the cattle.[19]

Capt. McNally [*sic*] had about thirty men in camp and after drawing rifles we started for this place which we reached on the first ultimo; on the route the captain had us drawn up in double ranks, and was informing us of what our duties would consist, when H—s, who is the most unfortunate man in the company, came charging down to take his place in ranks and was thrown clear over the line and lit on his head in front of the men much to their astonishment; some of them thought he had dropped from the clouds.[20] The captain said he would shoot the first man who ran from the fight, and I look upon my death-warrant as already signed and sealed; I am as good as dead already, for my only hope is cut off.[21]

Finally we arrived at Cuero, the present terminus of the Gulf, Western Texas and Pacific Railroad; this is quite a pretty town of about twelve hundred inhabitants, forty stores, one newspaper (the Cuero *Star*), one church, two hotels, three tailoring establishments, a school, and a money order postoffice, with an entry large enough for two men to get into at once.[22]

The town is situated almost in the centre of the county, near the banks of the beautiful Guadalupe river, as pretty a stream as there is in Texas. DeWitt county, as everybody knows, is bounded on the north by Gonzales, on the east by some county the name of which I do not remember, on the south by one which I do not recollect, and on the west by another, the name of which I have since forgotten.[23] Clinton, near which we are at present encamped, is the county seat, and contains about 400 inhabitants when they are all at home from "out of the hurly-burly."[24] They have a cute way to carry their six-shooters around here without breaking the law. Every man carries his coat tied behind his saddle, and in its folds is a peace preserver of the Smith & Wesson persuasion, ready at all times to demonstrate to any officious individual that his views on certain questions are not sound, and his argumentative position untenable unless he is behind a tree. Reports from here, however, have been much exaggerated; the citizens seem to be anxious for peace and quietness, and some are ready to fight for both at any time. This morning a party from camp were sent for to guard the prisoners while the jail was being fixed for new arrivals. I had supposed from accounts that Travis county jail could be pitted against the world for stench, filth and general nastiness; but I am assured by some of the boys that it is as much below the Clinton prison in the above attributes as a lightning bug is below Coggia's comet.[25] There are ten prisoners confined in it, and one very unjustly, as everybody thinks, for he simply attempted to kill his mother-in-law, which is, or ought to be, justifiable homicide. Court commences tomorrow, and we are told that if we are to have any fun, we will see it in a few days. If I live and do well, will write again in a week; if otherwise, *adieu pour toujours.*

"PIDGE"

Daily Democratic Statesman, August 11, 1874

[Both Lieutenant Robinson and Pvt. E. A. Northington wrote letters to the Statesman *on August 7, and a paragraph of each letter was printed in the issue of August 11.[26] Perhaps Pidge's letter was of the usual length but only one paragraph was printed.* —Volume editor*]*

FROM DEWITT COUNTY.—A letter from E. A. Northington, of Captain McNally's [*sic*] company, dated on the seventh, says:

Last night four of our men went out in the country to carry four of the Taylor boys home and when about eight miles from camp were fired on by the Sutton party, who numbered about twenty men. Two of our horses were killed, and one man was wounded, and another is missing. The Sutton party afterwards sent a man into our camp, who said they thought it was the Taylor gang they were firing into, and that they were willing to make amends to Captain McNelly. The Captain has gone with a squad of men to look for the missing man. The man wounded is named Clark [*sic*], and he is from Lampasas; he has a slight wound in the shoulder.[27] I am in Clinton this morning on business for the captain. We rather expect hot times down here, as the Sutton men say they intend to have the Taylor men we are protecting.

Below we give a short letter from "Pidge," which confirms and is substantially the same as the above:

CLINTON, August 7, 1874

Editors Democratic Statesman—Last night while three of Captain McNally's [*sic*] company in command of a sergeant were escorting John Taylor from his home, they were fired into by about twenty or thirty of the Sutton party, who claim to have mistaken them for the Taylors; one of the men from Bastrop, named Turner, is missing, and another named Chalk, from Lampasas, shot through the shoulder. Two of the men's horses were shot and left on the field.[28]

Daily Democratic Statesman, September 2, 1874

LETTER FROM "PIDGE"

CLINTON, August 28, 1874

Editors, Democratic Statesman—In my last I promised to write again in a week, but have been perfectly prostrated ever since the battle we had with Gen. Tomlinson [*sic,* Tumlinson].[29] The morning after the fight Capt. McNelly left to view the field, and ordered me to remain in charge of the camp; to be very vigilant and above all things not to sleep—the most difficult order he has ever given me; I have not entirely recovered from the effects of it yet, and I think am entitled to a life pension from the State; who among its early settlers and defenders, has ever made a greater sacrifice? As soon as I recuperated I was ordered to take a guard and escort John Taylor to what was formerly his home before he went traveling for his health. On the route we passed the battle ground; there had been differences of opinion among us as regarded the weapons with which Tomlinson's mob were armed, but all doubts are now removed; from the appearance of the fence behind which Taylor and his small guard took refuge, I should say they are provided with Gatlin guns. Some say they have *mitrailleuses*. I hope if they get after me with a *mitrailleuse* they may lose my trail. But, oh! remember us in your prayers! You ought to behold a few of the double-barreled ducking pieces which are carried by those who own the strongest horses; they have barrels about the size and length of the smoke stack on the press room engine, and when they go off they wake the dead. One would easily blow an ordinary sized individual clear out of DeWitt county, and M—n, of Austin, has sent to Austin for a life preserver—he does not expect to stop this side of the Gulf.[30] Tomlin-

John Milam Taylor, “when on foot, reminds one strongly of an old sundried bucket about to fall to pieces; when on horseback his powers of endurance are almost incredible.” Courtesy the Robert G. McCubbin Collection.

son goes about like Robinson Cruso with a gun on each shoulder and two Smith & Wesson's (No. 3) in his belt. I had the pleasure of seeing this gentleman a few days since; he has the frosts of sixty winters on his head, and green spectacles on his nose, and, it is said, can see with his naked eye farther than any hawk this side the Rio Grande; when he gets on his spectacles there is no telling what he can see, as he magnified five of the company who were traveling the road into an ambuscade of the Taylor party. The Cuero *Star* termed it the first square fight, which was all right, as they were four to one.[31] I did not approach very close to "Capt. Joe," as he is called by the DeWittians. I was fearful he might be hungry, and want a broiled ranger for breakfast, and it would have taken a long time to have properly cooked me, for as soon as he was pointed out the cold chills commenced chasing each other down my back and into my boots, and my stirrups rattled like the "bones" of a negro minstrel. I went to Cuero next day for some chill tonic, and was agreeably surprised to meet one of my former chums in the person of Frank W—, who had left Virginia in order to enjoy a quiet and peaceful life in DeWitt.[32] Calmly and serenely he packs up ammunition for the citizens, and is said to keep the best powder in the town, and, as for his rim-fire cartridges, they were never known to fail. He says this country is much livelier than Virginia, and I agree with him—it is livelier. In order to illustrate the tenacity of life among the men in this country, the people point with pride to Frank Frantz. The sheriff deputized a certain citizen, well known to the writer of this article, to arrest Frank, who had been enjoying the franking privilege long enough. In making the arrest, he blew one side of Frank's head off with a double-barreled shot-gun, and after taking him home for surgical treatment, returned and found it, but threw it away again, as it was so much hashed up with the buck-shot that it was no use to Frank or any one else. Mrs. Frantz wished to know who had been dispatched for the doctor; when told that Christopher —, well known around here, had departed on that errand of mercy, (the first he had ever rode,) she let down her back hair and screamed in a perfect ecstasy of rage and astonishment, "Why you infernal fools," bawled the woman, "don't you know he'll stop and brand every maverick he comes across between here and the Guadalupe river? Why Frank's head will grow back and be covered with hair before the doctor gets here." Mr. Frantz recovered of course, nothing short of a Whitworth gun, or a ten gallon can of nitro-glycerine [*sic*] has the least effect on a DeWittian who is "native and to the manor born," and is now in Bastrop jail, waiting to be nominated for the next

Legislature.[33] He says he can fill a representative's seat with half a head, equally as well as some who were there last session with no head at all. The three men who are now in camp, and who claim protection, consist of Tuggle, a brother of the man hanged by the mob not long since; King, a citizen of Clinton, and John Taylor, whose nephew is now imprisoned in Galveston, charged with killing Slaughter on board the steamer at Indianola.[34] Taylor, when on foot, reminds one strongly of an old sun-dried bucket about to fall to pieces; when on horseback his powers of endurance are almost incredible. I took a ride with him, recently, to look at some of his horses; he owns a great number, and I thought to trade "Buckephailus" for one who could travel faster than a crab. We *corraled* twenty or thirty; I singled out a beautiful gray, and Taylor's wild horse rider, a young man named Milam, roped him. After the life was nearly choked out of him, and he had pulled up three or four postoaks, they got the saddle on him; Milam mounted; and he shot out from the crowd like a bolt of lightning. The first pass made was at a buzzard sailing over, and he nearly succeeded in bringing him down—

> "By many a 'buckist,' I had been,
> And many a mustang's pitching seen,
> But never aught like this."

Milam sat him like a rock, and I considered his illustrious namesake as small potatoes compared to this Milam.[35] After he dismounted I was asked if I could see how he moved, and that when I was tired of the pomps and vanities of this wicked world, I would take an amble on him. We then started for camp; Taylor said he would lead like Mary's little lamb, and tied him to the tail of the pony I had borrowed for the trip, which was very small, but one of the most dignified horses in camp. He tied him securely; alas! too securely; the first step my horse made, the vicious brute towing astern got frightened and commenced tearing around and around like he was in a circus ring; he just lifted my pony up from the ground, all but his fore feet and spun him round like a tee-toturn in a few seconds there was a hole in the soft ground like some-one had begun to dig a well; he was up to his shoulders when the hair of his tail pulled out, and then came the tug of war for the saddle; already rendered so dizzy I could not see from the continual rotary motion, I was sandwiched in a pile of horses, saddles, ropes and raw hide lariets [*sic*], worse than the famed net of the *retiarius;* I finally made my escape more dead than alive, climbed a tree and awaited the finale; this beautiful gray tied himself up and lay on his back struggling and squealing as if he were possessed by the demon of evil.[36] I looked for him to kill himself, and was grieved that he didn't do it. I was so sorry that Sutton's men had not served Taylor like the Jews—killed him and all his stock, too; mortal man was never so mad "up a tree" before. We finally got him to camp, and every time I look at him I feel like joining the next mob and just cleaning out the whole Taylor generation. But that dignified pony! He was "a sight to see." His dignity and his tail were both gone forever, and he looked at me with a reproachful expression, as if he regarded me as the prime mover of it all. I could hardly refrain from asking his pardon. Everybody felt sorry for him, and he looked like he was sorry for himself. His tail was as bare of hair as the State Treasury was of money before Morgan bought the bonds, and his *ungotched* ear bit off close to his head.[37] I rode to camp on a sack containing the fragments of a once elegant saddle. It was an old Virginia saddle, one of the flat kind, and was the cause of this company being called "short horns" by the Cueroarens.[38]

About two weeks ago, a credulous and kind-hearted gentleman of Clinton told the boys he would give them credit for articles at his store, and the town was immediately charged by the whole company.[39] Thompson bought a lot of old iron, and C—k, of Austin, purchased seventeen dollars worth of fishing tackle. He anchored hooks and trout lines in the river for ten miles, and the people are afraid to bathe anywhere in this vicinity. Such purchases as were made by some of the boys would have astonished the oldest sutler in the United States army. "Cigarette Jim" has a guitar, on which he strums every night; but the boys say he is doing good service, as no enemy will ever approach the camp while he touches his light guitar. Adams has a cracked violin, and Northington a busted banjo.[40] Yesterday, Martin King came up to the captain's tent with tears in his eyes and told him he had sought his camp for protection from men who thirsted for his blood, but would now be compelled to leave and meet his fate, whatever that fate might be; that he preferred sudden death to a life of lingering misery, and would gladly take those promising young musicians to a place where they would *stretch their strings* for the last time.[41] They were sent on a scout and King's Winchester rifle has been taken away from him, as they are expected to return today.

Court has adjourned, and Tomlinson's trial is postponed till next term.

A negro killed a Mexican, with a rock, day before yesterday, near camp, and was captured after a long race and lodged in jail; no excitement nothing short of a pitched battle is ever noticed here.[42]

Must close, as the musicians are in sight, and the captain has told me to try to pacify King.

Adios,

PIDGE

P. S.—If ever the French adage, *L'homme propose* etc. was verified in this world, it is here in this country.[43] I thought they "proposed" enough in Austin, but I have heard it here till the repetition has nearly *dis*posed of what Taylor's beautiful gray left of me. That, and "lay out," have nearly laid me out, and I thank Heaven I have gotten through thus far without using either, and now think I am entitled to two pensions. If I do not get them I shall have the consolation of knowing that I have saved some poor devil from suicide.

Daily Democratic Statesman, September 24, 1874

LETTER FROM "PIDGE"

CLINTON, DEWITT COUNTY, Sept. 18, 1874

Editors Democratic Statesman:

"It was an ancient farmer man,
    And he stoppeth one of three:
'By thy Colt's improved and Henry gun
    I pray thee tell to me
If you belong to the Sutton gang
    Or the Taylor companie?'"[44]

Such is the momentous question asked of every resident in, or traveler through DeWitt. All things hinge on this, and the end, from appearances, will necessarily be a war of extermination. The people of both factions are men accustomed to righting their own wrongs, and they object decidedly to any interference, even should that interference be lawful. In any new difference which may arise between two men not previously connected with the vendetta, each takes his place with one or the other party, and in this manner recruits are gathered in the protecting aegis of a band which will defend them to the death, if need be. The leaders of each party make large calculations on the rising generation; they turn the cylinder of a revolver as a rattle for the infants of this country, and give them empty cartridge cases for teething rings; they are weaned on gunpowder and brandy, and learn to shoot before they can talk. A few days ago two men belonging to the opposing factions had some words in Cuero, and appointed the bridge over the river, three miles distant, as the place to argue the question, each member of the debating society to occupy the floor as long as he could pump fire from a repeating gun, and the decision to be left to the god of war; Capt. McNelly got wind of the affair and sent me a courier to have a dozen men mounted and in readiness by the time he got to camp; with some difficulty I mounted them, for every one wished to know where they were going, and for what purpose; I told them the time had come at last for them to strike for their halters and their fires and that, to use the words of the Father of his Country, I wanted them to remember for what they were about to fight for; an answering shout of "scrip and glory, and more glory than scrip," greeted me and it was with the greatest difficulty that I restrained them going alone. "We'll follow you; we will not wait for the Captain; a dollar a day in scrip nerves our spirits to deeds of daring, and a thirst for blood permeates our gizzards, which a holocaust of Taylors and Suttons will scarcely allay." I prevailed on them to hold in for a slight while, and when the Captain arrived, we started in a full gallop. That race I will ever remember, for it was far more exciting than any fox chase in which I had ever participated; a sensation of rapture, which is indescribable, came over me during that wild ride across the prairie, soon to be changed for one not quite so "rapturous."[45] On a parallel line, and nearer the river, I could see a small body of men in single file, making desperate strides towards the bridges; and they had the advantage of us, for they were on a nearer road; but we beat them—as we swept past the point at which they would *debouche* into the main road, they were about a hundred yards distant. Although personally acquainted with most of them, I did not recognize any of the party, and supposed that the Captain wished to prevent them from effecting a junction with a larger force on the other side of the river. When near the bridge he ordered me to halt and keep these men from crossing; I waited with an anxious heart to hear him tell some of the men to assist me in this labor of love, but I waited in vain. "Well," thought I, "he is compelled to sacrifice some one, and he has resolved it shall be the sleeping partner of this concern, and I will take my last *siesta* this afternoon. Here is an end to my rations and aspirations also; at the entrance of this bridge I make my exit and leave DeWitt, I hope for a more peaceful state of existance [*sic*]." I dismounted from my horse; he reeled as he walked; "Good-bye, Bucky!" said I, "I have the consolation of knowing that if you [are] a source of as much trouble and annoyance to your capturer as you have been to me, he will shortly follow me, for you will very soon aggravate the life out of him." I shoved a cartridge in my gun—it carries one about the size and length of a rolling pin and outkicks a Spanish mule. I never fired it but once, and then I carried my arm in a sling for three weeks. I brought it to bear on the foremost horseman. I knew I was good for him—at least I had a lingering ray of hope that it might kick me to the other side of the river. Splashed from head to heel with mud he rode rapidly toward me, and I discovered him to be a resident of Clinton, with whom I was well acquainted—felt as happy as when I left my creditors in Virginia. Napoleon, on the bridge of Lodi, never felt better or braver than I did then, and I trod the floor like it was the quarter deck of a line-of-battle ship, and I was the skipper.[46]

By the time we got to camp I was perfectly reckless, and remained so for four days; and during this time we received advices as to where we could find Wes. Hardin. This has cooled me down considerably, for I had heard of him before I ever came to Texas.[47] He kills men just to see them kick, and on one occasion charged Cuero alone with a yell of "rats to your holes!" and such a shutting up of shops has not been seen since the panic![48] He can take two six-shooters and turn them like wheels in his hands and fire a shot from each at every revolution.[49] There is a reward of eighteen hundred dollars for him, and it will be well earned when he is captured. He is said to have killed thirty men and is a dead shot. We started with twelve men for the settlement in which he was reported to be, with two guides who knew the country; they *did* know it too. They took a bee line, and we floundered through the bogs during that miserable night, which I will never forget as long as I live; bog, bog, at every step, until I thought that perhaps Hardin was in Asia, and the guides were looking for a short cut through. About daybreak we arrived at our destination, where Capt. McNelly divided the party, giving your correspondent one-half, with orders to surround a certain house, while he, with the other half, surrounded another. The two were situated about the distance of a mile from each other, and Wes. Hardin was said to be in one or the other certain. It was the first time I ever made a call so early in the morning, and a long ride to pay a visit; but I would not have been offended in the least if he had not been at home—in fact, I believe I would have preferred his absence, for I did not wish to see him particularly. I thought of sending in to him my card, marked "P. P. C.—Mr. Hardin, if you will give me a half minute to do it in."[50] We drew near the silent house; the ghostly looking moss, trailing from the trees, swept

John Wesley Hardin as he appeared in 1871. "I had heard of him before I ever came to Texas," wrote Pidge. McNelly desperately wanted to capture Hardin but never caught up with him. Courtesy the Robert G. McCubbin Collection.

across my head, making me think of Wes. reaching for my scalp. We dismounted and cautiously approached the building, which was as silent as an Austin hotel in August. Sending part of the men to the rear of the house, I advanced in front. I had orders to wait until nearly sunrise before making myself known, and to fire a gun if I saw Mr. Hardin, in which case the Captain would come down from the other station. I did not have to wait five minutes, for I had my usual luck, and was discovered by the time I had reached the fence. Forty-nine dogs—from poodles to Spanish blood hounds, from rat terriers to British bull-dogs—charged me as I crouched behind some old lumber, and it was as much as I could do to prevent them from tearing me into strings like jerked beef. The next thing I saw was a faint light, and the next was a bearded Texan, shading his eyes with his hand, and gazing very earnestly on the lumber pile. Then I heard him speak: "Bill" said he, "I think I see his bulk; look behind the door and bring out the patent DeWitt protector;" this was a murderous looking gun, the barrel of which would almost reach to where I lay. Then he encouraged his canine brigade to find out my exact position, called them off again out of range, and prepared for business. "Is she well loaded, sonny?" "Sartin, dad; a heaping pint cup full in each barrel, not counting the slugs." Slowly he brought her to bear upon me, and the barrels yawned like two Hoosac tunnels; "Hold on mister," I shouted "don't shoot; you might bring the Captain down here on a false alarm and then—you might hit me; besides I think I see Mr. Hardin asleep in the left hand barrel of that fowling piece, and I do not wish him waked up."[51] "What do you all want around my house this time of day?" "We are looking for a situation for a grocery, school house, cotton-gin, tan-yard, or any great industry calculated to develope [*sic*] the resources of a live State like Texas; we would like to discover a good mill site, or dam site" (of foolishness ever to go into this business) I added mentally. By this time the men had gathered around and I was as bold as brass again. The female population of the ranche were almost in hysterics, but I quieted their fears by assuring them that John Wesley was the divine we were following on this occasion.[52] But oh! how touching was the meeting between the guide, a Sutton man, and the owner of the double-barreled Columbiad, who belonged to the Taylor party.[53] David and Jonathan could not have loved each other more; Damon and Pythias, after having been parted for a thousand years, would not have been half as glad to see each other; we could only stand and gaze upon this ebullition of affection.[54] We were all deeply moved, but the time for marching had arrived and we must tear them from each other although we were fearful that it would break their hearts. Oh! it was a scene calculated to move the heart of a Stone or any other man; silently we parted them "from each other and their hearts are lonely now."[55] One of the strangest things about these two parties is the good will exhibited when they meet where there is no chance for a fight; they have nothing against each other; oh no, "go homes [*sic*] *mon ami*, and you shall not be disturbed," the individual who listens to these cheering and peaceful words, rates them at exactly what they are worth and remains in the brush. He lacks faith in these assertions, but he does not lack ammunition; he has no confidence in these premises, but he has in his Henry rifle, and he is right, for the lessons of experience are never forgotten. The trial of William Taylor commences Monday, and the Houston *Telegraph* of a late date has an account of a rescuing party of Taylor men on the way armed with "large sized, ivory-handled, silver plated, breech-loading, cartridge-shooting, double-sighted, central-fire, Colt's improved and still improving revolvers; 'Sweet spirit! hear my prayer.'"[56]

The folks of Indianola are gone up [grown up] if they can get pistols like these over the bar. However the Houston people discovered this well-armed party of Taylors to be a few cow boys returning from Kansas, and all is serene again. John Taylor, who has just reached camp from Indianola, having gone down to the trial of his nephew, tells me that he wishes they were his men, for with such pistols they ought to be able to kill men clear out of sight. He returns to court Monday and we will then hear the result of the trial.

Buenos noches,

"Pidge."

P. S. When I first wrote to you from here, I was not acquainted with the geography of the country; I have since been told by an old citizen of Clinton that it takes five large counties to bound DeWitt, and it is an awful strain on them to hold it all. P.

Daily Democratic Statesman, October 14, 1874

LETTER FROM "PIDGE"

CLINTON, DEWITT COUNTY, Oct. 18 [*sic;* October 13], 1874

Editors Democratic Statesman—Things seem to have taken a more quiet turn down here of late, though it may be the slumbering of the volcano before the eruption.[57] The Guadalupe river is the only thing that has been on a rise lately, and has interfered somewhat with the usual pastime of nightriding in this vicinity; it has been higher than ever known, except on one occasion in 1869. There was a perfect sea between here and Cuero, and people visited the town in boats. It is predicted that this country will now be unhealthy; but I had supposed it had been so for some years. They say that congestive chills will now be very prevalent, but they can scarcely be worse than the Winchester bullet fever, a disease which has been raging here for years, and which has carried off some of the best citizens in a very sudden manner. The physicians say it will succumb to no treatment, and powders only seem to aggravate the complaint.

The trial of Wm. Taylor has been postponed, and his uncle John has left our camp, where he has been staying for some time, and returned to his home.[58] He lives not very far from Capt. Joe Tomlinson, one of the earliest settlers of the country.

Joe has just sent to camp for a guard to keep the Taylors off. A guard is now at Taylor's to keep the Tomlinsons off. King wants one to keep the Suttons off, and we have to mount one in camp to keep them all off. I was at Taylor's yesterday; went there to arrest a young man from Bastrop named Turner, charged with serious crimes. He was a member of this company, and has acted while in it so as to win the respect and admiration of all his comrades. This was my first experience in getting the "drop" on a man, and I have not the highest respect for the practice.[59] However, I thought, like Don Juan's poet:

> "To do in Rome as Romans do, a bit
> Of conduct was, which I'll observe in DeWitt."[60]

That last line has an extra syllable, which destroys the metre, but let it go. DeWitt is entitled to all extras, and it is well calculated to destroy anything. We finally arrived at Taylor's, where this young man was on duty as a guard, and as I introduced the sheriff, I pulled my pistol, and the men under my command did the same.[61] Twice he attempted to draw his weapon with our leveled six-shooters cocked in his face.

I took position near a small post oak, and was sorry it was not one of those California twigs we hear of—twenty feet across the stump. There was another item which bothered me a little, and that was Mr. John Taylor. Not being acquainted with the Bastrop man, he might take a notion to join us in our little game. Had he put his hand on his pistol, I would have been back in Virginia before now. The sheriff supposed me to be an adept in the business, and wanted me to be his deputy. "Oh, bother,"

I replied, with a yawn, "I am tired of it. It is a tame occupation in Texas compared to capturing deserters in the Blue Ridge. Some fun there, for they were in forts, and had mountain howitzers."[62] He stared at me, and I thought to myself, "representative of the greatest and most [glorious?] uncertainty of the world, could you but form an idea how near I was being frightened to death, you would not stick to your opinion quite as tenaciously as some of the old martyrs did. In fact, you would change it as quick as I would have changed my position—had he gotten that pistol."

"You ought to go for Wes. Hardin," said he; "he might furnish you a little sport. John Wesley, like his illustrious namesake, has gathered many in his fold, and his converts never fall from grace but once."[63] I told him I had been for him once but to my great disappointment he was absent. Continuing in this strain, we finally reached Clinton, with the prisoner; I bade him goodbye with a heavy heart, for I had been strongly prepossessed in his favor; he may have been guilty of the crimes charged against him, but a better soldier never put foot in stirrup.[64] That evening I attended church in Clinton, and listened to a very good minister from Cuero, who took issue against scepticism [*sic*]; he fought with doubts and mosquitos [*sic*] for an hour and a half in a most able manner. One thing was deserving of notice—not an old man was seen in church, not a silver-head could be observed, and I suppose that old people are never seen in DeWitt. If they are not killed they hide out in a country above here called "the brush," where the words of the gospel will never reach them unless used as wads for a double-barreled shotgun.

To show you the reverence with which the law is looked upon in this country, it is only necessary to mention Mr. —, who lives near here, and for whom the sheriff had an attachment to attend court at Indianola: "Mr. — I have an attachment for you;" "You have?" "Yes—sir!" "Well sir, you may attach and be d—d; now attach; I'm waiting for you." The deputy handed him the paper. Mr. — very coolly put it in his pocket, carried it home with him, and the deputy made one or two trips up there for his attachment before he recovered it. The office of sheriff is no sinecure in DeWitt, I can assure you; almost any body could get the place, I think. It is a source of deep regret to me that I did not come straight to this point when I first landed in Texas. I would never have been out of a situation, as I was in Austin; all a person has to do in DeWitt, is to make his choice; and I am surprised at any one who will remain out of a place while such brilliant openings are before them as can be found down here, I never expect to leave as long as I live. It was a fortunate choice that took me out of the way of duns and debts, and the boarding house keeper who comes to this country will take his life in his own hand; I warn them in time and I always go well armed.

A few days since I was in Clinton, and while there one of the Sutton party asked Mr. —: "Please to talk to him in a friendly manner; to give him a private conference, for his heart was bursting with affection for him." Said he, "will you go with me to some retired place where I may be able to pour out my whole soul to you without fear of interruption? Go with me to some sequestered spot where we may speak as breatheren [*sic*], as friends. Accompany me Mr. —, and let me forget the Sutton party, while the remembrance of the Taylors is obliterated from your heart of hearts. Will you go, *mon cher?*" "You bet your britches I'll go," said —. "Yes, you may even venture your shirt. In fact you need not hedge on your whole wardrobe, for I have a Smith & Wesson and you glory in the possession of a Colt's improved. I will go with you anywhere you wish, and if it is agreeable to you, nothing but death shall seperate [*sic*] us. I know you love me, but you would love me better if I were dead, for "The love where death has set his seal," etc. is everlasting, and of as huge a growth as your hypocrisy.[65] Let us depart, and you can be my better angel—if you can get out your six-shooter first." Such is the sweet confidence, the perfect faith, the confiding trust they exhibit towards each other. This is also a family feud, and they are arrayed against each other in the opposing parties, from children of the same parents down to fourth cousins and step-neighbors-in-law, there are *a great* many strangers, too, among them, and one man informed me that he was just from Scotland. When I asked him why he did not speak with an accent, he said the captain threw his accent overboard, because it impeded the progress of the vessel, and that she sailed fourteen knots upon a tow line.[66] I have since discovered him to be a Scotch gentleman from Connecticut, with only a shoddy idea of [Tweed?], but (since he came to DeWitt) a vivid remembrance of "Old Mortality."[67] I asked him to sing me a Scottish ballad of ancient times, and he struck up one which sounded strangely modern, and I think must have been manufactured here.

"Then he drew his Smith & Wesson,
Large sized army No. three
And he gave Jim—his blessin,
Such a lovely sight to see,
For he had no business messin
Where he hadn't ought to be.[68]

"Hold on; in what part of Taviola [?] did you learn that!" "In Murderer's Gulch, on the Collett; it is a beautiful song and was sung by Bill—but before he was tucked up on the blamed postoak in Dead Man's Hollow."[69] A cold shiver went over me, and I said I thought that was sufficient; that I felt somewhat chilly, and did not think this to be a healthy country no how. He said that a great many people had also found it unhealthy, even on elevated situations; "but I am delighted with the country said, he," and

"Twas all for the sake of our spiteful king,
That I left fair Scotland's stand,
It was all on account of the Taylor ring,
That I e're saw foreign land."[70]

but my heart often yearns in this mountainous country for the level highlands of my native hearth. Land of steaks and snakes from henceforward I cast my lot with thee. The click of the six-shooter is music to my ear, and peace I abhor as I do the [?] of the Viscount of Dundee.[71] I may make a name in this country yet, and be as eminent as Wes. Hardin!" "Yes, Mr. —," said I, "you are unknown to fame as yet, and fame, and almost everything else, is unknown to you, but there is no knowing but what you may yet be exalted above the common herd if you get our due, which I sincerely hope you may. Continue in that path which you have marked out and you will be apt to reap your reward and rise superior even to a Christian, for you will secure it both in this world and in the next. Having been always conscious of the rectitude of your intentions, you will at some future day, perhaps, entrance a spell bound audience with your [?] until the very rostrum moves from beneath your feet." "Do you really think so?" "I do indeed, my friend, for, according to [?] account, you are a descendant of those [?] land veterans who passed their life like some gentlemen of this country in the stock business, but the stock happened to belong to other parties." I have not seen this young man since, but I am certain that if he has the shadow of an opportunity he will be certain to make his mark (and *brand*).

The Cuero Volksfest comes off tomorrow, and will no doubt be a grand affair, deputations from all the towns in adjoining counties are expected, and a very pleasant time is anticipated by all. The members of this company have received an invitation and expect to go, of course, and also, to use a Texas expression, "get away" with some of their good things.

This country can boast of a great many very handsome women and there are some Clinton belles whose beauty cannot be surpassed. We have been treated very kindly since our arrival here, by the members of both parties and what few neutrals there are left. All have vied with each other to make our stay as pleasant as possible, and we have had, considering all things, a very pleasant time so far, of course we have been beseiged [*sic*] by the henchmen of the opposing factions, but we only put on a wise and knowing look, shake our heads and say, in the well known words of the illustrious head of the nation, "let us have peace," gentlemen of the Taylor party, keep your selves calm and cool, friends of the Sutton band, do not fight, for there is nothing to be gained by it, we have come down here not to know any party, for the stock of both companies is at par with us, and we are here simply to accommodate the Governor, urged by duty and an empty stomach, we have come hither and we will not leave as long as there is bad feeling or beef in the whole country.[72]

Au revoir,
"PIDGE"

Daily Democratic Statesman, November 12, 1874

LETTER FROM "PIDGE"

CLINTON, DEWITT COUNTY, *Nov. 8, 1874*

Editors Democratic Statesman—"Nunc dimittis" "Now, Lord, let Thy servant depart in peace, for mine eyes have seen Thy salvation."[73] "Uncle Joe" has been convicted, converted, baptized; and received into the church, and is considered by his friends to be sincere. Some of the Taylor party, however, express some doubts about it, and say that it is "farewell, my hopes of court" for somebody, and that, before very long, or at least before court commences. Capt. Joe is considered a "soon one" by both friends and enemies; he is an old Indian fighter, and has a military head with no hair on it; he is sixty-four years old and can ride a horse over any ground, and when astride of his favorite horse, Gray Eagle, will beat the best cowboy in Western Texas. Wesley Hardin and his party have beseiged [*sic*] him in his castle on one or two occasions, but he hoisted his drawbridge, let fall his port-cullis, and bid defiance to all creation; then Wes. sent him word to remove the women and children, as he intended to bombard the fortress, demolish the stronghold, and sow the ruins with salt.[74] Capt. Joe would not surrender, and about the time the besiegers had prepared fireballs to burn the buildings, the sheriff arrived, and a compromise was affected. The Captain had sent Abracadabra, (called

George Culver Tennille was one of the few feudists mentioned by name in the letters (though misspelled): "A difficult job for the sheriff to get up a posse, for was not Wes. Hardin there? and George Tennell?" A Gonzales County posse killed Tennille on July 8, 1874. Author's collection.

"Ab." for short) through the lines to "carry the news to Mary, or any body else he could see, that we are all surrounded;" thus originated that well known song so popular a year or two since.[75] A difficult job for the sheriff to get up a *posse,* for was not Wes. Hardin there? and George Tennell [*sic*]'? and many more, who in the impressive language of this country, were "bad ones?"[76] He summoned Mr. . . . , from up on Big Sandy, who belongs to the opposing faction, and who, as a cussist, acknowledges no superior. "Wish me to go to Tomlinson's [*sic,* Tumlinson's] relief, do you?" he roared. "I would see you so far in the infernal regions that a streak of lightning, traveling at the rate of a million of miles in the millionth part of a fraction of a second, would be a million of years getting within a million of miles of striking distance of you, and then I wouldn't go. 'Be fined a hundred dollars?' All right; make it a thousand, make it ten thousand. I'll mortgage all my earthly possessions, and sell my soul to the devil for two bits, but I won't go, and you may just as well mark it down on your tablets in indelible ink." He finally concluded to go of his own accord, and the whole party, sheriff and all, were captured by Wes., who allowed the officer alone to go in and tell Captain Joe to surrender, and he would be protected. Joe told him that was as thin as the hair on his head, as transparent as the glass in his green spectacles, and he did not want any of it in his'n, for most of the posse were Taylor men. All hands, besiegers and besieged, finally adjourned to meet in Yorktown, where one of the famous compromises was agreed upon, and both parties came to Clinton to sign it. It was a beautiful compromise, well fixed up, and was warranted to last at least a month—if handled carefully; but it lacked three weeks of filling the time when they sang the same old song of "Le Roi Galliard qui s'appele La Guerre, C'est mon souverain tout debonnair," etc., and gathered the sixteen shooters, and came a volunteering for this king, whose authority, at that time, was the only one acknowledged in DeWitt.[77] Treaties of peace have been broken so often that they call them "comps" for brevity.[78] A certain gentleman near here received a letter the other day from a prominent editor, asking him to send a full and complete history of the war down here. He referred it to me, and I wrote to the editor that for ten thousand dollars in gold and my traveling expenses, I would get him up a history of deeds done here that would curdle the ink in his press fountain, and horrify the type till they would stand in the form without a lock. I could tell him tales which would make the hair stand on anybody's head except Capt. Joe's, but it would be very expensive traveling for the items. Some of the men whom I would have liked to interview were murdered, and some in Mexico; some killed, and some in Kansas; some hanged, and some in H—ades; but I would promise him a novel which I had originally intended for the New York *Dredger,* entitled "The Brigands of the Brush; or the Desperadoes of DeWitt."[79] Could give him the history of men through this section who wore the brand of cain upon their brow, and who would brand anything with a hide on, from a tambourine up to a buffalo; that the history of Wes. Hardin alone would fill the paper for six months—he is the man who can make Catherine-wheels of a pair of six-shooters and drop a man with every barrel. With a good retriever to go in the chaparral and get them out when killed, he can bag forty per day, and has done it scores of times. Could tell you of the ride for life which . . . made some years ago, escaping from the vigilance committee, during which he outran eight men, posted at the distance of a mile from each other on fresh horses, and finally escaped by leaping old "Bender" down a precipice fourteen feet high. "Bender had been sent to him by old man Rabb, a member of the committee, who, strange as it may appear for a vigilant, had some mercy in his heart. He afterwards saw the horse in Kansas, and with much emotion offered his owner an enormous sum for him. Could give him the exploits of Capt. Jack Helm, who kept his helm hard down on the people of this section, until Wes. one day, in a playful mood, gave him a broadside and sunk him.[80] Could give him the account of the escape of the Pace brothers and their run through the timber; where I saw the trees on each side of their course blazed with buckshot I supposed that Morgan's engineers were staking out a new railroad to San Antonio.[81] Of the kind forethought of the mobs, who hang men conveniently near to the cemetery, to avoid giving their friends unnecessary trouble.[82] Of one of the famous "comps" agreed to in Clinton which lasted a most unexampled length of time, six seconds by a stop watch, at the end of which time the popping of six-shooters had made the condition of the scarcely born "comp," precarious and not at all permanent. Of the amusements around here on New Year's day, when all Cuero turned out to see a pitched battle on the prairie between the two armies, and the unpopularity of the peace-makers who broke up the fun; and of many things which no one else had known or ever would know.[83] I have not heard from the editor yet, but I am certain he will not refuse my modest demand, for I would be stricken with age before I could get up a full account of a feud which has lasted for nearly twenty years. That he will close with my proposal is *une affaire decidee* and when I leave, the company quartermaster will swoon with joy. But in the eating line there are three men in this company who will be pitted against sausage mills for any amount. They would not want more than four days' time to create a famine in the Shenandoah valley. When guard duty at any citizen's house grows onerous, we always send this *dernier ressort,* this forlorn hope, and he wilts immediately. An aged citizen, with his white hair streaming in the breeze, came tearing into camp the other day and asked who was in command in a very excited manner. The Captain being in town, your correspondent was pointed out, when he clasped me around the neck and was, for some moments, unable to speak. I thought that perhaps somebody had murdered some of his family, and asked him the cause of his emotion. In a feeble voice, broken by sobs, he implored me to recall the guard. I repulsed the old gentleman with scorn, and demanded the cause of his applying for them. "I had something to guard then, my friend, but it is all gone now. They have cleaned me out completely, and like Oliver Twist, have tried to twist more out of me. I am plunged into misery, such as I have never experienced, since Jack Helm murdered my sixteen grandchildren. Take the destroyers back, and earn the blessing of one of the oldest settlers in this county. I start for Kansas in a few days. I have heard much of the grasshoppers and their doings up there, but after this experience, they have no terrors. Oh! it will be so consolatory to know in my exile, that the white robed angel of peace has spread her wings over my native county, for if this triumverate [*sic*] remains here long, there will be no subsistence for either party, and you will conquer a peace, which, if as strong as their digestion, and as lasting as their appetites, will be a peace indeed, for it will exist forevermore." They were recalled, and the next day the cussin'-master-general of DeWitt sent his in; also a message, which, if I were to repeat, would fill the remainder of this letter with blank spaces, and be a most desireable [*sic*] job for a new compositor.[84] He had attempted to get some work out of them, but made a signal failure; had given them scythes and expatiated to them hugely on the delightful odor arising from new mown hay. They told him they had contracted colds in camp, and couldn't smell worth a cent, even in scrip. He tried them on everything connected with his farm, and finally dismissed them as incorrigible. He says it is a matter of wonderment to him that they are not too lazy to draw their rations, their pay, or their breath.

We were recently visited by Uncle Jimmy . . . who was sent malignantly, and in cold blood, by some of our enemies, to talk this company to

Artist R. J. Onderdonk's version of the death of Jack Helm, "who kept his helm hard down on the people" until one day Wes Hardin, "in a playful mood, gave him a broadside and sunk him." Author's collection.

death, and he would have succeeded but for casually dropping a remark that the waving of arms would stop him as effectually as the pointing of arms had, many times previously, stopping other parties in De Witt. This lifted our souls out of the depths of despair, and we moved camp close to a windmill, ordered the miller to run it day and night, and when he could not raise the wind to call on us for scrip, but never to allow its arms to cease waving as long as we remain here. Uncle J. is a nice old gentleman, but he ought not to allow himself to be influenced by our enemies in this style. We never saw him before, and never did him any harm in our lives.

There was a beautiful illustration of that charming song, "two souls with but a single thought, two hearts that beat as one," on the railroad between Cuero and Indianola, not long since.[85] A passenger was implored by a badly frightened person in the baggage car, as he ever hoped for mercy to be shown him, to keep that murdering cut-throat in the rear coach from assassinating him. Passing to the rear of the train, he was warmly welcomed by another traveler, scared out of his seven senses, who asked him, tremblingly, not to allow the bloodthirsty villain in the baggage car to murder him in cold blood; this one was recognized as Knight, a witness before the grand jury here at the last term of court, and who was guarded in our camp for a long time; very appropriate was his name too, for he vanished between two days; he asked me before he left if I ever heard of the "Knight of Gwinne" and said that "he was him," for he was *gwine* as far as he could get; that parting from friends was so painful he would prefer not bidding them farewell, and that if he left in the day-time some of them had such an affection for him, they would follow his trail to the Rio Grande, just to get a lock of his hair—with his scalp attached to it. He left, and being out of a job went to Austin; somehow they all do this when similarly situated, which is the reason of the unparalleled good health of the city, for any one will be well as long as he has nothing to do and is not overgorged with food; I know this from experience. Knight went from Austin to Galveston, from there to Mexico, and is no doubt with Cortina this moment.[86]

The Volkfest at Cuero, not long since, was a success in the fullest sense of the word, and, in the name of this company, I return our thanks to the unknown correspondent of the Galveston News for his complimentary notice.[87] The most amusing thing I saw there was a couple of Teutonic whales, full of enthusiasm and beer, waddling down with a pair of large lanterns to see the display of fireworks, and singing, "Der Dutchen company is a goot company as ever coomed from Yarmany."A description would be stale at this date, or I would attempt one; cannot, however, avoid mentioning Mr. Hamilton's exhibition of dry goods and beauty, which was the observed of all the observed.[88] It appears to me that somebody has used that last expression before, but anyone who has aught to say of an affair of this kind has a patent right to it, and I don't intend to relinquish mine. Everything passed off pleasantly, and all returned home charmed with the entertainment. There was exhibited to the strangers from the adjoining counties and towns an illustration of how well DeWitt people can behave if they choose.

We were all delighted to observe the enlargement of the *Statesman.* It is now the largest in the State, perhaps, with the exception of Lieutenant Governor Hubbard, and your correspondent is charmed to witness evidence of its increased prosperity, for he was a stranger when the proprietors took him in and started him on the plank road to fortune, fame, and six dollars a week.[89] None but the kind-hearted employees of the office would have tolerated such a printer as yours truly among them, and the job compositor looked on me as his adverse star, his evil genius, whose destiny was to make him lose his situation, but I tried so hard to please him and keep him from using the patent Bogardus kicker of the office upon me, and turning me adrift, that he overlooked many doings of mine which could have been somewhat expensive to me at that time.[90]

"Capt. Joe's" guard has arrived—three of them—*the* three. He also sent a message to the effect, that they had cleaned *him* out—that he was sorry he had professed religion, for he would have liked much, so very much, to have said a few words to these men before they left. I thought of offering him the services of one of our Mexicans, to whom some of the men have been giving lessons in a national fine art, and who says that "*hasta luego,* bime-by, *poco tiempo,* pretty soon, can cuss *bueno* in Merikin lingwidge."

"Pidge"

P. S.—We have been invited to many social gatherings, and the last one, at Mr. B—'s, near here, was much enjoyed by the participants.

Daily Democratic Statesman, November 18, 1874

LES TROIS ETOILES

DeWitt, November 8, 1874[91]

Forgotten, so long ago,
Yet I know, in the days gone by,
That she fancies me worthy then
Of a smile, a glance from her eye;
And my tears fall bitterer when
I remember her and her pride.
Ah, me! I should have died—
She would think of me then, I know.

She is dead. She was dead to me
Before she was laid to rest;
And the last sweet kiss she gave,
Ere my name was a bitter jest,
Will be given again at her grave—
To the craven marble cold;
To kneel there, and say, "Behold,
I send this greeting to thee!"

She has brought me a brighter day,
And yet, is it best or worst?

Only the fates can foreknow.
Shall I count myself blest or curst
In this dream of the long ago?
Time was growing so kind
That I might have had hope to find
Content, tho' so far away.

Daily Democratic Statesman, December 9, 1874

LETTER FROM "PIDGE"

CLINTON, DEWITT CO., Dec. 5, 1874[92]

Editors, Democratic Statesman—Since my last, Capt. Joe Tomlinson has departed this life, after a short and painful illness, *de mortuis nil nisi bonum.*[93] He was one of the oldest settlers of this country, and participated in the last engagement fought with Indians in DeWitt; it occurred three miles west of here, at a place known as Indian Motte, and an account of the fight was given me by Mr. W. A. Blair, of this place, one of the survivors, and a great admirer of the *Statesman.* The fight occurred in the month of July, 1844; Capt. John York was then surveying land on the Coletto [*sic,* Coleto], and returning to the residence of Andrew Lockhart, found that Indians had passed down the Guadalupe in the direction of Victoria.[94] Sending a messenger to Capt. D. B. Fry [*sic,* Friar], the captain came to his assistance with a small party, and the combined forces elected York and J. J. Tomlinson (a brother of Joe's) as officers.[95] They soon found the trail and came up with the Indians, about forty strong, led by Big Scalper, who is to this day well known on the frontier. They were charged upon, and in the *melee* John Spear would have been sent to a world where Indians are not supposed to go, had not Capt. Joe Tomlinson given the noble red a passage to the happy hunting grounds. Two savages concealed themselves in the motte after the defeat, and dogs were sent forth to dislodge them. While a thoroughbred bull pup was holding to an Indian in the most approved style, Uncle Roderick, a slave of Andrew Lockhart's, blazed away, and with unerring aim killed both dog and Indian; of this party of frontiersmen, but five are now living—these are A. J. Bell, Andrew Neal, John York, J. F. Blair, and W. A. Blair.[96] A poem has been written on this encounter, but only a single verse is now remembered by the author:

> "Once the red savage took here his delight,
> Fished, fought and bled
> Now most of the inhabitants are white,
> With nary red."[97]

This was Capt. Tomlinson's last fight with Indians, but he has been fighting whites ever since, until recently; he is said to have had a presentiment of his approaching end and his illness, though painful, was brief. He was buried with Masonic honors and had many strong friends by whom he will be greatly missed. Everybody will miss him, I have no doubt, for he used to make things lively around here sometimes. The minister who converted him has been holding protracted services in Clinton until a few days since. He came full of ardor, he departed much depressed, for six shooters are the only arguments which move people here. Said he, "my friends, I have been in the Five Points of New York, I have visited the wharves of Boston, I even stayed a week in Washington City, I have trod the levees of New Orleans, and last, though far from least, I have perambulated the streets of Natchez under the hill, in her palmiest days, and I have always met with some encouragement until I anchored in DeWitt."[98] Seriously speaking, this is as desirable a county to live in as any in the State. Lawlessness has, in a great measure, subsided, and a man who can attend to his own business will do as well here, farming or stockraising, as he will anywhere. The people are quite sociable, and the ladies are beautiful. Clinton has always been noted for its handsome women, and social gatherings are of frequent occurrence in the village. Cuero, when we first arrived here, had a huge alarm bell and a home protection company of eight men.[99] This was on account of the playfullness of Wesley Hardin and some of his confreres, who sometimes rode into stores and amused themselves by shooting out the lights. No one knows where Wes. is at present, and I hope never will know, for Capt. McNelly seems to be impressed with the idea that I am suffering because I cannot get at him; but I am not; the one trip I made for him will satisfy me, I think, for some time to come, and if I never see him I will try to survive it. Cuero still sports its bell, but Clinton, though much smaller, has three bells. The *Star* has lately changed hands.[100] When the former editor came to see me in town one day, wishing to dispose of a Winchester rifle, two six-shooters, three derringers, a bowie knife and a pair of heavy boots with projecting soles, made expressly for kicking, I knew he was going to retire from business, and was sorry I could not purchase his whole arse-nel [*sic*]. The home protection company has disbanded, I believe, and [people] do not close up their houses now till it suits their convenience. Wes. formerly acted as mayor whenever he chose, and his commands could not have been more implicitly obeyed had he been the Sultan of Turkey. When he told them to get to their holes they *got,* and those who didn't stood a good chance to be carried to them. Wes. was a whale among little fishes, and was more dreaded than any desperado in the State of Texas. He killed a man in Cuero because he took his hands out of his own pockets when he (Wes.) told him not to do so.[101] Wes. might have thought he had something in them, but he will be badly fooled if he ever shoots me on the same supposition. After he disposed of this willful individual, who *would* take his hands out of his pockets, he went out on the prairie a short distance from town and slept, oh! so peacefully! Why, he deserved death—he took his hands out of his pockets. The assassination of this stranger was a mere nothing; he would take his hands out of his pockets. He ought not to have had pockets, or he ought not to have had hands. We can all understand how men, when goaded by passion, or with deep wrongs to avenge, can take the life of a human being, but the cold-blooded assassinations like those of old man Cox, Taylor, and others, of both factions, which have taken place here are almost incredible. The good citizens of this county, of whom there are many, deeply deplore the lawless deeds done in it, and which have made it a synonym for crime and desperadoism over the whole State. To a want of moral courage in denouncing wrong may be attributed some of it.[102]

We attended the Victoria fair, and to say that we were agreeably entertained does not half express our feelings. The Victoria people are certainly the politest in Texas. We arrived after nightfall, seeking quarters on our own hook, but finding them not; at last we were directed to the residence of a gentleman on Bustamente street, who, we were told, would pilot us. We found him, and may the blessing of Allah rest upon his household. "Would he go with us?" Certainly he would, and we took up the lines of march, unthoughtedly [*sic*] allowing him to walk. Street after street was traversed, this kind hearted gentleman leading the party, when he was suddenly seen to keel over in what Mr. Mantalini would call "a dem'd state."[103] We took him up tenderly, lifted him with care, and bore him into a neighboring saloon. (Right here I would remark that the Victoria people are certainly the politest in Texas.) He soon revived, and beckoned us to approach his bedside. He whispered feebly, "Victoria expected every man to do his duty; I have not failed in mine; I wish you to go to the committee of reception and tell them from me, that I went as far as I could; I have been on my feet all day, and positively could not ask a visitor for his horse; heaven bless you, and guide you to your quarters, which are now near at hand." He fell back upon his couch; there was the brightness of an inexpressable [*sic*] content upon his face, and, though broken by the deathrattle, we caught the last words of this second Wolfe: "I have done my duty, I die content."[104] The Victoria people are certainly the politest in Texas. He had walked himself to death, out of pure politeness, and perished a blessed martyr to his urbanity.

With the exception of the ladies' department, which was most creditable, the display of articles was small, but it being the first held for some years, the Victorians are excusable; they intend doing better in the future. A most excellent speech was made by ex-Governor Stockdale, which I intended reporting; but a perch on the dashboard of a buggy is not a favorable position for taking notes, and to the bright eyes of the two Victorians on the seat must be given the blame of my not hearing a word of it.[105]

A ball was given that evening at the Casino, where everybody had a good time and tripped it on "the light fantastic heel" till late in the night—I might have said till the "wee sma' hours;" but that is as bad as the "fantastic toe." And there are some patrons of the *Statesman* in this county who have suffered enough, of late years, and I do not wish to add to their misery. Why is it that no one within the memory of man has ever yet dreamed, thought, spoke or written of a dance without bringing in those two old and tiresome stereotyped phrases, is an incomprehensible mystery to me, and an evidence of the misanthropical [*sic*] malignity of all the Jenkinses.[106]

I had almost forgotten to say that a machine for cutting up turnips with lightning rapidity was considered a big thing by people on the grounds, and would have no doubt taken a premium if T . . . , of this company, had not placed his head under it, opened his mouth, and told the inventor to "start her." Had T . . . not missed his dinner the machine *might* have beat him, but as it was he "got away" with it. It was a dreadful scene; several ladies fainted, and the exhibitor hid his diminished head, and took the turnip cutter off the grounds. He afterwards said he could have kept T . . . in turnips, but did not wish to strain the machine. T . . . is one of the Fatal Three, the Immortal Trio, to whom "the earth before them is like the garden of Eden, and behind them a desolate wilderness;" one of that celebrated guard, the terror and *bete noir* of citizens, who, when they see them coming, leave all and take to the brush.[107] They are called the devastators, and a grasshopper who followed the trail would inevitably perish.

There was also exhibited an excellent saddle, made by a man who was suffering from some great affliction, but I have forgotten what it was. He was either deaf and dumb, or deaf and blind, or deaf, dumb and blind, or his mother-in-law lived with him, I do not recollect which, but he had suffered immensely. Do not know whether or not he got a diploma, but he certainly deserved one, for his work was almost commendable. We only stayed one day, but desire to return our thanks to the Victorian people for the uniform kindness and courtesy with which we were treated during the short time we were among them. Mission Valley was well represented, and I intend soon to go down, and give you an account of the mission founded there, the ruins of which are still to be seen; but like other neighborhoods in DeWitt an awful state of affairs exist therein.[108] I have been informed by a fair resident that in this Vale of Tempe, there are sixteen ladies and only one man, and he's a widower. It is said to be as much as an unmarried man's liberty is worth, to venture there alone. Thus it is for the unprotected stranger in DeWitt; dangers yawn for him at every step.

The district court commences here the day after tomorrow; the Fiery Cross has gone forth, and the clans on both sides are marshalling their forces and will be out in all the glory of hats with stuffed boa-constrictors for bands, sashes long enough to "put a girdle round the earth," and top boots with the moon and all the constellations of the heavens, worked on them in yellow morocco leather.[109] These are they which are called "bad ones" and "have come up through much tribulation" whenever the grand jury meets. When one of these dandies steps out for our admiration we are compelled to catch our breath, and say "be still, oh beating heart," and thrice blessed eyes, let not the sight wither you in your sockets; before the tide of immigration these marvellous [*sic*] sights will pass away; let us be thankful that we have the good fortune to exist in the present age."[110]

Adieu,
PIDGE

Pidge and the Rio Grande Frontier

The concluding paragraph of Pidge's last letter from DeWitt County ended on a note of optimism. Why his writing then ceased to appear in the *Statesman* is unknown; no additional contributions appeared there. There was no farewell from Pidge announcing his departure, as there had been when T. Chanders left Austin with other Rangers for the "seat of war" in DeWitt County. The company was temporarily disbanded in the latter part of February. The pay rolls identify an aggregate of seventy men comprising the company, including officers. Payment was through February 24, 1875, for those who had not previously been mustered out. The next document in the records is the muster and pay roll from the reorganization date of April 1 to August 31, 1875. Apparently the sentiment was that the company was no longer needed in DeWitt County, or perhaps simply that the funds to support it had ended.

The letter of December 9, 1874, was the last to appear in the *Statesman*. Whether there were others written but not accepted cannot now be determined. Why the correspondence stopped cannot now be determined either: presumably differences between Pidge and editor Cardwell caused the discontinuance. But readers in Austin could continue to enjoy Pidge's writings since they continued after McNelly's company arrived on the Rio Grande frontier, where it was sent to combat cattle thieves. The letters would now appear in the *Daily State Gazette*, edited by John D. Elliott. In the *Gazette* of April 17, 1875, appeared this brief item: "We have arranged with Capt. McNally [*sic*] for regular contributions for the GAZETTE and telegrams, from the seat of the west." Strangely the first letter would not appear until October 3, 1875. Were there others contributed but for some reason editor Elliott rejected them?

It is impossible to determine what Pidge did during the interim. There are few reports from McNelly that could provide information. His last report was dated November 30, 1874; other than this there are only pay vouchers. Consequently we know virtually nothing of McNelly himself or of any members of the company.

On January 10, 1875, McNelly wrote to General Steele that unless instructed to the contrary he would leave Clinton for Austin on either Janu-

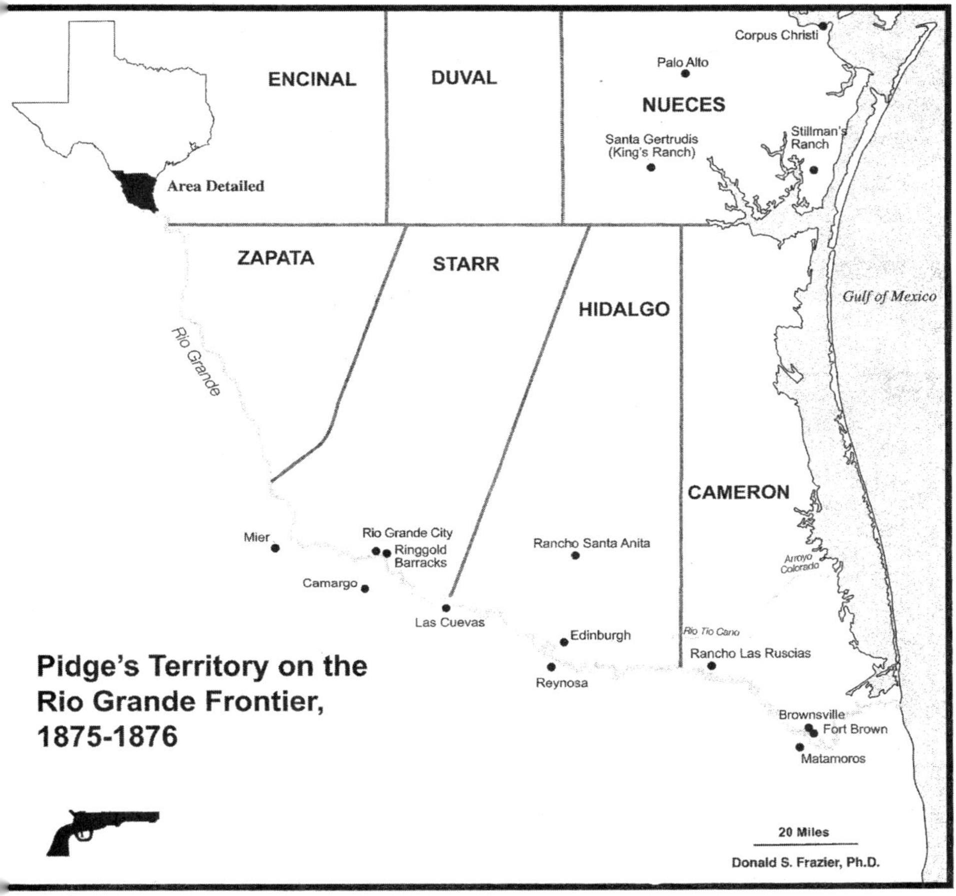

The Nueces Strip was contested ground between Texas ranchers and bandits from across the Rio Grande. Map by Donald S. Frazier.

ary 16 or 17. It is believed he did go to Austin, but whether his lieutenant accompanied him or remained in Clinton is not known. The lieutenant and some of the command may have remained in DeWitt County to determine if it was indeed proper for the company to leave the troubled area.

The captain was back in Clinton in March. On March 4 he wrote to General Steele that it was becoming more and more difficult for merchants to accept warrants because of the uncertainty of the length of stay of the company there. But his letter ended with an optimistic "All quiet."

Even though McNelly may have felt confident about the situation he

John Elliott edited the *Daily State Gazette*, which published Pidge's letters from the Rio Grande frontier. Courtesy the Austin–Travis County Collection.

was leaving in DeWitt County, some felt quite differently. In the *San Antonio Daily Express* of March 26 appeared a negative report. "Frontier Protection Falls Through" was the headline of the article:

> The State Troops, organized with such a flourish at the beginning of Coke's reign, are to be withdrawn soon and disbanded. The Legislature gets the credit of doing it, because they failed to make the requisite appropriation to keep these troops in the field.
>
> During the winter there was little use for these troops on the frontier, and Coke used them as a kind of State Police force to regulate some of his unruly partisans in DeWitt county and elsewhere.

Whatever inactivity the Washington County Volunteer Militia Company experienced during the winter was to be made up for on the border. San Antonio's *Daily Express* kept its readers well informed of McNelly's activities, eager to find opportunities to use these as a vehicle to condemn Coke.

The company reorganized on April 1, 1875, and started for the Rio Grande frontier on April 10. The *Daily Express* of April 24 reported that the company had arrived at Corpus Christi. In this tense situation

McNelly found not only Mexican raiders but armed groups of Americans as well, eager to take the law into their own hands. There was considerable fear on the part of many Americans as on March 26, a mere month prior to McNelly's arrival, a band of raiders had attacked settlements only a few miles from Corpus Christi itself. One of McNelly's first moves was to publish an order that all armed groups of civilians, unless in company of an officer of the law, would have to disband or else be treated as outlaws. The *Daily Express* complained that McNelly issued his orders like an emperor, and that tone is certainly evident. The order was headlined "The McNelly Pronunciemento," first published in the Corpus Christi newspaper and then in other area newspapers.

> HEADQUARTERS CO. A. VOL. MILITIA
> GORILLAS RANCH, APRIL 27
> Special Order, No.—In consequence of the most recent outrages committed in this portion of the country by armed bands of men acting without authority of law, I find it necessary to notify all such organizations that after the publication of this order I will arrest all such bands and turn them over to the civil authorities of the counties where they are arrested, and nothing but the actual presence of some duly accredited officer of the country or State will protect them from arrest.
> L. H. McNELLY
> Capt. Co. A., Vol. Militia

This was also printed in the *Daily Express* of May 8, with the following editorial comment:

> This is an extra-ordinary proclamation emanating from a Captain of a Corporal's guard sent by the so-called Governor of the State to the Rio Grande to extinguish the Mexican raiders. It seems to be directed, not against the Mexicans, but against the Americans, who are characterized as "armed bodies of men acting without authority of law." He also threatens to arrest the offenders if found with arms in their hands. Does this mean that the volunteer citizen companies have been burning ranches and killing Mexicans, just in the way of retaliation[?]
>
> This high handed way of ordering citizens to disband by a Captain of Police, exceeds anything that ever happened under the Davis police; martial law had some semblance of authority, but McNelly

issues his orders like an Emperor. And it is all right with the Democracy, nobody is hurt in their feelings, no one's liberties invaded, no protests, no indignation meetings, no hanging of harps upon the willows, no lamentations.

Just how tense a situation the Rio Grande was can be appreciated by the frequent newspaper reports detailing violence. For example, a certain Mr. Swearingen of Live Oak County on April 29, 1875, gave the *Express* a "detailed account of the ravages on the Rio Grande border." He reported great excitement and alarm prevailing over the area and that armed bodies of Mexicans were crossing the river to raid. It was reported that at least one hundred Mexicans had been killed by the raiders themselves as well as by revenge-seeking Americans.

A Dr. Fell, described as "an extensive ranchman of north-eastern Texas," in the *Express* of May 3, only six days after McNelly's "pronunciemento," estimated that there were three thousand Mexican bandits crossing over the river in parties numbering from fifty to two hundred. He reported it was the intent of the Mexicans that "no American shall live between the Nueces and the Rio Grande." It was the common belief that the controlling force behind the raiders was Juan Nepomuceno Cortina.

As if to show the young and relatively inexperienced ranger company that the violence it had entered into was of a much more serious nature than that of DeWitt County, the raiders shed additional blood on May 13, the day prior to McNelly's arrival at Edinburg. A Reynosa citizen named Treviño, apparently singlehandedly, cornered three of Cortina's raiders. In the ensuing gunfight one was killed, one wounded, and the other taken to Reynosa a prisoner. In a display of strength Cortina gathered 135 men and demanded the release of the prisoner. His demand was refused, and in retribution Treviño was shot and the Reynosa *alcalde* (or mayor) was hanged.

Cortina was born in 1824 in Camargo, Tamaulipas, the son of an unpretentious *ranchero* and an heiress to great Spanish land grants surrounding Brownsville. He grew up uneducated and illiterate but possessed a great natural ability to lead. During the Mexican war in the 1840s he served in the forces of Gen. Mariano Arista, who opposed General Taylor at the battles of Palo Alto and Resaca de la Palma in May, 1846. In 1875 Cortina's raiders would engage McNelly's Rangers on the old battle field of Palo Alto.

Juan Nepomuceno Cortina, raider, general, governor, and patriot; Texans considered him the head of a large group of raiders who pillaged ranches on the Texas side of the Rio Grande for many years. Courtesy the Robert G. McCubbin Collection.

After the Mexican war Cortina gathered a great following and was leader of these raiders until the middle 1870s. For years he raided in and controlled the Brownsville area, flying the Mexican flag on United States soil. Not until 1859 were U.S. forces able to force him back across the Rio Grande.

In his report to Governor Richard Coke, dated August 31, 1875, Adj. Gen. William Steele had this to say about the influence Cortina held:

> Cortina is the recognized head and protector of all the cattle thieves and murderers, from Camargo to the mouth of the Rio Grande. He takes them from the hands of any officer who is bold enough to arrest them; they, in turn, support him against all powers that may be brought against him. It is impossible to conceive, without having heard from many and undeniable sources on both sides of the line of Mexico and Texas, of the extent of the power of this great robber chief. It is a well known fact, that not only Cortina himself, but even his mistress, gives orders to judges, as to their decisions in cases, either civil or criminal, and such orders are obeyed. His armed adherents are said to number over two thousand. He has around him most of the time seventy or eighty of his trusted men. The police of Matamoras, of which city he is mayor, is composed entirely of ruffians, ready at any moment to commit murder or any other crime, at his bidding.[1]

General E. O. C. Ord pressed his investigation into Cortina's depredations to the extent that the Mexican government took Cortina into custody in July, 1875. He never again regained power in Mexico. He died on October 30, 1894, and was buried in Mexico City with full military honors.

McNelly and his company were stationed ten miles from Edinburg. On May 14 he wrote to General Steele of his initial impressions. He had met with Ranger Neal Coldwell, captain of Company F of the Frontier Battalion, and suggested that Coldwell had not been successful fighting the raiders as he was "disinclined to take chances in crossing the river." The act of crossing the boundary was against international law. This statement by McNelly prefigured events that would follow in November. McNelly concluded his report: "Cant Say anything yet about the condition of affairs here. everyone Says that the stealing is going on constantly but Capt Coulwell [*sic*] seems to think most of the reports are false. Will write you in a few days a full report of marches & information received & its credabillty [*sic*]."

In mid-May McNelly was at Brownsville gathering information regarding the movement of thieves. It is assumed that Lieutenant Robinson was in charge of the company during McNelly's absence. McNelly reported that he had "received information on the crossing of three droves of stolen cattle within the last week. Stealing horses, cattle and oxen is going on from Ringgold to Fort Brown."[2]

The stealing from Texas ranchers was done in complete contempt of the law because of the strength of the raiders and the fact that the Rio Grande provided a natural boundary line that American authorities could not legally cross. No attempt was made at secrecy as it apparently was common knowledge when raids were expected and how many beeves were contracted for by Cortina. The following item came from Brownsville on May 31, while Captain McNelly was conferring with General Steele at Corpus Christi:

"There is a man here purchasing beeves for the Cuban market. He is to get two thousand from Cortina. A vessel is lying off to transport them. American stock are being driven back from the Rio Grande on the Mexican side." A Brownsville report of June 4 reported the reaction of the people: "The appearance of the State Troops on the Rio Grande has produced great excitement among the people on the Mexican side. The residents of the ranches above Matamoras have organized to resist invasion. They have sentinels at the crossings of the river and the roads. In some ranches the women and children do not sleep in the houses at night. The cattle drovers are much alarmed."[3]

McNelly sent out scouts in groups of four or five to gather information on possible raids. This action finally brought about an engagement with the raiders that brought permanent fame to McNelly's men, now known as the Special Force, as it resulted in the destruction of a group of raiders who were highly esteemed by Cortina himself. There are conflicting reports as to exactly how McNelly learned when and where to strike the raiding party. Brig. Gen. Edward O. C. Ord stated in his official report of September 10: "The success of Captain McNally [*sic*] of the State Troops, in striking the party of Cortina's men in possession of a stolen herd recently, was due to his accidentally capturing two straggling robbers, who, by the use of the only effectual means known in such cases, but not legitimate enough for regulars to apply, were compelled to betray the position and strength of their band." McNelly did make excellent use of Mexican spies within the raiding parties, paying them an amount dependant on the results of their acts of betrayal.[4]

McNelly reported that on June 8 Lieutenant Robinson and eighteen other rangers had captured a raider named Rafael Salinas. From the prisoner it was learned that a raiding party of sixteen men under the command of Camillo Lerma and José María Olguine were under Cortina's orders to gather cattle from the La Parra area. On June 11 another raider was captured, Incosnascion García, whose story agreed with that of Salinas. The raiders had three hundred head of cattle in their possession and intended to cross the Arroyo Colorado the night of June 11 and to drive on to the Rio Grande the following day. Although the manner of learning the whereabouts of the raiders may be argued, they were sighted by the Ranger force on June 12 and were almost annihilated in a gun battle fought on horseback and on foot, covering many miles. Only one ranger lost his life, the youngest of the command, L. B. "Berry" Smith. Smith remained the youngest Texas Ranger ever to die in the line of duty. L. B. Wright achieved some recognition as a fighting man when with a single shot he killed two raiders mounted on one horse.

A report of the battle appeared in the Brownsville newspaper on June 12:

> To-day [McNelly] made a forced march of twenty-five miles. The raiders saw they would be overtaken, and drew up on the bank of a wide slough and opened fire. McNelly moved at a trot, and ordered his men not to fire. The raiders ran when he was within a hundred yards of them. He pursued, and succeeded in flanking them with three men. They halted and fought desperately. McNelly's horses were jaded, and but seven men were able to get into the fight. All the raiders, twelve in number, were killed. Berry Smith rushed in the midst of them and was shot by their leader, Camalo [*sic*] Lerma. The rangers had but two horses killed and two wounded. They took 250 beeves, most of them Captain King's. The fight occurred twelve miles from Town.
>
> Captain McNelly arrived this evening with the body of Smith, which will be buried at the expense of the city. The beeves will soon be here.
>
> The heartfelt thanks of a bleeding and suffering people are due Captain McNelly and his brave boys. Three times three for our gallant rangers.

There are a number of accounts of this battle on the Palo Alto Prairie written by men who participated. George Durham and William Calli-

Capt. Richard King suffered frequent losses to the raiders from the south side of the Rio Grande. His influence caused Gov. Richard Coke to send Captain McNelly to the Nueces Strip, with Pidge as his lieutenant. Courtesy the Texas State Archives.

cott both left important accounts of the action, although written years later. Contemporary accounts are sparse. Callicott wrote of the battle and Robinson's participation as follows:

> [The raiders] then broke out in full speed across the Palo Walto [*sic*] prairie towards the Rio Grande River. Lieutenant Robinson and us behind them and Captain and old Casuse [Jesus Sandoval] and his men on the side till they got past the timber. Lieutenant Robinson

> had 14 of us with him. He had got close to them always running in line of battle in case they should turn to the left or scatter in any direction. We had them straight ahead of us headed towards the Rio Grande River with not a trace in sight, only now and then a little bunch of Spanish daggers. When we got within one hundred or 150 yards of them Lieutenant Robinson shouted out to go for them, boys, go for them. Every man slapped spurs to his horse giving him all the speed he had. I rammed both spurs to Old Ball at once opening up his throttle [;] he made such an unexpected lunge that he jumped from under my hat and come near going from under me. We soon got up with them and then the battle opened up right. As fast as we overhauled one we would shoot him, killing him or his horse.

McNelly and company arrived in Brownsville later that day. His report to Governor Coke included the following paragraph: "This morning I came up with a band of twelve raiders. They attacked me when I over took them. It was a running fight. After that I got seven of them engaged and killed all. They fought desperately. I lost one man, Benj. Smith, and two horses killed and two wounded. I captured 250 beeves. To-night I go for another party. Men all trumps."

Unfortunately McNelly was unable to lead his men after the second party as his horses could not recover in time. The leader of the second group of raiders was identified as Ricardo Flores, who would later be mentioned in a letter written by Pidge and published in the *Gazette*.

On the same day Brownsville City Marshal Joseph P. O'Shaughnessy, with a detachment of U.S. Cavalry, searched the Palo Alto Prairie to recover the bodies of the slain raiders.[5] In an affidavit sworn on June 16 before Judge F. J. Parker, clerk of the U.S. District Court, he indicated that although only eight bodies had been found, he knew there were others.

On June 16 Pvt. L. B. Smith was buried. A Brownsville reporter described the funeral in a special to the *Galveston Daily News* dated June 14: "There was a large funeral procession—citizens and soldiers turning out. Col. Merriam, of the regular army, and Col. [John S. "Rip"] Ford were marshals. He received a military burial, and was honored by citizens and soldiers." Curiously, Pidge made no mention of the burial or of the Palo Alto Prairie fight in any of his writings. William Callicott recalled the funeral vividly:

> The next morning bright and early we all started for Brownsville to attend the funeral of our dead Ranger boy. The funeral was to take

> place at 3 P.M. We got there early in the morning. . . . It was getting to be about 12 o'clock A.M. The Captain told Lieutenant Robinson to take charge of us and to remain at the [Richard] King house until time to go to the undertaker's department, and to leave our horses there and to attend the funeral on foot, and that he would have to attend it with his wife and son, Rebel, who had come all the way from Washington County, his old home, to see him, and that he wanted to be with them as much as possible.[6] He told the Lieutenant to keep us from scattering over the town, that he didn't want him to touch a drop of anything to drink, or us either. Said that if we did it would spoil the whole thing, and said for him to go to the undertaker's where everything would be in shape by half past three P.M.
>
> According to orders Lieutenant Robinson and old Casuse Sandaval [*sic*], our Mexican Ranger that wanted to show all Mexicans that might be over on this side to view the dead bandits that he had got a few of them. At half past three P.M. Lieutenant Robinson and old Casuse and the balance of us marched up to the undertaker's where we found the hearse ready with two big fine black horses hitched to it, two U.S. bands of music, 2 companies of U.S. Regulars to march in with us to the cemetery. We marched by a church and took him in and had his funeral preached. We then marched to a cemetary [*sic*] that was but a little distance off. There people had gathered from far and near to see the last of our 18 year old Ranger boy laid to rest in the northwest corner of the Brownsville Cemetary, July [*sic*, June] 13, 1875. The U.S. Regulars fired the farewell shot over his grave and today our 18 year old Ranger boy sleeps in an unknown grave on the Texas bank of the Rio Grande.

According to Callicott the following participated in the battle: Captain McNelly, Lieutenant Robinson, Spencer J. Adams, John B. Armstrong, William Callicott, George Durham, Horace Mabin, R. P. Orrell, William Rudd, Jesus Sandoval, L. B. Smith and Smith's father, Thomas Sullivan, Lawrence B. Wright, and Linton L. Wright.

The following day McNelly telegraphed this report to General Steele, revealing his good feelings over his success: "Had a fight with raiders, killed twelve and captured two hundred and sixty five beeves. Wish you were here." In his September 30 report McNelly corrected the death count, saying that fifteen raiders had been killed and one wounded. He also reported that in July he had recaptured three hundred head of cattle

William Crump Callicott joined McNelly's Ranger force and was with him in the battle on the Palo Alto Prairie as well as during the invasion of Mexico. This is how McNelly's Rangers appeared: a belt full of cartridges, swivel with Sharp's carbine, and knife. Courtesy the Walter Prescott Webb Collection, Briscoe Center for American History, Austin.

and that in the three-month period of June, July, and August he had recaptured forty-three horses.

Robinson probably had additional paperwork in late July, as this brief item appeared in the Austin *Statesman* on July 28: "Capt. McNelly has received a reinforcement of twenty-six men—splendid looking scalp hunters."

Occasionally documents concerning the Special Force do provide us with knowledge of Robinson's activities and whereabouts. On August 4, Rangers E. A. Northington, C. W. Depriest, A. S. McKay, and C. W. Howery wrote out a statement of indebtedness acknowledging a debt in the sum of forty dollars each to Ranger Josiah Turner for horses purchased from him. This statement was written at El Baston and witnessed by Robinson and G. A. Hall.[7]

On August 5–12 McNelly and possibly Robinson as well were on a seven-day scout. Some of their activities are learned from this letter to Steele from Brownsville, dated August 13 and riddled with spelling errors:

> Had information three weeks ago of a contemplated raid from Comargo & the Cuavas, had spies with the thievs [.] Kept myself posted in all their movements. & in fact I know through my Spies all the general movements of the raiding parties on the other Side from Matamoris to Comargo, received a telegram on the morning of the 4" that they would cross at the Cuavos on the Sixth. I knew the point of meeting ("The Magotee of Don Jaun") & the time they were expected to arrive. I left camp after dark & traveled, by trails, all night (the 4") & the 5". laying in the brush during the days [.] reached a point of timber twelve miles from the Magotee of Don Jaun on the morning of the 6" & remained there until the night of the eleventh when I learned from one of my spies the reason they had not come over. . . .
>
> There has been no determined attempts at driving off cattle Since you were here & no crossing below my camp. the mexicans wont *ride* across Palo Alto Prairie after dark. most all the leading Spirits have gone up to Comargo & above, three crossings were made above Edinburo one July 20 one 22nd & one on the 27" small parties & but one got back with cattel & they crossed near "Rancho Davis." . . . If this party that has been making So much preperations to cross fail

> & backs out there will be no further use for my company down here. I have Kept up such an active System of scouting that they are continualy reporting my company in four or five different places at the same time & these theives have become disgusted with the country & are moving up the river.

The next known activity of the company took place in September when it was en route for Laredo. McNelly telegraphed Steele that it was "very necessary" that he go to Brenham at once, reason not provided. Lieutenant Robinson was left in charge of the company.

The preceding summary accounts for some of the activities of McNelly's company on the border. During this time it must be assumed that Pidge's mind was at work on his creative endeavors as well as on being a fighting Ranger. Nothing had been published since the letter from DeWitt County appearing in the *Statesman* of December 9, 1874. The first printed work from the border was a poem titled "Rio Grande—1875." One other poem would come from the border region, "Hynes Store—Santa Maria—1868." Besides these two poems, five letters were also printed, all dealing with the situation on the border. They provide a valuable record of McNelly's—and Robinson's—experiences on the Rio Grande frontier, including the Texas Ranger invasion of Mexico.

Daily State Gazette, October 3, 1875

RIO GRANDE—1875

By night he sought the ranger's camp.
Admitted by the sentinel—
"Pass weary stranger—all is well:
Go in, the midnight dew is damp."

Beneath the canvass well he stood,
That ancient man so stern and gray:
"Stranger, when I have said my say
You'll learn that aye avenged is blood.

"The pallid ghost of one I slew,
In former years, has followed me
Around the world, by land, by sea—
The sun itself was not more true.

"O'er Afric's sand, through desert waste,
I bent my steps—'twas with me still;
Through Polar's snows, Siberian blasts—
The form of him I could not kill.

"Four days ago I looked upon
The Rio Bravo, rolling wide,
And for the last time by my side
Appeared the shade, with hollow groan:

"Live here in peace; henceforth thou'rt free:
Thy suffering's o'er, thy penance done.

"I've driven thee from many a land,
Have followed fast and followed well,
But I had rather live in h—ll
Than anchor on the Rio Grande."
"PIDGE"[8]

Daily State Gazette, October 16, 1875

RIO GRANDE FRONTIER

September 20, 1875

Editor State Gazette:

I would have written you long before now, but we have kept so constantly on the move that it was impossible. We have rode by day and by night over this whole country, and there is not a ranche, no Mexican or American in four counties who does not know every man in this company as well as he does his own brother. If we did not keep constantly on the move, we would soon be a broken community, for the Mexicans seem to regard us as their own property, to be cheated, robbed and extorted upon generally, to the fullest. The day you arrive they sell you beef for two cents; next day it has *riz* to four cents; next day to eight, and then we sound boots and saddles and leave for some other point where the process is certainly to be repeated. One rooster who resides on the road to Rancho Davis wished to charge fifty cents per head for company horses occupying a corral for two hours, hardly large enough for them all to stand in; this was a case in which it was thought that P—'s knowledge of profane history would be of more service than any argument, so he was told to converse with the ranchero in his native tongue.[9] "I know very little of *his native tongue,* but I will do my level best; no man can do more." "Well heave ahead P—; be smart, we've a long ride before us." The boys fell back out of range, for they knew that the air in P—'s vicinity would soon be too thick to breath[e] with comfort, and then commenced a scene which would have filled the stoutest heart with horror: *"Caramba!* you charge too mucho; *Carago! V es una ladrone. Per todos los santos!"* I can't work this foreign piece any longer," said P—; "I'll have to open on him from my own battery. You d—d punkin-colored descendant of a Falstalan traitor, you wretched representative of a revolutionary and turbulent race of perambulating pepper pods why—your heart is black as your *frijoles*—your conscience as stretchy as your *tortillas;* to charge us a dollar *and* a half per cubic foot for the air breathed by our horses, and no oxygen, to speak of, in it, at that?[10] Have N—sound the assembly, I can't do this subject justice; if it was any common rascality I could expatiate on it, but this gets away with me; fall in line, *muchachos;* he says we rented it for the day, and we'll just carry the little corral along with us; each man take a post and fill his saddle-pockets with dirt, and we can easily move it; I'll serve you out, d—n your Mexican eyes!" bawled old P—, as he laid hold of a post and caused the picket fence to tremble.[11] This brought the Aztec to his senses, and a compromise was effected. *"Quiedado,* my dirt-colored rooster!" said P— as the column went by, "you live in a community whose reputation for honesty is as low as that of the Canal Ring, or the Indian-Ring, or the Whiskey Ring; so look out, my ring-tailed roarer, that the ring of a carbine doesn't ring you into eternity; for, by the jumping John Rogers, if we catch you in the cattle business, you'll be willing and glad to pay any price for air of any kind."[12] This is only a speciman. I do not suppose that people in the interior have the smallest conception of the difficulties experienced by a detached command in such a country as this, or how (when off the river line) entirely isolated from all creation [as] we are; life is a perfect blank; news of any kind, except of raiding movements, is a thing unknown to us; we accidently heard of the death of President Johnson six weeks after it was published in the newspapers.[13] The only nice time we ever had was during the Beecher trial; we missed *that* infliction, and it is the only good fortune we have experienced since we left.[14]

Scouting duty is very arduous and we have lately returned from one in which some fun was *very* confidently anticipated, but disappointment awaited us; information which was considered perfectly reliable was received that a party of raiders would be at a certain place, at a certain hour, on a certain day, *certain;* in order to not disturb the congregation by arriving fashionable late, we repaired thither two days before the appointed hour on that miserable time! We laid in the hot sun two days without food, and getting water by stealth, at night, from a well five miles distant; at last word was received from our Mexican scout that they were near by, forty strong; then "there was mounting in hot haste," and the captain made the men a speech, very short and sweet, and we started in columns of fours across a desert of sand; as we swept on in a plunging trot, a warlike soul in the rear of the column, waved his six-shooter above his head, informed me confidentially that he was a "whizzer from Bitter Creek," and asked permission to go to the front; I told him I had no doubt of his having formerly resided on that classic stream, nor of his having been an ornament to its bank; but it was necessary for the preservation of a strictly A No. 1 formation that we should keep his present position until the command wheeled into line, when he would have the opportunity so ardently longed for of "whizzing" to the devil if he did not keep a sharp lookout.[15] Far off, by the aid of the glasses, we could see our Aztec Arabs wheeling and galloping in every direction; one is seen coming in a full run directly toward us; "close up—gallop—march" is the order; pistols are in their holsters, and carbines taken from their slings; Capt. M—s face is flushed with the joy of battle; all is ready, and we look for the bugle notes to ring out short and sharp in the charge, but alas for the "whizzer!" It is a message of peace that is brought by the scout. The Forty Thieves are discovered to be a party of Capt. King's *vaqueros,* and "slowly and sadly we all marched back;" all, except your correspondent, were deeply disappointed; to me it was glad tidings of exceeding great joy, but they all seemed *so very* much put out about it that I thought it would appear strange if I did not do something so I raved and frothed at the mouth like a first-class maniac.[16] But the "whizzer"—ye gods the "whizzer!"—he was a picture; all that good courage had to be thrown away, and like Bob Acres his soul was filled with grief on account of it; his lamentations were loud; he had been absolutely thirsting for Mexican blood and was inconsolable under the last great affliction; "drive a bullet through a heart torn with anguish," said he, "and end a miserable existance [*sic*] which has experienced nothing but ill fortune," striking an attitude and opening his vest; "git on your horse, you d—d fool," said old P—; "a Mexican boy with a quirt would tone you down *mighty* quick." *"Esta hombre es muy valiente,"* said Sandoval, our Mexican guide.[17] "You're right," explained P—, "bad ones come from here; it's the h—l-teariness place in the State of Texas." *"Si Senor!"* Betare Creek! he must be *une* lettle *rincon chiquita* of h—l herself." "It is, *mi amigo;* yet if yer take the denizens of that bunch on the squar, they won't fight a crippled chinch." The "whizzer" left soon afterwards, carrying off a carbine and pistol belonging to the State, and Bitter creek stock is below par in the company. Jesus Sandoval is a trump—a perfect Chesterfield in politeness; he puts us to shame by the elegance of his manners; as to the number of robbers he has put "up a tree," their name is legion: scrupulously polite in every day intercourse, his urbanity on these extraordinary occasions is boundless.[18] Beau Brummel would have blushed with shame and hid his diminished head, could he have witnessed Sandoval officiating at a "tucking up;" the comfort and convenience of his *amigos,* as he calls them, is his sole thought; not a word which could jar their feelings, not the slightest reproach, not a single allusion as to their method of raising the wind, is allowed when he is acting as master of ceremonies; their own mothers could not be more tender; their own children no more respectful; his countenance is illustrated with a heavenly peace as he "works them off," and he is *so* kind and *so* considerate that it is almost a pleasure to be hanged by such a nice gentleman.[19] Cortina, before his arrest, would have given his right arm to have caught Sandoval on the Mexican side of the Rio Brave [*sic*], and even now it is as much as his life is worth if he should be seen in Matamoras; he is very popular with the Americans on the river, and Squire Joe Hynes is his particular friend; they may be partners perhaps, for the first thing that greets ones eyes on entering Hynes' premises is three or four second handed coffins piled up along-side a miscellaneous mass of old cart wheels, plows, cotton and hay pressers, broken buggies and the smashed and battered timbers of an old wrecked steamboat.[20] The American flag flaps defiantly over Joe and his plunder, and when I told him that he ought to take his coffins out of the weather, he replied, "well, there is no telling at what moment they may be needed, perhaps in the night, and they can open the gate and get one without disturbing me; keep 'em just for the accomodation [*sic*] of my neighbors; don't make a cent on one." "But they'll warp Squire and be in a dilapidated condition." "Well, you may just bet your soul's salvation that they will be in any more of a dilapidated condition than the men who fill them. I tell you my innocent June-bug, that a natural death was never died on this river, and a fellow's in huge luck if his fragments are not gathered up in a hamper-basket and transported in a sack on the back of a Mexican *burro.* I have not seen the Squire for some time, the command having lately moved in the vicinity of Edinburgh.[21] There are strong rumors that Don Pedro Martinez, General Trevino, Nuevo Leon and Canales, Governor of Tamaulipas have "pronounced" against the general government, but nothing definite can be obtained.[22] The 9th cavalry (colored) are enroute to New Mexico; the 8th (white) will take their place at the military posts on the river and at Fort Brown.[23] The Rio Grande has been on a huge bender but is now within its banks; however it is always a huge "bender."[24]

More anon,
PIDGE

Daily State Gazette, November 6, 1875

RANCHE "LOS BURROS"

H'dalgo [Hidalgo] Co., Texas, Oct. 1875

Editor State Gazette:

Translated, the above means "Ranche of the Asses"; it was quite appropriate too were one to witness the scene which I beheld therein this morning; I had read of such superstition among Eastern half-civilized natives, but never dreamed of seeing among the citizens of Uncle Sam, even the Mexicans. Two of the men visited the ranche on some errand, and had not been in camp after their return more than fifteen minutes, when a *vaquero* arrived "bloody with spurring, and fiery red with speed."[25] After the interpretation, a work of some hours, I learned that one of the two had "cast an evil eye" on an infant at the Ranche, and they wanted him; some considerable time elapsed before any one knew what this meant, 'till some body suggested that it was a superstition of the Aztecs.[26] Then H. and W. were told what they had done to the young Montezuma the hope and pride of the family; it was a rich scene; the interpreter translating literally told W. that the Mexican said he had "put an eye on the child."[27] "Why you lying thief, I never touched the child!" "H. did it then." "I never" said H. "I never put my hand on the dirty brat, nor wouldn't for a months pay, and if he says so I'll put a *head on him.*[28] Punkin-colored prevaricator depart: depart with muchas speedas; leave the camp; cut sticks; in your lingo, vamouse! We never touched the yaller cub, and I can prove it." At this juncture there appeared on the scene a young man who had read Byron, and looking on W—, exclaimed: "I knew him by the evil eye; that aids his envious treachery."[29] Then W— understood and buckling on his pistol, said he: "There is no telling what the dodblasted fools will do in such a lay-out as this appears to be;" told Mexicano he was at his service. F— went along also and I attended through curiosity. Arrived, we found about two dozen women crying and wringing hands over an infant, which as F— said appeared to be "pretty d—d sick." W— and F— were told that it was impossible to ascertain which of them had cast the evil eye, and they would both have to take a swallow of water in their mouths and inject it into that of the child. W— did so; no perceptible change in the condition of the infant. Then F— rose in his majesty: "Let me get a squirt at him; I think I can fix him if there's any virtue in this water cure." Filling his mouth as full as it would hold F— approached the bed-side—about seven feet high and his cheeks distended till they appeared like toy baloons [*sic*]—placed his mouth to the infants, and then the fountains of the great deep seemed to have broken loose; the woman gave a scream of terror; all who were near said afterward's that A—'s mouth must have contained at least three quarts [F— here becomes A— and remains so throughout]. The house was flooded; the wretched baby gave one feeble gasp, a shiver, and then I thought he had gone to a country where evil eyes are unknown. The women "were too much horrified to speak, and could only shriek, shriek," while in their midst stood A—, smiling benignantly, and asking them "if it was enough."[30] It was more than enough; they look on A— now as a phenomenon, and wonder how one mouth could hold the water with which he deluged the building; the boys tell A— that with his glorious mouth and an evil eye to back it, he can capture Mexico single-handed, and be an emporor [*sic*] if he chooses. The Senor General Juan Nepomucino Cortina is expected soon in Matamoras when we will have some fun, I reckon, for his henchmen will flock to him like vultures to the slaughter. They are scattered at present, and only come over in small parties; some *rancheros* cap [tured] three last week, and through fear or because they did not want to be troubled with them, allowing them to go free.

I have been out here six months, and I say it with pride, know a dozen words of the language. At this rate I will speak it well enough for business purposes in about four hundred years. Oh! if I was only as apt as a Mexican gentleman I saw not long since, while on the road to Fort Brown. He was quick at learning a language. He learned English thoroughly—orthography, etymology, syntax and prosidy [*sic*]—all in three fourths of a second, and the way it happened was thusly: Capt. McNelly and I saw him at the door of a ranch, and though the Captain knew him from description, and knew he could talk English, I did not; so we came up to him; "Talk English." *"No intende Englesha, Senor!"* "Not a word?" 'No *Senor.*" "He can't understand us," said the Captain, "and we might as well shoot him where he sits as to"—talk about celerity! We really did not have sufficient time in which to ask him if he liked the language, that he comprehended so well. "From the way he run, I think he knows our language, Captain." "From the manner in which that blouse stood out behind, I think he has some little knowledge of it," replied the Captain.

Has the Convention met yet?[31] Like poor Joe, we don't know nothing here, and have no earthly way to find out.

More anon,
"PIDGE"

Daily State Gazette, November 21, 1875

HYNES STORE—SANTA MARIA—1868

Rio Grande, November, 1875[32]

I.
He passed the gate, he entered in
Where Joe beneath his fig tree sat;
The Squire arose; he touched his hat.
With "Bill, are you for war agin.
With this here old Falstaff brigade
Of broken-kneed and spavited steeds?
Oh! William great must be your needs,
To start with these upon a raid."

II.
"Hast heard the news?" said William B.?
"Two hundred men are coming down,
And burning ranche and tower and town;
I go on a forced march, you see?"
And at these words a heavenly cast
Lit up Joe's honest countenance
He grasped Bill's hand, commenced a dance,
And yelled, "he's told the truth at last."

III.
"By *Gad,* he's told the truth at last;
A straight, unvarnished tale from him—
Lord! what a shock—mine eyes grow dim—
I faint—I fall—I'm going fast—
Yes, William B., the march is forced.
It couldn't well be otherwise;
Above your steeds the vulture flies—"
Here William ripped, and swore and cussed.

IV.
"I know *these* cannot make the trip,
But H— and I we gallop fast
And *cut them off;* these come at last—"
"Sebastian, bring me out a nip!
Peaceful I rest with slumbers soft."
Here Joe laid down and closed his eyes,
"So perish all our enemies!
Bold William rides to *cut them off.*"

V.
Bold William never heard the last
Of this bold ride, nor ever will;
'Tho years have flown, rancheros still
Enquire if Bill above has passed.
And little Greasers jeer and skoff
And wriggle fingers from the nose.
And point to Bill where 'er he goes,
And shout, *"he starts to cut 'em off."*
"PIDGE"

Daily State Gazette, January 19, 1876

CAMP TEXAS RANGERS

Laguna de los Calabaso,
Jan.15, 1876

Editor State Gazette:

I would have sent you an account of the invasion long, long ago, but was compelled by special orders to write out a *true* account of it, which has been awful straining to the mind; I am not accustomed to this, and have scarcely recovered from it yet; besides, I think I must have been sun struck in Mexico, or received some kind of shock; I have not felt well since; it may be the effect of the heavy dew on the river, but every time a shot is fired in my vicinity, a disagreeable chilly sensation starts with lightning speed from the back of my neck, and comes out at my boot heels.[33] Dew is awful heavy in Mexico; the two nights we were over there it was amply sufficient to have cast a damper even on a person's courage.[34] Orders were received from Capt. M— at 1 P.M. to ride rapidly to *Las Cuevas*. alias Robber's Roost.[35] We obeyed them to the letter; we rode rapidly; fifty-five miles in six hours, each man carrying one hundred rounds of ammunition. Had Mr. Micawber been a ranger, he would have seen in the countenances of the rancheros on the road that "something had turned up;" such a woe-begone looking lay out was never beheld; most of them are in sympathy with the raiders from the other side, and naturally supposed from the appearance of things that the waltz was drawing near its finale; in fact, that the jig was up, and they sorrowed sorely, like unto those who have no hope.[36] As we came into the main telegraph route, we could see where the detachment from the gallant Eighth had passed, and heard from the frightened rancheros that the fight was still progressing.[37] A little further, and swung to the tree in full view of the road, was a hideous object waving in the night breeze, fearful to look upon; the "boys" did not seem to mind it much, however, and while one quoted,

> "Of an outlawe this is the lawe,
> That men tayke him and binde;
> Without pitie, hanged to be,
> And waive with the wynde,"[38]

another, who had music in his soul, and a little mescal in his canteen, sung:

> "He sleeps his last sleep, he has stole his last cattle.
> No sound can awake him to plunder again."

Two more weary miles, and we came upon the United States Cavalry, pleasantly camped in the dusty road at the Rancho *Lomo Alto*, or High Hill. Capt. M.— was impatiently awaiting our arrivel [*sic*].[39] "Have the horses well groomed," said he; "they will go into the river at midnight; I suppose you have rations with you." "No, sir; but we have sixty rounds of carbine ammunition and forty of pistol—." "You certainly have brought bread?" "No, sir; but we have lots of car—." "No salt?" "None; but just dead loads of cartri—." "So I suppose the men have nothing but coffee in their haversacks?" "They haven't got that even, but they've got a hundred rounds of—." "Well, don't this beat the devil!" said [McNelly]; "there is nothing to eat this side of Ringgold Barracks, and you've come up here without even a grain of coffee; how do you expect to live when you get across?" "Don't expect to live long Captain, but in these two belts I have a hundred rounds of—." "Oh, go to h—ll with your cartridges." "Well," thought I, "that's just where you've ordered me to go." "Are your horses much fatigued?" "They've got plenty of metal on them if they haven't *in* them," I answered; "each saddle has strapped to it a hundred rounds of metallic—." "If you mention cartridges to me again," said the Captain, "I'll put you in arrest and leave you on this side of the river." I thought it would look too bad to *say* anything, but I handed him a box of Winchesters, with a mental prayer that he *would* put me in arrest. In single file and leading the horses, we gathered at the beautiful, the beautiful river and in silence commenced the embarkation; on each side of the crossing crouched the men, gun in hand, to protect the passage of the first boat; from below at another crossing echoed the sullen roar of the Springfields, where the regulars were making a feint, while we went over undiscovered; with a very little assistance I could have made a feint myself about that time. After crossing two horses and getting them through the quicksands, it was calculated that with the best of luck and no accident all of them could be safely landed on the Mexican bank by Christmas Eve. This mode was then abandoned and we left them, I for one with many misgivings that I should ever mount mine again. Captain M— had advised me, that as I was to come over in the last boat I might improve what few shining hours remained to me by leaving directions as to what disposition should be made of my personal effects. He seemed to take a malicious delight in causing me to feel as badly as possible. I was not very long in writing my will—simply directing that my effects should be packed in a cartridge box and sent to the Second Sergeant (then in hospital at Fort Brown), to be by them distributed among the poor.[40] I went down to the boat with a happy heart, and feeling like the widow of mite-y memory—if I had not set my house in order, it was because I had no house to set, and the cartridge box I knew to be just stuffed and crammed to bursting. "Heaven bless the poor people," thought I, "wont they have a [measure?]!" I reached the vessel that was destined to "waft me from the silent shore." Shade of Noah and Dollinger! what a tub to cross Jordan in! it kept four men busy bailing to keep the nose of the man who paddled above the water.[41] It only carried four; it might have carried more had there been room enough for them to bail, but there wasn't; the bow was as sharp as an Austin lawyer, and the stern as broad as a ship of the line; one could punch a hole through it anywhere with one's finger, and the bailers were compelled to be very particular to keep from bailing out what little bottom was left to the craft; the labor they performed was fearful, had one ceased bailing for a single second, the ship would have gone down in mid-ocean with all on board. The "boys" called her the "Sinking Fund," when I went on board she was full up to the gunwales; we bailed, and bailed, and bailed, but it was of no use; the water ran in as fast as we threw it out, and we were in a quandry [*sic*], when a brilliant idea and one only common to the mind of a man of genius, struck the boatman, who proposed hauling her out on the bank until the water ran out, then launching her quick, and all hands to the pumps immediately.[42] "Avast there! shouted R—, of Austin; "shiver my timbers! I've thought of a better plan; turn her over—bottom side upwards—wrong side out—put her on her beam ends, and by G—d we'll make the trip in single rank upon her keel; won't have to work our passage and keep equally as dry as we would a bailing; gracious goodness, what perils we poor Rangers encounter by land and sea."[43] The boatman thought this *una* notion *grande*, and after much blasphemy in Spanish, German and English, we arrived on the *alotra lado* in safety, without the knowledge of the bandits, who were all down on the crossing below, thinking that, if any, would be the point of attack. We laid upon our arms till the dawn of day, and then marched to Las Cuevas, said to be one mile distant; after we had walked about three, we concluded there must be a mistake somewhere, or that the town was marching too; a little further and we ran full upon the ranche Las Ancharvas, which we did not know was on the road, the Cacharassers popped it to us pretty lively for a while; Seven were killed and nine wounded we heard afterwards.[44]

Some of them were smoking cigarettes and looking on with *sang froid* while the others fought; they were a cool set sure; the old woman in the *jacale* did not stop pulling *tortillas*. We continued the march to the main town, but we made no *entree* there; the alarm had been given, and out from the houses poured the robbers by hundreds; in a strong *corral* immediately in our front two hundred men, well fortified, awaited our coming; beyond this was another full to overflowing, from every side they were pouring in on foot and on horseback, and estimates of their forces were made by "the boys," according to the view each had ranging from two hundred to twenty-seven thousand; to the right and outside of the fortifications, I caught a glimpse of a column of cavalry, in sets of fours, which seemed to me to stretch to Matamoras. When Capt. M— gave the order to fall back to the river, I was awfully fatigued, but I scorned to let this interfere with my duty, and stepped up with much alacrity; such fiendish yells I never heard, but I could see very little; where the smoke came from the guns it hung like a pall, and I was not sorry to leave, for it had a very offensive odor to me. Back to the river we went, and waited further developments. The infantry arm of the service did not appear to be a favorite with the men on the return, and many a fervent prayer went up in the style of Richard III.[45] Poor fellows! They knew not what was still before them. Pickets were put out, and all was quiet till I went out to visit them, when "the Americans came down, like the wolf on the fold," and I left on double time; could I have left on *treble time,* I would have had no hesitation in doing so; about thirty were close at the heels of little M— and I, shooting at every jump I knew they could not hit little M—, for he is no larger than a good sized carrot, but I thought it was a considerable distance to the river; on the Texas side were some of the Eighth Cavalry, and a Gatling gun, and just here I would like to remark that if there is an inanimate object in this whole world for which I have a pure and unadulterated veneration, respect and love, that object is a Gatling gun; if Mr. Gatling has a daughter I would marry her to-morrow, if she would have me, for the sake of her father—and the gun.[46] The Rangers, the Regulars and the Gatling opened on the Mexicans simultaneously, and they did not stay much longer than I did at the piqquet [*sic*] post; as they retired, we advanced, and ran them into the chapparal [*sic*] and were then reinforced, paradoxical as it may appear, by volunteers, from the regulars but they swam over in a much better ship than ours. I have a very faint recollection of what happened for the next three or four hours; worn out with hunger and thirst, and cold and heat, and riding and walking, and running and fighting, I tried to get a little sleep in a hole in the mud, but they bothered me so with the firing that I was in a state of semi-somnambulism, and knew no more than if I had been wide awake.

Then a flag of truce came down and informed us confidently that the party who ran in the piqquet and charged the Gatling gun and everything else, came down for the purpose of making peace; we were so much obliged to them for this information—we never would have known it otherwise. They brought a lengthy communication from the Agun—something or other at Camargo, and addressed to the "Commanding officer of the forces invading Mexico."[47] This Capt. M— refused to receive, as he only came over to receive property stolen from Texas, and if possible capture the robbers; all the time during the treaty they were concentrating forces in our front, but finally a cessation of hostilities was agreed upon till 9 o'clock next morning. We slept on our arms and legs too, that night, for he had heard of Mexican truces before. Next morning we threw up intrenchments [*sic*] and made a beautiful little fort, but it was terrible hard ground to dig. I heard one man say that he did not think anybody on earth could have been in so many different arms of the service in a brief space of time; he had a field glass in his hand and was watching the chapparal at the moment. "Since yesterday morning," said he, "I have belonged to the cavalry, the navy, the horse marines, the infantry, the [?] and [?], and now I'm in the signal corps. The United States troops had been ordered to the American shore the previous night and we were left alone in our glory; our ferry rope was hauled to the Texas side and I thought "the last link is broken that bound me to thee."[48] Texas never looked so charming to me before, said one of the men, "I will wager six months pay against a *tamale* that there is more love for Texas, more pure admiration for the State in this little band of Rangers than in all the rest of the citizens combined." "Who is in charge of the Gatling gun?" said I to the last one of the cavalry, as he started to the boat; "Sergeant O'Conner, sir," said he, touching his cap.[49] "Well, give my compliments to the sergeant, and tell them when they come, to try to turn his machine as fast as possible; that I would advise him to have plenty of assistants, as he might get tired or something, and above all things to point her high—give her plenty of elevation, for Heaven's sake; I had much rather stand in range of double-geared chain lightning, or an earthquake, or a first class volcano, or a tidal wave, than a machine that grinds out death and destruction at the rate of two hundred and forty shots per minute, and if he *should* [two lines illegible]. He promised to carry my directions and I returned to my hole under a bank. "We are going up the Great Spout now; a second Alamo, but not half so romantic in name; just fancy being killed at the *Rincon de Cucharras;* in plain English, the spoon corner.[50] "If Ben Butler commanded the party I could die happy," said a Ranger, who formerly lived in New Orleans.[51] "Gentlemen," said the first sergeant, limping forward with one boot on, "I do hate to start on my last long journey with such a sore heel; but the Lord's will be done. Alas," he remarked to me.[52] "Celestin will wait in vain for the wheels of our chariots."[53] Things *did* have quite an azure appearance about that time. At 10 A.M. the officers of the Aya—whatever-it-was, arrived, and the captain to prevent them from finding out what a forelorn [*sic*] hope we really were, hid us in the chapparal near, and went forth and talked to them as if he had as many men and ships as Xerxes.[54] When he called for the corporal's guard, half the company went forth. The Mexicans gazed at the chapparal thicket, and no doubt thought like Col. Sellers, "there's millions in it;" at last they agreed to deliver seventy-five of the stolen cattle at Camargo the following day, and then an escort was furnished them to the piqquet post; from there they bore off the body of Major Don Juan Flores Salinus [*sic*].[55] This was the rooster who led his battalion to the charge on the previous day, and who emptied his six-shooter at your correspondent in his laudable endeavors to preserve peaceful and friendly relations between Texas and the Mexican Republic. No one was more anxious for peace than I, and determined not to be outdone in a virtuous action by a greaser, even if he was a Major; I helped him to the best of my poor ability.

After the commissioners left, the U.S. people brought us down an elegant boat to come home in, and proudly I stepped upon her deck and bade adieu to a country in which I was not acquainted in the least, but whose inhabitants had vied with each other in giving, not me alone, but all my friends, a very warm reception. The Turkish bank of the Boryslines [*sic*] had no more charms for Mazeppa than the Texas shore of the Rio Grande for me.[56] I climbed the steep bank and horror of horrors! my little sweetheart Miss Gatling Gunne, had eloped with Sergeant O'Conner; being gone, they told me, six hours, and I fondly imagining she was there in her bewitching, coquetry to throw kisses across the river! I was glad I had no knowledge of her departure, for it would have broken my heart. I saw her afterwards in the camp of the regulars, but had no reproaches to give her. She never would have gone with the Sergeant had he not enticed her with four large American mules and orders from the general. I heard the only married man in the company wish for his mother-in-law: "Yes, fellers," said he, "I believe I could kiss her now." Next morning the Captain with ten men left for Ringgold Barracks to receive the stolen property, and was informed at the hour appointed that they were really so very busy with matters of the utmost importance they did not have time to attend to the affair that day, and to call again. He sent them word that "business was business," but he thought the present of about as much importance as any they could have, and wanted to know what they were going to do about it. Then the beeves were sent down, but they wanted assistance to cross them, and the ten Rangers went over for that purpose. Here a new difficulty arose; the Mexican Customhouse officers wanted a permit or they could not allow them to cross; this was, to say the least, sublimely cocky—appealingly so. They went over without any permit and it was *surmised* that they might return in the same manner. Capt. M— exhausted all arguments with these gentlemen, except one, which he reserved for the very last, and which, as a *dernier resorte* in this country, is considered "a clincher;" then he exhausted that; "Prepare to load with ball cartridges—load!"[57] The ominous "kerchack" of the carbine levers as the long, murderous looking cartridges were chambered home, satisfied them as to the permit and the cattle were allowed to cross over without one; such is the power of a fifty calibre argument, such the authority of Sharp on International law.[58]

Were there forces sufficient on the Rio Grande frontier to follow these murderous bandits to their secret haunts in Mexico, robbery would soon be too precarious a mode of gaining a livelihood; a few more such lessons as this one given them by Capt. M— would teach them that on their own side of the river they are not always *perfectly* safe, as they have heretofore considered themselves; they have been accustomed to yell and jeer across the river at citizens of Texas, whom they have despoiled of their property, and who stand upon the bank and look on huge herds of their own stock taken by the strong band and driven over their very eyes, impotent of any redress. Once over the river, and pursuit and inquiry is ended. Let the policy inaugurated at the Ranche *Cuevas* be followed on vigorously, and there will be some hope for Texas' citizens and some security for their property.

"PIDGE"

P.S.—You will see from the date of this letter that we are at *Laguna de la Calabuso;* this simmered down in English means "Pumpkin Lake." I have often thought that it was the language which causes these people to be so polite. A man who would ask *Senor Don Ricardo Flares,* whether or not he would take sugar in his'n, would kick plain Dick Flowers out of the office for bothering him during business hours.[59]

N.B.—We heard from a reliable source afterwards that in *Las Cuevas,* at the time of our attack, were six hundred men.

FROM OUR REGULAR RIO GRANDE CORRESPONDENT

Camp Texas Rangers,
Cameron County, March 4, 1876

Editor State Gazette[60]

It is stated in a late New York paper that if Gen. Porfirio Diaz had four dollars and twenty cents, he would start the most fearful revolution ever heard of on the border.[61] I understand that he has received the above amount and perhaps a little more, and the next telegrams will no doubt bring the clash of resounding arms; "clash of resounding arms," is about all that happens in a Mexican revolution. They yell, and bawl, and whoop and halloo, and fight day and night, for a week, and the list of killed, wounded and missing, is put on a postal card and forwarded to Department Headquarters, with the recommendation that the survivors of both factions be hung and the sender appointed military commander of the district. The authorities of Matamoras, however, are considerably alarmed, and the Commandante of the city came over the other day to see if he could enlist the sympathies of Fort Brown's commanding officer in his behalf, enough to stop the "doing" and let him draw his quarter's pay in peace with his fellow men; he met with no success and returned in much mental anxiety.

If Diaz should succeed, Cortina will be Governor of Tamaulipas, and then, in the language of the border, "things will be whooped up" on this side of the river; beef will decline in price in Matamoras, and hides will be a drag on the markets. There are a few Micaubers in Fort Brown who do not expect to wait much longer for something to "turn up." Don Porfirio, it is stated, will offer a bounty when he arrives on the *alotro lado;* an enterprising spirit will necessarily be compelled, in order to jump the bounty, to also jump the river. People out here have a small opinion of revolutions, generally speaking. The other day I was at Squire Joe Hynes, in the village of Santa Maria, when I heard the booming of artillery in Matamoras; much excited, I asked the Squire what it meant. "Oh," said he with a yawn, and lighting another cigar, "I suppose they've started their dam, little, old revolution; it's nothing, have 'em every month or two; here's hoping it may prove a Kilkenny cat contest, and the rest of the people will be better off.[62] When they are busy cutting one another's throats, they don't steal quite as much from the citizens of Texas; here's h—l to 'em—both sides—and a bloody war and a sickly season." The firing proved to be a heavy salute in honor of President Lerdo de Tejado, and the anniversary of his inauguration.[63] Notwithstanding the prevailing contempt on the border for a "dam, little, old revolution," the one in embryo at this time will no doubt assume a grave aspect. The interior is said to be ripe for a revolt, and the border is never otherwise; Diaz is reported to have able backers, and the present administration is seriously alarmed. Your correspondent saw a number of breech loading small arms in Brownsville with ammunition, etc., belonging to Don Porfirio; among them was the delectable Spencer rifle which Guadalupe Espinosa emptied at him on the historic field at Palo Alto.[64] Somebody belonging to Lerdo's army will strike for home when this piece opens on him if it causes him to feel as wretched as it did me; he will not stay long, even there, but will fly from his wife and blessed babes, if he has any, and "put" for the silver mines.

I wish that Captain Kells of the U.S.N. was here to see this war break loose, for he has a keen appreciation of such things, and enjoys them to the fullest extent.[65] The first time I ever saw the Captain was on board his ship, the Rio Bravo, when he entertained me with a description of the terrible storm experienced by the vessel while crossing the gulf from New Orleans.[66] "Do you see two guns on the forward deck?" "After my anchors were carried away while off Sabine Pass, I was compelled to fasten cables to those pieces and heave them overboard in order to save the ship from Davy Jones' locker."

"On what man-of-war were you stationed Captain, before you assumed command of the Bravo?" "Cannon, I cuss," he replied, looking intently at one of the guns.[67] "I would not have thought it of you Captain," said I, "especially after it has been the means of saving your vessel." The captain heaved a sigh, "come in the cabin," said he, "out of the sunshines; you might wilt out here on deck." He never replied to my inquiry, but I heard afterwards that he was appointed from the U.S. sloop-of-war Canonices, stationed at Pensacola. Every one was sorry when the Captain was ordered away; he was immensely very popular, possessed the happy faculty of squelching a bore and was a blessing to society. "Shall we annex the Zona Libra?" said one of those and afterward when Kells was preparing for a trip up the river; "I don't care what you do with it so I get my launch ready for Edinburg," was the reply.[68] It was on the same voyage that having tied up his boat for the night near a Mexican village, the inhabitants came down to see it and comment thereon. Have you *eggies?* said the captain. "*No senor. Chickies? No senor. Yo no intiende!*" Then Kells clapped his hands like a rooster does his wings and crow[ed] to let them know that he wanted "chickies." Supposing from this that he was ignorant of Spanish, they commenced telling each other how they could finish up the steam launch; they could riddle it with rifle balls; they could sink it with brick-bats; they could do anything and everything with it. Kells said nothing until they had finished, and then pulled tarpaulin from the Gatling gun; "Now," said he, "suppose you try that on a little; just a little; and by the tail of Jonah's whale, I'll make you think that h—ll has broke loose in Georgia! "*Caramba!*" "*Carago!*" "*Entiende Va bien el Hispaniola!*" "You *bet* I do; and I understand how to work that Gatling *tambien* and will be most happy to show you at any time." They had enough of this *gringo,* and went back somewhat crestfallen at being so taken in.

A great many fandangos are held in the large ranches along the river, and I have attended several. The dance is carried on in the open air around a pole, in the centre of which is a cross; every stationary article in the whole country has a cross on it, even down to the sugar mills. The dancing consists of all the modern dances—waltzes, redowns, polkas, and ([?]!) the old Virginia reel. I was so pleased to see the last that I took down the costumes of some of the senoritas present in my note book. "Senorita *Panchita R—* wore a be-autiful *sola* of black silk, *catines de ceda, tren—s* of black velvet; the *decollete* corsage was caught at intervals with long narrow *epingles;* there were several of them, perhaps more, and a large *aigrette* and *bouquet de corsage* of the same; her's was the most *recherche* toilet in the whole ranche. Senorita *Rosita C—* wore a *tunica de musilina (en train)* no ornaments to speak of. Effect mild, but delightful. Senorita *Concepcion V—* wore a *tunica* of white *fallie,* handsomely embroidered (there was about four inches space between the body and the skirt, but this was in perfect taste for the place was warm); *rebosa* of black gauze. Effect stunning and gorgeous. Senorita *Eugene S—* wore a *tunica* of cream-colored *ceda,* richly trimmed with gauze the same shade; [?] of gold, a magnificent [?] of the same metal, striped *medias,* tied with red [?] (she kicked rather high and I saw them); a *polon* [?] with extra stuffing in it and *rizas pos t—is.* Effect terrific. The gentlemen all wore shirts and six-shooters.

Now I will leave it to you as a man of honor, to say if any Jenkins that ever cursed a suffering world can beat the above?[69] I have received the congratulations of the command and they will back me for the championship of the world, and for any amount in State paper.

I saw from a late GAZETTE that Capt. McNelly would soon return; many thanks to you for the information.[70] We had heard nothing from him; the military chest was empty, credit down to zero, and in another week would have been compelled to invade Mexico or perish through starvation. We are at present encamped on the *Laguna de las Flores,* where if ticks do much abound, chegoes [*sic*] do more abound; a stranger coming into camp would think the whole command afflicted with St. Vitas' dance.

The robbers have lately transferred their attention to horses and have crossed a goodly number; it is only accidentally that one hears of these raids, and the Mexicans of the country will not give information until too late to accomplish anything; there are a few who would do so, but they are afraid.

Adios.

"PIDGE"

P.S. Have just this moment received a dispatch from Fort Brown conveying the intelligence that the "dam little old revolution" commenced yesterday. Col. Magill Pena with his command has taken Reynosa and Camargo.[71] He expects to capture Mier to-day. The national guard are under arms; troops are hurrying up the river; the customs collectors at Camargo have fled with their books and papers and money to this side of the river; the friends and adherents of Diaz are thickly swarming in Matamoras, which is quiet as yet, but on the eve of outbreak—the interior is in revolt, and it is expected that Pena, after capturing Mier, will move down on the "Heroic City," and will be joined by Diaz on the route.[72] No matter which side is successful, Texas will be the loser; the vanquished will fly to this side and stock will suffer hugely. No patriotic citizen can help joining Squire Hynes in his immortal toast—"Here's h—ll to 'em, both sides."

SECOND DISPATCH

N.B. A few were killed in Reynosa; three fourths of the Republic is said to have joined the *pronunciamento.*

P.

Daily State Gazette, March 19, 1876

FROM OUR REGULAR RIO GRANDE CORRESPONDENT

Camp Texas Rangers,
Laguna de los Flores,
Cameron Co., March 9, 1876

Editors Gazette:

Did you ever hear of *quien sabe?*[73] We have heard nothing else for a year; it is the everlasting and never failing response to all inquiries as to distance, routes, directions, forage, water, weather, state of the country, characters of the people, soil, climate and productions. A person who remains here six months will have the tiresome old phrase stereotyped on his brain until he seems to breathe a perfect atmosphere of *quien sabe.* Its literal translation is "who knows," and it is the general opinion of the whole population; description conveys but a faint idea of its comprehensiveness, the expressive gestures which accompany the *quien sabe* are dreadful to contemplate, especially when one has lost his way or is very hungry. When we receive recruits, they are always informed of what they will suffer from the *quien sabe,* and its nameless horrors are generally unfolded to them, otherwise they would desert the service or commit suicide. The third sergeant of the company is relieved from all duty, in order to prepare the new man for the terrible ordeal through which they are to pass. He drills them in what is termed "Instructions in the *quien sabe,*" and relieves it of some of its horrors by teaching the recruits retaliation on the Mexicans.

The men being formed in single rank, without carbines, the instructor commands: 1. *Squad.* 2. *Quien.* 3. *Sabe.* At the first command, carry the toes of both feet outward at an angle of 185 degrees; (two) bring the hands in front of the body as high as and opposite to the shoulders, fingers extended as wide as possible; (three) make a frightful grimace at the same time elevating the right shoulder and depressing the left; look as much like an idiot as possible. The recruits resume the position of the soldier at the remark, "what a lot of d—d fools!" The average interpreter in this country regards neither orders or entreties [*sic*] in the discharge of his official duties; these duties consist of holding a most interesting and highly diverting conversation with the Mexican addressed, regardless of time, place or circumstances; often and often at the forks of a road with which I was unacquainted, have I been edified with perhaps a dissertation on the aborigines or Central America, or a discussion as to the probable duration of the Cuban War; I have sat in my saddle and listened with a feeling of such utter helplessness, such entire wretchedness, mentally apologizing for ever being in existance [*sic*], utterly ignored by both ranchero and interpreter. I have wondered on those occasions whether I possess any rights which any human being was bound to respect; I have felt at these times as if I was of about as much importance as a newly born Mexican infant, or its blessed *madre*. Although the proposed route may be [?] or better, I [?] to guess at what is said or go on without the information, the average interpreter does not care; he looks with a lofty scorn on a person who cannot speak Spanish, and pities him, I have no doubt, he deserves it too. I did I am certain. If Job had been comforted in the Spanish language and had then employed a Rio Grande interpreter, the old gentleman who is supposed to reside down below, (and who, whatever else may be said against him, never deserts his friends in adversity) would have a much easier *job*, he would have had no trouble whatever.

Never shall I forget the time I was ordered with a detachment of twenty men to report to the sheriff of — county, and follow a marauding party; he spoke Spanish, his friends also spoke Spanish, several guides were along and they spoke Spanish. We were scarcely noticed at all by any of the party. Not a word was deigned us by anyone as to where we were going, or for what purpose; as meek as lambs to the slaughter we followed in rear; we would have as more dared to join the party then if we had been escorting the Emporer [*sic*] of all the Russians. We followed in their august wake for about forty miles, like little dogs after a cart, had marched eighty on the previous day and were not in the best humors. At last I called a halt; the advance guard were so entirely absorbed in Spanish conversation that they rode two miles before they were aware of the loss of their soldiers. We had dismounted and unsaddled before they returned. "Why did you stop?" said one. "Oh," said I, "from the appearance of different things, I have become convinced that he is not in this section of the country." "Hello—where." "I do not know—anybody—Sir John Franklin or Dr. Livingstone, or Charly [*sic*] Ross, or Boss Tweed, or the wandering Jew, anybody, it don't make any difference with us; we are paid for this, and I follow the trail of the old serpent himself, from here [?] Straits, and then ferry over to the Eastern Continent, and keep on till the day of Judgment, only stopping then, for roll call; only let us know what it is you are after and we will go on a few thousand miles further; we ask your forgiveness, on our bended knees and full of thorns besides, for not being able to speak the lingo, we feel like bloody villans [*sic*] on account of it.[74] We know we are serving death by the law, but we entreat you to spare our miserable lives, which shall, in future, be devoted to the study of the languages—that it is a language of which the speaker never tires. We are well aware from to-days performance in our front, and yet there is an English session which I have heard repeated rather often in the last two hours among the men of this detachment, which I am informed has no equivalent in the Spanish tongue. They must have guessed what it was, for they immediately gave us all the information we desired. Perhaps some of them heard it, for although short it is very strong.

I have heard no news from the revolution since I last wrote you. The Diaz party are daily expected to move down on Matamoras. The authorities of the city brought the old lady who edits the *Vox de Publico* to the Santa Cruz ferry, chucked her in a boat and sent her to this side, with a warning that if she returns they will tear all the stuffing out of her bustle.[75] The *Vox de Publico* is the paper which has been so friendly to this command, calling us bloody, murderous [*sic*], stick at nothing everything to do pirates.[76] It also "whooped up" your correspondent on the occasion. A letter copied from the GAZETTE was published in a Brownsville paper, and the editress of the "*Voice of the Many headed,* "went into spasms and smashed her patent palpitators.[77] She said that Capt. Kidd, yes, even the murderer of W. Moore, Esq., "that bloody pirate bold, who gathered in the gold as she sailed," was a being of angelic sweetness compared to Capt. M. or any of the company.[78]

Another rooster, collector of customs at Santa Cruz, received information on Sunday afternoon last, that the air of Texas would be healthier for him, and he got to this side in time to see the squad of cavalry arrive at his lately vacated office; they insisted on his returning but he stood upon the shore.

And he cussed 'em o'er and o'er, finally winding up with a stave of "On Jordan's stormy banks I stand," and is at present in Fort Brown, meditating upon the instability of affairs in general and Mexican affairs in particular.[79] The adherents of Diaz are jubilant and confidently anticipate victory; numbers of families are preparing for a move to the Texas bank of the river; things look squally, but nobody seems to know much about movements on the other side. Will keep you advised from time to time if there is anything worth writing about.

In haste,

"PIDGE"

P.S. Have just heard that the Diaz party has captured Mier; do not know the truth of the report; they might capture all Mexico before we would know it, as we are so far back in the chapparal.[80]

P.

Daily State Gazette, March 31, 1876

FROM OUR REGULAR RIO GRANDE CORRESPONDENT

CAMP TEXAS RANGERS,
LAGUNA DE LOS FLORES, M'ch 16, '76

Editors State Gazette:[81]

Like Joaquin Miller's Pilgrims of the Plains, we have been out here in the desert until we have

"Learned to read the sign of storms,
The moon's wide circles, sunset bars.
And storm-provoking blood and flame:
And like the Chaldean shepherds came
At night to name the moving stars:
And in the heavens, pictured forms
Of beasts and fishes of the sea;
And marked the great bear wearily
Rise up and drag his clinking chain
Of stars around the starry main."[82]

This service has its advantages and disadvantages; if we never see an English speaking female, cannot we console ourselves with the reflection that this is Leap Year, and bless an all-wise providence which has removed us from the perils of the interior? Should we be struck by lightning have not our friends the happy, consoling thought to comfort them, that lightning alone was the cause of our death, and that we were never called on by an agent of the patent, silver-tipped, insulating, combination, thunder and lightning company? If we tear our clothes in the brush, we mend them; we do not listen for hours to a lilly [*sic*] handed, side-whiskered "galoot" expatiate on the heavenly attributes of Singer's new

Captain McNelly died in September, 1877, survived by his wife and one son. In appreciation for his success in fighting cattle thieves Capt. Richard King had this impressive obelisk placed on McNelly's grave near Burton, in Washington County, Texas. Author's photo.

back-action-front or rear shuttle-lock switch sewing machine, with combined hemmer, feller and tucker, warranted to saw through tissue paper or the armor of an iron-clad with the same needle. If we have no library, we are never called upon to endure a book agent. No committee of ladies fair ever came here with a subscription list for the purpose of buying "our dear minister a new set of furniture," for the dear minister himself is a rather scarce article in these parts; the supposition is, that good feeding is seldom found; if you know of one who is out of a job, recommend him to us. Let him arise and make application to the Adjutant General for a chaplain's birth, for there is not a man in the company who has seen the insides of a church since last June. The man who does the barbering business for us, will never succeed in a city; he has been too much snubbed and imposed upon. A Ranger who wishes to be shaved, seats himself, draws his pistol and tells the barber that the first word about the Centennial, or the Republican nominee for the next President, or the third term, or anything else, will be his death signal, then and there.[83] We very seldom get the papers and are not bored with an account of an agricultural hall, or any other hall except the first sergeant, and occasionally one on the stock of some hapless ranchero.[84] We never have our hair cut or sit for our pictures. We do not know where Mrs. Woodhull is lecturing, or what hapless town in inflicted with Theodore Tilton.[85] If the infatuated Mrs. Southworth, of the North, or the inexpressible and irrepressible Augusta—h Evans, of the South, publish one of the "current" novels for which they are so famous, we thank God, we are far removed from the remotest probability of an infliction.[86] Even the New York Steetzer has not be[en] seen for a year, and the name of Sylvanus Snob is seldom heard.[87] Oh! we have much for which to be thankful, and we *are* thankful; when the wolves howl about our lovely camp we bless the stars that they are not politicians; when the tiger prowls around, we congratulate each other that it is not the tax collector; when the panther screams, the only married man in the company rises from his blankets, falls on his knees and returns thanks to his Creator that he does not have to get up, strike a light, take the panther in his arms and walk him around. One can visit a ranche where there are young Mexican ladies as often as he pleases, without being "supposed to have 'serious intentions;'" the "padre" does not send his son to you with an enormous club to inquire if you are going to leave Susan Mariar to die of a broken heart; the old lady does not tell you how terrible smart Susan Mariar is around the ranche, and that she could not possibly get along without her; mother does not cry and howl when Susan Mariar gets married and off her hands; she does not go into hysterics and tumble over like an American matron, yet no doubt she is equally as glad. Don Pedro, or Don Juan, or Don who-ever-he-may-be, puts Susan Mariar on a Spanish pony, takes her home and presents her with a brand new *mantale* as a bridal present; she sits astride of this, goes to preparing *tortilles* for the griddle, and never stops till she dies. What does she know of women's rights? (or lefts?) Nothing. Perhaps she has never heard of Mrs. Cady Stanton; if so, let us rather envy her than otherwise.[88] Lydia Thompson must, at some period of her eventful life have traveled through here, for the women generally wear the style of hose introduced by that charming actress; we, poor *gringos* that we are, supposed their stockings to be of yellow silk at first, but that is a mistake common to new arrivals in the country.[89] The Eighth Regiment of U.S. Cavalry from New Mexico, are posted along the river and in Fort Brown; it is a splendid regiment composed of officers and men accustomed to frontier services; the men of this command swears by "D" company and its gallant Captain, Randlett; he is the officer who came to our assistance when we were so hard pressed at *Los Cuevos;* he earned my everlasting gratitude on that occasion, and he has it; he always will have it.[90] I expected you to furnish me a first class obituary notice with poetry *a la* G. W. Childs thrown in, and to tell everybody what a promising young man I was; this, however, would have been superfluous, for some of the citizens of For[t] Brown, have been holding my notes for a considerable amount for a considerable time.[91] I will depend on you to do so if I ever *am* dishey [?] and to make it strong.

As an evidence that history repeats itself it is only necessary to introduce an extract from an account of the Scotch and English borders during the fourteenth and fifteenth centuries. "What manner of cattle stealers they are that inhabit these valleys, John Leslie, a Scotchman himself, and Bishop of Ross, will inform you.[92] They sally out of their own borders in the night, through in-frequented by-ways and many intricate windings; all the day time they refresh themselves and their horses in lurking holes they had pitched upon before, till they arrive in the dark to those places they have a design upon. As soon [as] they have seized upon the booty, they in a like manner, return home in the night, through blind-ways and [avoiding?] many a [company?]. The more skillful any Captain is to pass through them wild deserts and crooked turnings his reputation is the greater, and he is looked upon as a man of an excellent head. And they are so very cunning that they seldom have their booty taken from them," etc. This is a perfect description of robber tactics on the Rio Bravo at present. The *Magote de San Juan,* about forty miles from our present camp, is a favorite rendezvous for the marauders; this is a jungle of chapparal, situated in a large open prairie, and elevated; it contains water, and from this point they sally forth and gather small bunches of cattle until a sufficient number are collected, when they drive them full speed for the river. These raids are generally made at the full of the moon, the robbers arriving singly on a certain day at the point previously agreed upon.[93] They have a little business on the Mexican shore of the river to engage their attention at present, all of our particular friends from *La Bolsa, Las Cuevas* and other robber dens having taken service with Gen. Diaz and the revolutionists. The latter are not doing much at present, and each party seems to be dodging the other; very few have been killed as yet, and it is regarded as very fortunate by people on this side. The cavalry from Fort Brown have gone out several times to dispense revolutionists said to be on this side, but found them not. I heard last evening that they had demanded the surrender of Matamoras; do not know the truth of this report.

In haste,

"PIDGE"

P.S.—I see that some carpet-bagging idiot from Connecticut, who happened to get into the Virginia Legislature, has introduced a bill taxing all persons who chew tobacco, smoke, drink whiskey, or "cuss."[94] I am going home to spend my pay; shall leave on next steamer; will write you from New Orleans.[95] Heaven knows I *ought* to pay it out for "cussing;" I "cussed" enough before I got a part of it.

Au Revoir,

P.

The Last Gunfight

Lieutenant Robinson wrote his last letter to *Gazette* editor Elliott on March 16, 1876, in the Ranger camp at Laguna de las Flores. Signing off "In haste," he added a postscript containing a rare personal comment: "I am going home to spend my pay, shall leave on next steamer, will write you from New Orleans."

Why did Robinson leave the ranger command and return to Virginia at this particular time? He knew there were troubles at home, although he could not have known the full details of the troubles. But Lizzie May had just sent this telegram, a cry for help that he could not ignore: "I am in dire distress. Come home immediately." If he had been thinking about a return home, this appeal from his sister was all he needed to finalize his decision. He felt compelled to return, knowing it was a family obligation he could not refuse.[1]

His last weeks in Texas can be only partially reconstructed. On March 16 he was in camp. Two days later he was in Brownsville, as a special telegram from that city of that date and printed in the *Galveston Daily News* of the following day informed its readers: "Capt. McNelly and family are in Brownsville. Lieutenant Robinson also."

It is not known how long Robinson stayed in Brownsville; probably no longer than necessary, as he was eager to return home. Perhaps he went to the city cemetery to visit the grave of Pvt. L. B. Smith once more. It is probable that he left Brownsville within a few days, taking a steamer to Galveston and continuing his journey on another steamer to New Orleans, probably one of the Morgan line. Galveston had six possible steamer departure times to choose from: the *Whitney* under Captain Hopkins left on Sundays, Wednesdays, and Fridays at 2:00 p.m.; the *Clinton* under Captain Staples left on Tuesdays at midnight; the *Hutchinson* under Captain Talbot on Thursdays at midnight; and the *Morgan* under Captain Lewis on Saturdays, also at midnight. One advertisement, appearing regularly in the *Galveston Daily News,* stated that the Morgan lines were "carrying passengers, connecting to New York, Philadelphia, Baltimore, St. Louis, Chicago, and all points North and West." Would it not have been appropriate for Robinson to start his journey of revenge on the *Clinton?* It was on that steamer two years before, almost to the day, that William Sutton and his friend Gabriel Slaughter had attempted to leave a feud but had been cut down at the last minute by their enemies, two of the Taylors. Pidge Robinson was certainly aware of this, after dealing with the feuding factions back in 1874. Now Robinson was leaving Texas—as Sutton and Slaughter had intended to do—but to settle an old feud of his own.

Since Pidge had indicated he would send an additional letter from New Orleans it is understood that he wanted to spend some time there. He may have intended to write of whatever experiences he found of interest in his passage or of the exciting city of New Orleans. At any rate from the time it is known he was in Brownsville, Texas, on March 18, to when it is known he was home in Campbell County, Virginia, two weeks passed. He may have not left New Orleans until March 31, the same day his last letter would be read on the streets of Austin in the *Daily State Gazette.*

This advertisement appeared regularly in the *Times Picayune* of New Orleans: "The Mobile line, The Great through Route to the East, North and West via Atlanta and via St. Louis, carrying the U.S. mail / Trains depart and arrive from depot, foot of Canal Street. . . . Pullman Palace Cars daily, to Louisville, Nashville, Lynchburg, and Baltimore, without change, and only one change to New York and Eastern cities." The ticket office was located at the corner of Camp and Common streets opposite the City Hotel. The express left at 7:30 a.m. daily. From the steamer's deck at New Orleans to the rails of the Mobile line, Robinson was heading home, where he arrived on Saturday, April 1. He was accompanied by a friend, Whitfield Clark, but whether this companion had made the journey with him or they had met at Lynchburg is uncertain. Although he likely wanted to see Pidgie E. Mitchell, he could not have done so openly, as her brother Jesse was still there. Probably he spent most of the first day and evening with his father, whom he had not seen for at least two years.

But on the morning of Sunday, April 2, Robinson no longer thought of spending his pay, or visiting his father, or seeing Pidgie. His thoughts focused on his avowed purpose—that of shedding blood, the blood of his old enemy Jesse E. Mitchell. With his experience as a Ranger fighting outlaws, he must have felt confident challenging a former clerk in the Piedmont House of Lynchburg who was now working as a gauger for the U.S. government.[2]

Robinson began searching for Mitchell. For weapons he had with him his Navy Colt, property of the State of Texas, and a concealed derringer. Although the various newspaper accounts reported what happened as a "duel," it was not a formal duel in the traditional sense of the word. There had been no seconds arranged to guarantee the observance of dueling etiquette; and duels were illegal at that time. A correspondent from the Lynchburg *Star* was probably among the first to arrive on the scene, possibly having attended a service at the nearby Providence Church.[3] The *Star* files have not survived, but its report was reprinted in the *Lynchburg Virginian,* with an introductory paragraph. If not an actual eyewitness, the reporter must have talked with several people to gather information. This, the most complete report of the gunfight, is presented here in its entirety.

TRAGIC AFFAIR—A BLOODY ENCOUNTER

On Sunday morning a desperate shooting affray took place near Providence Church, about eight miles from the city, on the Campbell Court House road. The parties were two young men, named Truxton Robinson and Jesse E. Mitchell, who lived in the neighborhood. Robinson, it seems, has been absent for two or three years (in Texas, we believe,) and only recently returned to his father's. Some domestic trouble is said to have been the cause of the difficulty between the parties. The circumstances of the shooting are given as follows by a correspondent of the *Star*:

> On Sunday morning, as above stated, he [Robinson] saw Mitchell at a cabin on his father's land, in which some colored persons live, (about three hundred yards from his father's residence,) and started to where Mitchell was. Mitchell says when he saw Robinson approaching he started from him in the direction of his father's house, (Jas. S. Mitchell, Esq.) When Robinson had approached to within twenty paces of Mitchell he cocked a large Navy pistol. Mitchell, being strongly impressed at that moment with the first law of nature, drew his pistol (a five-shooter) and fired when Robinson was about fifteen paces off, and Robinson firing instantaneously with him.
>
> Robinson was struck in the abdomen, the ball taking a downward direction and lodging near the surface on the left hip. Mitchell was struck on the right hand, the ball entering the right cheek, and passing to the back part of his head, rendering him unable to shoot any more. Robinson advanced and fired the second time, the ball enter-

> ing the breast of Mitchell on the right side, ranging across just below the collar bone, escaping on the other side, inflicting a very dangerous wound. Mitchell says he then received a pistol shot in the bowels from a derringer in the hands of Robinson when it was so close to him that it burned his clothing (which your correspondent saw.)
>
> Drs. A. I. Clark and T. E. Stratton, of Rustburg, were instantly called, and are doing all they can to relieve their sufferings, but the recovery of either of them is extremely doubtful.
>
> Both are young men of honorable and respectable parentage, and this community deeply sympathizes with them in their afflictions.[4]

Since the coroner's report has not survived it is impossible to determine who may have been called as witnesses to the shooting. We have only Mitchell's version of the shooting, and possibly the "colored persons" were asked about what they may have seen or knew. Since it was a Sunday morning and fairly close to the church, there may have been worshippers close to the scene.

Robinson was clearly the aggressor, advancing on his enemy with his Navy Colt cocked. Mitchell then drew his weapon and fired, *first.* If the *Star*'s article was correct in its details, Robinson received a shot in the abdomen, the only shot Mitchell fired. Mitchell received a shot on the hand which then passed through his right cheek and then to the back part of his head. Then he received a shot on the right side and a shot from a derringer in the bowels, fired at point blank range.

The *Lynchburg News* provided essentially the same coverage of the shooting with a few additional details. The reporter was either aware of the feud or else the wounded men revealed to him the cause of the shooting, as he wrote: "The fight grew out of an old feud between the parties concerned, of several years' standing, and which seems not to have suffered by time."[5]

Two physicians—Dr. Hobson Clark and Dr. Thomas E. Stratton—provided what medical care they could. On Monday, April 3, Dr. H. Grey Latham of Lynchburg visited Mitchell and found him "very dangerously injured, though not necessarily fatally, no specifically unfavorable symptoms having as yet developed themselves." Dr. Latham did not see Robinson, but from what he had heard, saw "but little show of his recovery."[6] Latham's view that Robinson would probably die proved accurate. The news was telegraphed from Richmond and reprinted in many newspapers around the United States, including the *Galveston Daily News,*

New Orleans Times Picayune, New York Times, St. Paul Pioneer Press, and *Baltimore Sun.*

> Richmond, April 3.—Thaxton T. Robinson and Jesse Mitchell, young men highly esteemed in Campbell County, Va., met to-day, at New Providence Church, near Rustburg, in that county, to settle an old feud with pistols. Robinson was shot in the abdomen, and the other received one shot in the hand, which glancing went through his cheek and lodged in the back of his head. Another shot took effect in the breast. The latest report states that Robinson is dead and Mitchell could not survive. The difficulty is understood to have been on account of a woman.

The *New York Times* headlined it: "A Fatal Duel in Virginia." The *Picayune* chose "Settling an Old Feud" and added this paragraph: "Robinson was lieutenant in the United States army, and has been absent several years on duty on the Texas frontier, and Mitchell had recently been appointed gauger." The *Galveston Daily News* headlined its report: "Settled with Pistols / Mortal Combat between Two Young Virginians." Clearly, the press of the day considered the encounter between Robinson and Mitchell a duel rather than a chance encounter that ended in gunplay. The *Daily Herald* of Dallas stressed this aspect, adding a French idiom for additional color: "A duel a l'outrance was fought yesterday near Richmond [*sic*], Virginia, between T. Robinson and J. Mitchell. The former was killed and the latter mortally wounded."

The only official record of Robinson's death appeared in the Campbell County Register of Deaths. This reveals that Robinson, incorrectly identified as Thos. J. Robertson, died on April 3, 1876, giving his occupation as a farmer of that county; noting that he was single, twenty-eight years of age, and the son of Thomas J. and Harriett Robertson; and recording the cause of death—"Shot." This information was provided by a friend, Booker Smith.[7]

Numerous additional items appeared in print in the week following the shooting. The *Lynchburg News* reported that Robinson had "died about 1 o'clock yesterday morning, after intense suffering, and that Mr. Mitchell's condition, though serious and critical, was not hopeless." The coroner's inquest held on April 4 rendered its verdict that Robinson had come to his death by a pistol shot fired by the hand of Jesse E. Mitchell. Commented the *News:* "We have felt justified in suppressing much of the information in relation to the circumstances leading to the unfortunate difficulty, and while both the young men have been obviously wrong in the matter, it is much in Mitchell's favor that his assailant returned home with the avowed purpose of shedding blood, and attacked Mitchell without any previous warning. We still hope that Mr. Mitchell may recover from his serious wounds."[8]

It is most frustrating from a historian's viewpoint to learn that a newspaper deliberately suppressed much of the information concerning the circumstances of the shooting. One aspect of the suppressed news was exactly why Mitchell forbade the Pidgie E. Mitchell–T. C. Robinson love affair to flourish. It is interesting and curious that the *News* declared Mitchell and Robinson both "obviously wrong," even though Robinson had advanced on Mitchell with his pistol cocked and ready to fire.

It is impossible now to determine to whom Robinson had confessed his avowed purpose of shedding blood. It seems doubtful he would tell his father; and doubtful he would tell his beloved that he was coming home to kill her brother. Perhaps he confessed it to his sister Lizzie May, or to his friend Whitfield Clark, who may have been along to act as a second if indeed there was the intention of staging a duel. By confessing that he intended to kill Mitchell, did he not realize he would be charged with murder? Perhaps he believed he would be acquitted if forced to go to trial.

Strangely the *Richmond State* newspaper believed the duel had occurred on April 1 and hinted that the reports were an April Fool's joke. Commented *State* editor John Hampden Chamberlayne: "We will do the people of Lynchburg the justice to say that when they go to fighting they mean business. Cowhides are voted too thin when the object is to thin out the population. But it may be an April Fool joke."[9]

Responded the Lynchburg *News:*

> The Richmond *State* seems to be in a fearful muddle in relation to the fatal duel in Campbell county, and all from not reading the NEWS, which distinctly stated that the affair came off eight miles from this city. Robinson, who came home for the openly expressed purpose of shedding blood, is dead and buried, and Mitchell will probably die before this paragraph reaches the *State* sanctum. The duel did *not* take place on the 1st of April, and if there is any "April Fool" joke about it, we fail to see it.[10]

The contemporary reporting indicated that Robinson's attack on Mitchell was clearly in the open. Interestingly there is an oral tradition in the Rustburg area that it happened quite differently. Gladys Perrow

Scrogham related the version that her grandmother, Olivia Glass Perrow, had grown up believing: that Jesse Mitchell "knew of Robinson courting his sister and he didn't approve of it. One night Robinson knew Mitchell was going to travel the road that led to both families' homes. So Robinson lay in a ditch along the side of the road and waited for Mitchell to come by. When he came by Robinson shot at him. I don't know if Mitchell was hit with the shot but he didn't die. Mitchell fell to the ground and Robinson thought he was dead. Robinson got out of the ditch and when he did Mitchell shot and killed him."[11]

Some months after the shooting Lizzie May wrote a letter to a friend in Austin in which she discussed her brother's death. The unidentified friend shared it with the *Daily State Gazette* editor, who printed an excerpt:

> Miss Lizzie May Robinson, sister of our correspondent "Pidge," who was shot in a difficulty sometime since in Virginia, in a letter to a friend in this city, says all who witnessed the difficulty between her brother and Mitchel [*sic*], say that he [Mitchell] did not fire, that a shot from the pistol of Pidge struck the trigger of Mitchel's pistol cutting off his right finger, discharging the weapon and the ball mortally wounding her brother. The case was brought before Justice Jas. Walton, whom "Pidge" had cowhided before coming to Texas. Walton acquitted Mitchel.[12]

Was this Justice Walton's way of having his own revenge on Robinson for being cowhided by the deceased—to acquit Mitchell? If there were eyewitnesses to the shooting, the discrepancies indicate that no two witnesses see the same thing in the same way. It would be of interest to know the name of the friend in Austin to whom Lizzie May wrote the letter describing her brother's death.

It is not known how Captain McNelly received the news of the death of his first lieutenant. By telegram? By reading of it in a newspaper? And it would be interesting to know if he had been aware of Robinson's true intention in returning home to Virginia at that time. In all probability *someone* in the ranger camp was aware that Pidge was going home for a purpose other than simply spending his pay. On the reverse of the company's April return appears the list of those who had enlisted, had been discharged, and had deserted. This also appears: "*Died* T. C. Robinson Lieut. At Campbell County, Virginia April 4th while Absent with leave." This is not in McNelly's handwriting. The next time Robinson's name appears on a McNelly document is on the reverse of the June 1876 monthly return. Robinson is listed as still owing the State of Texas one pistol. He had taken home the Navy Colt, property of the state, valued at $16.50. That amount was deducted from his pay.

In the spring of 1876 Lizzie May Robinson and her father were the only ones left of the immediate family. Mrs. Robinson had died in 1869 at the age of sixty-three years. Lizzie May's father, Captain Robinson, was eighty years old. The question of what to do must have been in their minds; their home was on 180 acres, which Captain Robinson had acquired in September of 1843 from Bennett A. Henderson and his wife for $1,800. This was "one Certain tract or parcel of Land lying and being in the County of Campbell Containing One hundred and Eighty acres be the same more or less bounded by the lands of Edward B. Withers, Stephen Perrow, Wm. A. Staples and the lands of the Estate of John Murrel deceased." The acreage was "about four miles from the County Seat of Campbell County."

In July of 1879 Captain Robinson died. Lizzie May was the only surviving member of the family. Now she was to experience a different type of trouble, again involving Jesse E. Mitchell, but now he was working with accomplices. In reality it was only a continuation of the troubles her late brother had intended to resolve and had lost his life trying to settle. The Robinson land was to change hands to pay for a debt. The Deed of Trust, written in elegant longhand, begins:

> This Deed made the 28th day of August 1879 between Lizzie May Robinson of the first part William E. Glass Justice of the second part and Jesse E. Mitchell of the third part. Witnesseth:—Whereas the said Lizzie May Robinson is justly indebted to the said Jesse E. Mitchell in the sum of Seventeen hundred & Seventy-five Dollars and interest as evidenced by her bond of Two thousand three hundred dollars as of the 12th day of August 1876. Subject to a credit of Twenty-five Dollars as of the 21st day of December 1876 and also of Five Hundred Dollars as of 7th day of August—The payment of which bond & its interest the Said Lizzie May Robinson is anxious to secure.[13]

The justice of the peace before whom this deed was signed was none other than James C. Walton.

The same record of deeds shows that on December 12, 1879, Lizzie May sold the 180 acres of land to George V. Harlow:

> Lizzie May Robinson does hereby sell and convey to the Said George V. Harlow the tract or parcel of land of which her father Thos. Robinson died Seized & possessed being in Campbell County near Providence Church. It is agreed that ⅛ acre shall be preserved for a Grave Yard as the place where the family are buried, with right of ingress & egress thereto.[14]

Although Jesse Mitchell survived his wounds he was not satisfied, as he now determined to inflict more misery on the Robinsons, this time with partners in the venture. Having already taken her brother's life, he was determined to take from Lizzie the property the Robinson family owned. Mitchell continued his persecution. Instead of a pistol his weapons now were extortion and blackmail. Lizzie May's version of events is preserved—and we have only hers, not Mitchell's—from court testimony. Her troubles that ultimately caused her to beg help from her brother in Texas had begun years before. Robinson himself had had his problems with the legal system, although exactly what they amounted to is undetermined, and Lizzie May had assisted "in the escape of my brother," as she described her actions.[15] Troubles increased from the day when she was visiting the residence of William E. Glass, a neighbor. There she met Jesse E. Mitchell. She recalled that this was in 1874, and at that time she did not deny helping her brother escape from the law.

After Pidge had left for Texas Mitchell began his scheme of blackmail. He accused Lizzie May of aiding her brother to escape and threatened to reveal this information to Judge Walton. He convinced her that she would wish she had denied having been involved in her brother's escape, as Judge Walton would hear of it and would charge her, try her, and send her to jail. But Mitchell promised that he could prevent this from happening. How and why would he stop it? Only if she promised "never to receive another letter" from her brother, nor ever again to be visited by or visit her friend James Booker Smith. Mitchell claimed this action was because he had been sent out of her father's house and that now he "intended to be revenged on me."

Sometime later Mitchell sent Lizzie May word that he wanted to see her, "on a matter of importance to me and mine," as she testified. They were to meet at a certain spot a quarter of a mile from her home. She agreed, and from there her troubles only increased. Mitchell claimed he had "observed" that she continued to receive letters from her brother, and also continued to receive visits from Booker Smith, and that he would "have his revenge [even] if it cost him his life." He further told her that "he could prove that I had given birth to a child" and inquired "what I had done with it." At this point Lizzie May wanted to leave, but then Mitchell revealed a surprise. He said, "Gentlemen, you have heard the conversation," and a voice from the brush answered, "Yes."

Mitchell refused to reveal the identity of the "gentlemen" who were hidden from view when this conversation occurred. He admitted watching "everything that went on in my house through a spy-glass." This had taken place when she was "alone and unprotected." The place of this "interview" was at Mr. Given's field on a neighboring hill.

After the "interview" Lizzie stayed "closely at home never going out but Mitchell was observed." The household in early 1876 consisted of herself, her father, and "a small colored girl."

At this point in her life Lizzie May Robinson was nearly helpless. Then Mitchell again had an "interview" with her, claiming that he could prove whatever he wished to prove against her and she would be jailed. He had her in his power. She admitted: "I knew my fate." He convinced Lizzie to sign a "confession" or else he would go to Judge Walton. Mitchell at this point "laughed a sneering laugh" and informed her that her brother would come to her relief "and a happy time we would have in jail together." She signed the false document.

But even then Mitchell's vengeful maneuvers did not cease. He sent another note, now demanding five hundred dollars and a bond for an additional thousand dollars. If she complied he would "shut the matter up." William E. Glass was the witness for this bond. But she had had enough. She telegraphed her brother in Texas to come home immediately. These threats and blackmail brought Pidge Robinson home. Perhaps Lizzie May thought her brother and Mitchell could somehow resolve matters if they met; she could not know the encounter would be lethal.

Pidge's death did not satisfy Mitchell. In the fall of 1876 he wrote to Lizzie May demanding an additional two hundred dollars. She replied that she had no money, but in turn Mitchell now demanded her father's gold watch, as proof that she would somehow get the money, the watch to be held as security, to "show a willing mind to do something." In spite of her entreaties not to take the watch, "that it was of no value to him, and I prized it very highly," she did send him the watch.

Jesse E. Mitchell now had money, a promissory note, and a gold watch, but he wanted even more. Lizzie May's testimony on March 9,

1880, ended with: "My father died last July; he left a tract of land of 480 acres. I gave up the watch and certificate because I was afraid not [to]; [Mitchell] always wrote me he had my confession and witnesses to it. I never owed him anything in my life." Lizzie May held up very well against the "searching cross-examination of the counsel for the defense." Her "sad countenance and quivering lips at the mention of the murder of her brother or any allusions to her having given birth to a child," according to the *Virginian* court reporter present, was "calculated to excite the sympathy of all observers."

One thing made clear was that between Lizzie and Mitchell there "had been no friendly intercourse" since 1874. The confession Lizzie May had signed was produced in court, with the following note appended:

> The above is my confession to Jesse Mitchell, and I gave it to him rather than he should expose me, this the 30th day of May, 1875, which he promises not to do, provided I keep Booker Smith from visiting me or speaking to me at any time, and the rest of my family, and that I should never go to their house again. Should I keep this promise he is never to expose this confession. Lizzie May Robinson.

She further testified that she was present when Mitchell was ordered out of her father's house. Her statement continued: "I was at one time intimate with him. These were lover-like attentions, I received them kindly. These relations were first broken in the Summer of 1873." Then the "unfriendly feeling" between Mitchell and her brother began. "I know of no other cause for his being ordered out of my father's house; I have no reason to believe that the difficulty then had any connection with me."[16]

The court record leaves one feeling compassion and sympathy for Lizzie May Robinson. The troubles between the two families had started after the Robinsons had acted the Good Samaritan part of aiding the injured Jesse Mitchell after his accident with a saw. Then Mitchell was ordered out of the Robinson home; her only brother had to leave home; the threats and blackmail were made against her; and the loss of her father weakened any combative spirit within her. It was all was more than Lizzie May could deal with sensibly. Finally she brought an attorney into the picture and court proceedings began against Jesse E. Mitchell, William E. Glass, and James C. Walton.

Additional testimony revealed that Lizzie May recalled being "a very small child, probably 10 or 11 years old, when Mitchell first commenced paying me attention as a lover." She reckoned he was fifteen years older than she. Charges were brought against the trio: Mitchell, William E. Glass, and James C. Walton were charged with extortion of a deed of trust; Mitchell and Glass were charged with extortion of a bond of $2,300; Mitchell alone was charged with extorting $500 and a gold watch from Lizzie May Robinson. The jury, after hearing all the evidence and arguments of prosecution and defense counsel, returned a verdict of guilty against Jesse E. Mitchell. His term of punishment was fixed at five years in the penitentiary. The others were allowed to provide bail.[17]

Many questions remain. What happened to Lizzie May Robinson immediately after the ordeal with Jesse E. Mitchell was concluded in the court of law? Her confessed intimacy with Mitchell seems to have been the reason the troubles began in the first place. If Captain Robinson had discovered an improper relationship developing between Mitchell and his daughter he would have ordered Mitchell out of his house and had every right to do so. Lizzie May's initial acts of intimacy with Mitchell eventually resulted in Texas Ranger T. C. Robinson, lieutenant of Company A of McNelly's troop, returning home to settle what had become a feud—with pistols. Ironically, Lizzie May's brother had similar feelings toward Mitchell's sister, Mary Elizabeth R., commonly known as "Pidgie."

In spite of the threats against her, Lizzie May did continue to see James Booker Smith. On June 23, 1880, they were married.[18] Twenty years later they were living in the Bolivar and Sandy Hollow of Augusta County, some seventy miles north of Rustburg, Virginia. There were no children from the union, and details are of the couple's later life are not known.[19]

Pidgie E. Mitchell, the inspiration for Robinson's *nom de plume,* did find some degree of contentment in her life. On November 16, 1881, she married William E. Glass, one of the "gentlemen" who had hidden in the brush to hear Lizzie May's "confession."[20] From Campbell County they moved some fifty miles northwest to Amherst County, residing in the county seat of Buena Vista, in the Blue Ridge Mountains of Virginia. Although he had been involved in Jesse E. Mitchell's extortion scheme, Glass became a successful businessman and respected member of the community; Pidgie E. Mitchell Glass presumably enjoyed the fruits of his labors. She died on Sunday evening, January 28, 1923. No glowing words of praise were offered in her obituary; only that she was a member of the Methodist Church.[21] William survived her for three years, pass-

The site of Pidge's last gunfight was near the old Providence Methodist Church near Rustburg in Campbell County, Virginia. Author's collection.

ing away on April 1, 1926, "after an illness of a few weeks." His obituary described him as "a hard worker" who "managed to gather much of the world's goods about him. He was an upright, honest man, standing four square in all his dealings."[22] In his will he provided significant funds for the local Masonic Lodge as well as for the local Methodist Church.

No punishment was meted out to Jesse E. Mitchell by the legal system for killing Pidge Robinson. But he paid the price of extortion and blackmail with five years behind bars. In 1880 he was in the county jail in Rustburg when the census taker visited jailer William T. Clement. In addition to Mitchell, Clement had seven other prisoners in his care and three servants within the jail to assist him with his official responsibilities. Mitchell's occupation was given as a grocer, and was forty years of age.[23] Little else is known of the man. After serving his time he married Mary T. Flynn, a thirty-five-year-old widow, on January 21, 1891, in Campbell County. He was ten years her senior.[24] They moved to Lynchburg, only a few miles north of where Mitchell had killed Robinson, and established their home at 710 Fillmore Street. The couple had one son, Richard, born in February of 1893. After a lengthy illness Jesse died at home on May 16, 1900, at the age of fifty-four years. The funeral was held at his residence.[25] His widow Mary survived him for some twelve years. Her exact death date is not determined, but the city directories carry

Pidge's headstone in the family cemetery shows a hand holding a pistol, and his epitaph commemorates his service with the Texas Rangers. Author's collection.

her name as the widow of Jesse; she is last listed in the 1912 edition. A modern apartment building now stands at that address. Jesse and Mary Mitchell were both buried in the Spring Hill Cemetery of Lynchburg, in a plot then owned by her father, David T. Farley. The graves of Jesse E. and Mary T. Mitchell are unmarked.

Today, midway between Lynchburg and Rustburg, just a few hundred feet west of Highway 501 and almost directly opposite the site of the old Providence Methodist Church, is the eighth of an acre of land set aside as the Robinson family cemetery. No sign alerts drivers to its location. Within the bucolic setting, out of sight from the highway, is what is officially known as the Robinson-Green Family Cemetery. Few headstones remain, and there appear to be numerous unmarked graves. The stones that mark the final resting place of Captain Robinson, and that of his wife Harriett, are standing, as is the stone of their only son, Thomas C. Robinson. It stands tall and erect although at some point in the past it was cracked. Curiously, the name Thomas C. Robinson does not appear on the headstone. Instead of the kind of inscription one might expect, such as his name and "Gone but Not Forgotten," an unusual engraving marks the stone. At the top of the three-foot-tall key-slot marker is the following inscription:

In Memory of
"PIDGE"
Lieut. Co. A. Texas Rangers
Born Nov'r 27, 1846
Died April 3, 1876
A devoted Son and Brother,
A True Friend and brave
Soldier rests here.

Green be the turf above thee,
Friend of my better days;
None knew thee but to love thee,
None named thee but in praise.

At the top is a hand holding a pistol—not, as one might expect, a weeping willow tree or an open Bible, or a closed book signifying that life had closed, but a carved representation of the Navy Colt, property of the State of Texas.[26]

Notes

INTRODUCTION

1. Sonnichsen, *I'll Die Before I'll Run,* 60–61.

2. Although the census records and newspaper articles dealing with his family and his death consistently use the initials T. T., I have used the initials T. C., as those were used by Robinson himself in signing all of McNelly's official correspondence. I have been unable to determine a reason for the discrepancy between the sets of initials.

3. Wooten, *Comprehensive History of Texas,* 350.

4. Jennings, *A Texas Ranger,* 121.

5. Webb, *The Texas Rangers.*

6. Durham, *Taming the Nueces Strip.*

7. Wilkins, *The Law Comes to Texas.*

8. Utley, *Lone Star Justice,* 328 n.27.

9. US Census, Campbell County, Virginia, 1850.

10. US Census, Campbell County, Virginia, 1860.

11. US Census, Campbell County, Virginia, 1870.

12. Ibid.

13. Campbell County, Common Law Order Book no. 29, December 11, 1867, 232. Campbell County Court Records, Rustburg, Virginia.

14. Ibid., March 10, 1868, 353; August 10, 1868, 399; December 15, 1868, 450 and 452. Campbell County Court Records, Rustburg, Virginia.

15. US Census, Campbell County, Virginia, enumerated July 16, 1870, by Samuel P. Holt, 59.

16. The quotes are from the *Democrat and Ranchero* of Brownsville, Texas, February 28, 1880, reviewing the subsequent troubles of the Robinsons. The *Democrat and Ranchero* covered the news because Robinson had spent time in Brownsville as a ranger and many people were familiar with him and his writings.

17. Ibid.

18. The date of Robinson's departure for Texas is from the testimony of Lizzie May Robinson, appearing in the *Lynchburg Virginian,* March 11, 1880.

THE AUSTIN LETTERS

1. Unfortunately it cannot be determined exactly when Pidge arrived in Austin or was employed by the *Statesman.*

2. The term *mooley* was a dialectical variation of *muley,* which referred to a hornless animal. Devons described any of a breed of vigorous red dual-purpose cattle of English origin. The muley animals tended to congregate when bedded down and usually isolated themselves from the horned cattle.

3. *Calzoueros,* or properly *calzoneros,* was a word of Mexican origin, describing trousers that were opened on the outer sides of the leg from the knee downward but that could be closed with buttons or silver conchas.

4. The expression "like a wolf on the fold" is a paraphrase of a line from Lord Byron's "The Destruction of Sennacherib," which begins:

> The Assyrian came down like the wolf on the fold,
> And his cohorts were gleaming in purple and gold.
> And the sheen of their spears was like stars on the sea,
> When the blue wave rolls nightly on deep Galilee.

Pidge paraphrased the line again later in the letter published in the *Daily State Gazette* of January 19, 1876.

5. Europa was the daughter of Agenor, King of Phoenicia. In Roman mythology Jupiter was king of the gods and was the god of thunder, lightning, and rain. He was known as Zeus in Greek mythology. He changed himself into the form of a bull and abducted Europa. The reference to peanuts is the first clue indicating what occupation Pidge may have been engaged in prior to leaving Virginia. The peanut as a crop originated with early Virginian colonists, and Virginia soon became one of the leading states in peanut production.

6. These lines are paraphrased from Alfred Lord Tennyson's long poem "Maud." The following, which provided the inspiration for the paraphrase, appeared as stanzas 6 and 7 in section 27:

> Prophet, curse me the blabbing lip,
> And curse me the British vermin, the rat;
> I know not whether he came in the Hanover ship,
> But I know that he lies and listens mute
> In an ancient mansion's crannies and holes:
> Arsenic, arsenic, sure, would do it,
> Except that now we poison our babes, poor souls!
> It is all used up for that.
> Tell him now: she is standing here at my head;
> Not beautiful now, not even kind;
> He may take her now; for she never speaks her mind,
> But is ever the one thing silent here.
> She is not of us, as I divine;
> She comes from another stiller world of the dead,
> Stiller, not fairer than mine.

This poem, first published in 1855, related the history of a man saved from selfish despair by a pure love. My thanks to Dorothy Eagle, editor of *The Oxford Companion to English Literature,* for this quotation.

7. It is probable that "Dreams" was inspired by Lord Byron's masterpiece *Childe Harold's Pilgrimage.* Compare Pidge's poem with canto 1, stanza 10:

Childe Harold had a mother—not forgot,
Though parting from that mother he did shun;
A sister whom he loved, but saw her not
Before his weary pilgrimage begun:
If friends he had, he bade adieu to none.
Yet deem not thence his breast a breast of steel;
Ye, who have known what 'tis to dote upon
A few dear objects, will in sadness feel
Such partings break the heart they fondly hope to heal.

The term "Self-exiled I" of line 14 certainly refers to his troubles in Virginia with Jesse E. Mitchell. Note that line 21 speaks of his deceased mother. Her headstone in the family cemetery reveals that Harriett B. Robinson, wife of Capt. Thomas Robinson, died on October 22, 1869. "In life beloved / In death lamented." She was sixty-three years of age.

Byron's *Childe Harold's Pilgrimage,* canto 3, stanza 16, referred to the hero as being self-exiled, wandering forth with no hope:

Self-exiled Harold wanders forth again,
With nought of hope left, but with less of gloom,
The very knowledge that he lived in vain,
That all was over on this side the tomb,
Had made Despair a smilingness assume,
Which, though 'twere wild—as on the plundered wreck
When mariners would madly meet their doom
With draughts intemperate on the sinking deck—
Did yet inspire a cheer, which he forbore to check.

The 1870 Campbell County census spells the family name *Robertson,* showing Thomas Robinson as being seventy-two years of age with occupation as a farmer. His only son, Thomas T., is listed as twenty-three years of age, and "works on farm"; daugther Mary E. is listed as twenty years old, without occupation. The senior Robinson listed real estate valued at $4,000 with a personal estate of $500.

Thomas Robinson's headstone accords him the rank of captain: "In memory of Capt. Thos. Robinson / Died / July 15, 1879 / Aged 84 years." This epitaph appears:

Farewell dear father take thy rest;
God called thee home. He thought it best,
T'was hard indeed to part with thee
But Christ's strong Arm supported me.

8. It has not been determined which ranger captain this may have been, if it was based on an actual incident. It is not a veiled reference to Captain McNelly, for Pidge and the captain did not meet until July 17.

9. The *Great Eastern* was a British iron steamship launched in 1858, the prototype of the modern ocean liner. It was four times greater than any ship then afloat, was designed to carry four thousand passengers, and was almost 700 feet long. After brief success in laying the Atlantic cable in 1865–66 it was retired and became an exhibit. It was scrapped in 1888.

10. The expression "King of Terrors" originated with the Old Testament. In Job 18:5–14 appear these lines: "The wicked man's light must certainly be put out, his brilliant flame cease to shine. Disease devours his flesh, Death's First-born gnaws his limbs. He is torn from the shelter of his tent, and dragged before the King of Terrors."

11. This is a reference to an actual accident that took place on April 8, 1874, at the small community of Manor, approximately fifteen miles north east of Austin. It was reported in the "Locals" of the *Statesman* of April 10. Reportedly every car left the track but none was badly damaged, and only a brakeman and one passenger were slightly injured. Reported the *Statesman:* "The accident was caused by a defective tie, which gave way as the locomotive passed over it, spreading the rail to such an extent that the other cars could not pass over. It was fortunate that the train was moving slowly at this time, as it had just started down a heavy grade, and one minute later might have made the casualties very serious." This may have been written by Pidge himself, since he did contribute locals to the *Statesman.* Unfortunately the identity of the writer of the locals was never provided. The term *local* refers to both the item itself and the person writing it.

12. This is a reference to an article the Waco *Examiner* had taken from the *Statesman* without giving proper credit. The *Statesman* of June 2, 1874, accused the *Examiner* of having "copied an article of ours in its editorial columns without credit. But conduct is in keeping with a paper which like the bird of gay plumage struts and airs itself, but has not one musical note—one original idea. If all our exchanges exhibited the same amount of stupidity as the *Examiner* does, we would favor an exchange of editors for Balaam's ass." Additional comments relevant to this exchange were printed in the *Statesman* on June 6 and June 8.

13. At this time the *Statesman* was edited by John Cardwell and John D. Walker. After beginning as a twenty-column tri-weekly it grew steadily in size and popularity and soon became recognized as a leading newspaper of the state. The *Statesman,* after the Democratic Executive Committee chose Cardwell to be its editor in July, 1871, became prominent in the campaign of 1873. It was then that the carpetbag regime under Governor E. J. Davis was defeated. Cardwell and Walker became joint editors in January, 1873. Cardwell was editor and proprietor for fifteen years. The man who started Pidge "on the plank road to fortune, fame, and six dollars a week" was born on January 28, 1837, in Lexington, Georgia. He was educated there and then in colleges of the East and Europe. During the war he was a financial agent of the Confederacy to Central America. After the war's end he spent several years in Brazil. Under the Cleveland administration he was sent as consul general to Egypt, remaining there for four years.

When Harrison became president, Cardwell was replaced and he returned to Texas, where he engaged in planting in Wharton County. He died on April 17, 1893, after a two-week illness. The *Houston Post,* in writing of his life, noted on April 20, 1893, that "his powerful pen wielded a masterful influence in the politics of Texas. He was perhaps the strongest writer that the Texas press ever had."

14. This is a paraphrase of the poem "Excelsior" composed by Henry W. Longfellow on September 28, 1841. Its intent was to describe the life of a man of genius who resisted all temptations, laid aside all fears, ignored all warnings, to press on to accomplish his purpose. The first and last stanzas follow:

> The shades of night were falling fast,
> As through an Alpine village passed
> A youth, who bore, 'mid snow and ice,
> A banner with the strange device,
> Excelsior!
>
> There in the twilight cold and gray,
> Lifeless, but beautiful, he lay,
> And from the sky, serene and far,
> A voice fell, like a falling star,
> Excelsior!

15. The poem "To Miss F.W., of Virginia" is perhaps a paraphrase of some other poem, but if so I have not located the original. In the same issue of the *Statesman,* dated June 24, appeared this item relevant to Pidge: "OUR readers will be pleased to read another poem from 'Pidge.' He is a young man of fine talents, and only needs a little encouragement to make him as famous as some of the celebraties [*sic*] who have mounted the hill of fame upon much less brain capital. We shall be pleased to receive other poems, and locals too, from him. By-the-by, we see that the Bastrop *Advertiser* has published Pidge's "Dull Season," which appeared a short time since in the *Statesman.*"

Unfortunately no copies of the June 1874 issue of the *Advertiser* have yet been located. Conceivably some additional information about Pidge may have been printed in an introductory paragraph.

16. It has not been possible to determine who "Short Stop" was. So far as is known, no other writings of this individual were published during the period when Pidge was a contributor to the *Statesman.* The "Soliloquy of a Drone," authored by Short Stop, was actually a paraphrase of another poetic work that had appeared in the *Statesman,* "The Soliloquy of a Female Hamlet." This had appeared in the issue of June 5, 1874. No author was identified. The latter work was a paraphrase of Hamlet's "To be or not to be" soliloquy. In the *Statesman* of June 25, along with Short Stop's "Soliloquy of a Drone," appeared this brief item: "SHORT STOP makes an appearance today, and confronts 'Dull Season' with very pertinent queries." "Dull Season" was referring to Pidge himself. Here follows

"The Soliloquy of a Female Hamlet," which appeared in the *Statesman* on June 5, with no author identified.

To wed or not to wed, that is the question;
Whether 'tis nobler in a girl to suffer
The slings and arrows of an old maid's fortune,
Or married be, and so plunge in a sea of troubles
From which naught saves her? To wed—to flirt
No more; and by a husband say, we end
The heartache and the thousand natural shocks
That nerves are heir to–'tis a consummation
Devoutly to be wished—a maid—a wife;
A wife! Perchance t' obey; aye, there's the rub;
For in that married state what orders come,
When we have shuffled on domestic bliss,
Must give us pause; there's the respect,
That makes our pining in a lonely life.
For who would bear the whips and scorns of time,
Mrs. Grundy's sneer, the mean man's contumely.
The pangs of repressed love, a woman's wrong,
The insolence of striplings, and the spurns
The spiteful spinster of the old mat[r]ons take,
When she herself might airs and graces get
With a rich husband? Who would men forswear,
To have hysterics in a single blessedness,
But that they dread love, honor and obey.
The unbearable control, from whose bourne
The spinster may escape, puzzles the will
And makes us rather [?] us all,
And this the native hue of resolution
Is sicklied o'er with the pale fear of man,
And marriage of great pith and brilliancy,
With this regard are often brought to naught,
And lose the chance of binding. Soft you, now!
The rich Senator—Jones in my meditation
Be all thy mines remembered.

Short Stop's "Soliloquy of a Drone," dated June 23 and composed in Austin, was printed in the *Statesman* on June 25 and follows:

To work or not to work, that is the question—
Whether 'tis nobler in the "dull season" to suffer
The slings and arrows of fastidiousness,
Or to take one's coat off, like a man,
And, by opposing indolence, end it? To work, to sweat,

No more; and by the sweat of work to say we end
All board duns, and the thousand natural shocks
That idleness is heir to–'tis a consummation
Devoutly to be wish'd. To work, to toil
To toil, perchance to labor! Ay, there's the rub,
For in hard toil of life what soreness may come
When we have shuffled off aversion to toil
Must give us pause; there's the respect
That makes soft jobs the joy of life.

17. "Tip Top" was also the name of a medicine prepared by D. W. C. Baker, druggist, and may have been the inspiration for this term here. According to the advertisement in the *Statesman* of August 21, 1874: "This medicine is coming into general use, and is said to be a sure remedy for lichen itch, ringworm, and tetter."

18. Baseball was becoming a more and more popular sport. In the July 1, 1874, issue of the *Statesman* appeared the following local, which may also be a contribution from Pidge: "BASE BALL.—There is some little interested [*sic*] manifested among the young gentlemen of Austin in regard to the revival of base ball playing. A report has reached this city that the Galveston batters are fixing up their playgrounds elegantly and that they will ere long send our challenges. The Austin boys ought to be prepared to 'give them a riffle.'"

19. In the last lines of "Droning" Pidge uses a nautical metaphor, a type used several times in his later contributions. The "hawse" is that part of a ship's bow containing the hawse-hole, through which run the cables. "Thwart your hawse" would thus mean to change the course. The "raws" of Shakespeare refers to those lines before they were refined. The "wise saws" are familiar sayings, proverbs, or maxims. This is also a reference to a long quotation from *As You Like It,* beginning:

All the world's a stage,
And all the men and women merely players.

Shakespeare then described the seven ages of man. The fifth age is Justice, "full of wise saws and modern instances."

20. Elsewhere in the July 11, 1874, issue of the *Statesman* appeared this item bringing the reader's attention to the letter describing the visit to the Lunatic Asylum: "'PIDGE's' communication will be read with great pleasure. If you are dull, read it; if you are lively, read it; and if you are lonesome, read it often. It is spicy and crisp, good for old and young." The reason for Pidge's visit to the asylum at this particular point in time may have been that the improvements on the buildings were progressing. The *Statesman* reported in the issue of June 12: "The work at the Lunatic Asylum, as we learn from Col. Cook, is steadily progressing, and perhaps there are but few persons in the city or State who are apprised of the proportions of the improvements going on there. The ell now being

added to the Lunatic Asylum building is one hundred by forty feet, and is to be three stories high, and built in a very substantial manner. The first story of the building is already up, and the job is to be completed during the coming fall." Col. Abner H. Cook (1814–84) was a North Carolina native who arrived in Texas in 1839. His skill in designing and construction soon earned him a reputation as a master builder. His style of Greek revival can be seen in pictures of the governor's mansion and the Old Main building of the University of Texas.

21. Dr. David Richard Wallace (1825–1911) served as superintendent of the State Lunatic Asylum from 1874 to 1879. He had received his medical degree in 1853 from the New York City Medical College. He went to Bastrop, Texas, in 1855 and was on the staff with the opening of Waco University in 1861. He served as a surgeon throughout the Civil War. In 1883 he helped establish the North Texas Lunatic Asylum; he was appointed superintendent there and resigned in 1891 to return to private practice in Waco. Wallace believed the insane should not be hidden away but should be treated as suffering from an illness that could be cured. In this respect he was a pioneer in the field of psychiatry in Texas. See Merle Mears Duncan, "David Richard Wallace," in Tyler, *New Handbook of Texas,* 6:809.

22. The term *jubus* is a variation of "tuberous," an alternative of "dubious." In the South especially it meant doubtful and hesitating.

23. The expression is correctly spelled *dernier ressort,* or "without appeal"; Pidge used it several times. William Lewis Moody was the chair of the Finance Committee appointed by Texas governor Richard Coke. Coke had promised that his plan of retiring state warrants to await redemption from the sale of bonds would provide $1,000,000 of bonds required to be sold for payment of the floating debt. This promise was made March 19. On June 19 Moody left New York, having failed completely to accomplish the promise of the governor. The *Statesman* had been in opposition to the plan. Its June 25 headline read: "Governor Coke's Financial Scheme Crowned with a Failure," and the article concluded with: "State Financial [Agent] Moody . . . is now on his way to Texas without having effected one thing for which he was appointed. He has neither been able to sell bonds or borrow money upon them."

24. The Bible verse comes from Philippians 4:7: "The peace of God which passeth all understanding."

25. Of further interest, Edward King toured Texas in the 1870s and also visited the Lunatic Asylum. His published account of his travels in King, *The Great South,* 127–28, included this description:

> Under the rich glow of the February sun the white walls of the structure formed a delicious contrast to the foliage of the live oaks near at hand, making it seem more like a temple than like the retreat of clouded reason. In wandering through the wards I came suddenly upon a group of idiot girls, seated on benches in a niche before a sunny window. These poor creatures cowered silently—grimacing now and then—as I stood gazing upon them, when sud-

denly, one or two of them, doubtless excited by the presence of a visitor, rose and began dancing and shrieking. The suddenness of the transition, and the fearful, mysterious nature of these idiotic saturnalia, appalled me. I avow that I could hardly drag my limbs to the door, and when once more in the sunlight I felt as if I had come from Dante's Hell. The cheery German physician in charge complained of the overcrowded condition of the asylum, adding that as the majority of the cases brought him had already become chronic, it was a hopeless throng with which he had to deal.

In a yard of the asylum, comfortably inclosed, and covered by a picturesque roof upon which a vine had been trained, I saw the sty in which 'Queen Elizabeth,' a filthy and dreadful old negress, wallowed all day long. Behind green lattices neatly set upon the walls of another building, I could hear the furiously insane groaning and shouting. It is said that there are more than 1,200 insane in the State, for most of whom an asylum is necessary.

PIDGE AND THE DEWITT COUNTY FEUD

1. Rose, *The Texas Vendetta,* 31.

2. Capt. L. H. McNelly to Adj. Gen. W. Steele, August 3, 1874, Adjutant General Papers, Texas State Archives.

3. Quoted in Rose, *The Texas Vendetta,* 47. The *encinal* is an area between the Nueces and Rio Grande rivers. The region is a sandy ridge with water easily obtainable, with heavy growth of *encinos,* or live oaks, from which it obtained its name. Many Mexicans crossed the Rio Grande into the region and built temporary shelters of sticks and mud (*jacales*). By their locality they were able to give considerable aid and information to their confederates in crime on either side of the river. These squatters were no doubt who Rose had in mind with his use of the term *Chevaliers d'Encinal.* He thus erred by referring to the DeWitt County feudists with this term, as they had nothing in common with the Mexican desperadoes whom McNelly would later fight in 1875 and 1876.

4. McNelly to Steele, August 8, 1874.

5. McNelly to Steele, September 2, 1874.

6. Mayfield, "Capt. W. L. Rudd of Yorktown," 561–66.

7. Callicott, "Reminiscences," 1.

8. McNelly to Steele, August 7, 1874.

9. McNelly to Steele, October 20, 1874.

10. Another quotation from Lord Byron, this time from the extremely successful poem "Mazeppa." The title character had been caught seducing another man's wife. His punishment was to be tied to the back of a wild horse, which was then let loose on the prairie for what was intended to be his certain death. He survived and avenged himself on his foe. The character Mazeppa early described how he had met his love, Theresa:

I loved her then—I love her still;
And such as I am, love indeed

> In fierce extremes—in good and ill.
> But still we love even in our rage,
> And haunted to our very age
> With the vain shadow of the past,
> As is Mazeppa to the last.

The line Pidge here uses is from strophe VI, beginning with line 232:

> We met—we gazed—I saw, and sigh'd,
> She did not speak, and yet replied;
> There are ten thousand tones and signs
> We hear and see, but none defines—
> Involuntary sparks of thought,
> Which strike from out the heart o'er wrought,
> And from a strange intelligence,
> Alike mysterious and intense.

Pidge later again refers to "Mazeppa" in the letter written on January 15 and published on January 19, 1876, in the Austin *Daily State Gazette.*

11. It soon became apparent that McNelly would not allow drinking among his recruits. His attitude toward drinking was later printed in the *Daily State Gazette* of August 10, 1876: "[McNelly] refused to enlist any man who drinks consequently will have an entire temperance command. He has but little faith in whiskey fighting. The smell of burnt powder tends wonderfully to sober a man, and this done, the man who fights only under the influence of whiskey becomes demoralized, and don't [*sic*] make a good man for frontier services." Before the close of 1874 three of those who had enlisted with Robinson had been dishonorably discharged. Of additional interest is that an item appeared in the Bastrop *Advertiser* regarding Robinson's and McNelly's attitude toward drinking. The item originally appeared in the *Colorado Citizen* of Columbus, Texas (date not determined), and was reprinted in the *Advertiser* of August 21, 1875. Because there are so few items concerning Robinson in the contemporary press, this item is reprinted in full:

> A writer in the Colorado Citizen, going out with recruits for Capt. McNally's [*sic*] command on the Rio Grande, relates, after being drawn up in line, as follows:
>
> "Gentlemen, I make it a rule to allow no gambling in camps, no cursing, no drunkenness. I will at once release him from his obligation to the State."
>
> Whereupon five timid hearted ones wisely concluded to 'return to their dwellings, a lonely return.' The remainder of the company being more than satisfied with Capt. McNelly, the condition of their obligation, &c., were ordered by him to take up a line of march for our present camps thirty-five miles from Brownsville, where we met the old company, under command of Lieutenant T. C. Robinson, an officer of fine deportment and bearing."

It is of particular interest to note that this reporter could not avoid quoting a line from some unidentified poetic work. Knowing Pidge's penchant for quoting or paraphrasing poetry in his writings, one wonders if Robinson himself wrote this item.

12. The gleaning from the *San Antonio Herald* may have been a reference to the article reprinted in the *Statesman* of July 19, 1874, and earlier quoted here, about the young man who said his men were "derned well heeled."

13. "R. of Austin" is certainly Howard G. Rector, who enlisted with Robinson. Rector served under McNelly from July 25, 1874, to October 31, 1876, and later served under McNelly's successor, Capt. J. L. Hall.

14. This is a quotation from Charles Dickens's *Dombey and Son,* book 1, chapter 7: "He's tough, ma'am, tough is J. B. Tough and devilish sly." This work was first published in 1848.

15. The "D. H." initials refer to "Death's Head" or human skulls. The eighteenth century especially had an intense interest in the macabre. The expression *rampant regardant* is a heraldic term describing a lion (or other animal) rearing up on the hind legs, with forelegs or forepaws extended, and with head turned backward, all displayed from the side. Interestingly, the expression was used in a letter published in the *Cuero Star* of March 6, 1874 (five days before the killing of William Sutton and Gabriel Slaughter), written to the editor from "Near the Cow Pens on Sandies" by one signing his name "Juris Consultis." Consultis condemned the practice of mavericking, which allowed young boys to develop a good-sized herd of cattle in a short time. He wrote: "This system of things is the curse of our State, the death's head, which frightens thousands of good citizens from our borders. Its baleful influence is felt in every department of society. The whole community is *particeps criminis,* in this maverick business; for the actors in it can not be punished by law, are received in the best circles, and virtually encouraged in their pursuit." Could Pidge have read this very article?

16. Bucephalus was the horse of Alexander the Great. The name suggests any riding horse of an especially spirited and mettlesome nature. Pidge is using the term ironically here. Pidge became familiar with this term from Byron's "Mazeppa," as lines 101–106 reveal:

On the earth
So fit a pair had never birth,
Since Alexander's days till now,
As thy Bucephalus and thou:
All Scythia's fame to thine should yield
For pricking on o'er flood and field.

17. There is probably a double meaning in this expression. The verb *to guy* meant to make an object of ridicule, thus Robinson and Thompson would be ridiculed. Also it may be a word play on "guide," or "direct."

18. This is a reference to the Houston and Texas Central Railway Company.

This originated as the Galveston and Red River Railway, chartered in March, 1848, to build from Galveston Bay to the Red River. Four years of inactivity resulted in Houston citizens chartering legislation to permit the road to start at Houston. By the end of 1856 twenty-five miles were in operation, and the name was changed to the Houston and Texas Central. Fifty-five miles more had been built prior to 1861 when the Civil War stopped construction. The Houston and Texas Central would not build a line from Hempstead to Austin as expected, thus the citizens of Washington County decided to build a road from Hempstead to Brenham, the seat of Washington County. The Washington County Railroad was chartered in 1856 and completed in 1869. In 1869 the Houston and Central bought the Washington County Railroad and by 1871 had extended it ninety-four miles to Austin.

19. The newspapers of the 1870s have frequent references to lightning-rods and rod salesmen. Much humor evolved around the new phenomenon at the expense of the salesman. A poem had been published in the *San Antonio Daily Express* of August 19, 1873, by "Joe Jot, Jr." and could possibly have been read and enjoyed by Pidge.

20. Two men in the company could have been "H—s," either A. R. Hendricks or M. L. Hoplans. Since Hendricks was a sergeant it is assumed that "the most unfortunate man in the company" was Private Hoplans.

21. Frequently Pidge alludes to his own cowardliness and fear of death. Earlier he had joked about his search for a situation being probably a "permanent place"—that is, a place for his burial. Frequently allusions to death refer specifically to death by hanging. Of course this is not surprising for that time and place, as Texas was notorious for the frequency with which prisoners were tried, found guilty, and hanged through mob activity. Pidge was certainly aware of the recent occasion when a trio of prisoners had been lynched in DeWitt County: the lynching of R. P. "Scrap" Taylor, Jim White, and Alfred "Kute" Tuggle during the night of June 21–22, 1874. They were reportedly in the employ of John Wesley Hardin as cowboys. This had been reported in the *Statesman* of June 27. Earlier, during the night of June 7, 1874, three other Hardin associates had been lynched in Comanche County: brother Joseph G. Hardin and cousins W. A. "Bud" and T. K. "Tom" Dixon. This had also been reported in the *Statesman*, in the issue of June 11, 1874.

22. Cuero, on the east bank of the Guadalupe River only a few miles from Clinton, became the county seat of DeWitt County in 1876. At the time of Pidge's letter the town was to be only a temporary terminus of the Gulf, Western Texas and Pacific Railroad (GWT&PRR). In May, 1870, New Yorker Charles W. Morgan had announced his intention to build his own railway westward from Indianola through San Antonio and western Texas to California and the Pacific. The railway reached Cuero in March of 1873 but was not continued. There are occasional references to Morgan's engineers in the letters, and they are allusions to this scheme (see letters of August 28 and November 8, 1874). The director of the

GWT&PRR was ex-lieutenant governor Fletcher S. Stockdale, a prominent Indianola lawyer, who is later mentioned in the letter of December 5, 1874. Clinton, on the west bank of the Guadalupe River, had been named county seat in 1850, but with the arrival of the railroad at Cuero in 1873 Clinton's prosperity declined. As a terminus Cuero quickly eclipsed nearby Yorktown, which had been an important stage and wagon stop on the road from Indianola to San Antonio.

The weekly newspaper the *Cuero Star* began publishing in June, 1873, with Rudolph Kleberg as editor. The *Star* reported on May 21, 1874, in its forty-first issue, "Our enterprising and worthy postmaster, Dr. R. Frank, has made arrangements for a money order office in connection with the Postoffice." The Prussian-born man was still the postmaster, as the 1880 DeWitt County census shows him in that position. It is not known if Rudolph Frank was indeed a doctor or if the title was an honorary one.

23. DeWitt County had been considered the center of the Sutton-Taylor feud, so much so that it could easily have been termed the "DeWitt County War" rather than the Sutton-Taylor Feud. The surrounding counties that Pidge carefully chose to forget were Gonzales to the northwest, Lavaca to the northeast, Victoria to the southeast, Goliad due south, and Karnes to the west. DeWitt was in the center, some ninety miles south of Austin, which is in Travis County. Burton, county seat of Washington County, where McNelly resided, was some ninety miles to the northeast.

24. Pidge is here thinking of these lines from Macbeth:

> 1st Witch: When shall we three meet again. In thunder, lightning, or in rain?
> 2nd Witch: When the hurlyburly's done, When the battle's lost and won (act I, scene i, lines 1–4).

25. Reference to the jail was most timely as during the preceding month there had been a great demand for a new Travis County jail. The *Statesman* editorialized in its issue of July 10, 1874: "The present condition of this building, which consists of but a single room without air or ventilation, infested with vermine, reeking with abominable stench and crowded with a suffering mass of suffocating human beings, who strip themselves naked because of the intolerable heat and closeness—we say the present condition of the jail should bring a blush of shame to the cheek of every citizen in our county. It is a disgrace to the age and a crime against humanity." In the July 12 editorial the *Statesman* was pleased to learn that the new jail committee would soon issue a call for sealed bids. It was assumed that "no time will be lost in contracting for the construction of a prison which shall not also be a piece of torture to the 'miserables' there held in durance." It was not until July 26, 1876, however, that the prisoners were removed from the old to the new jail.

The following humorous suggestion had been printed in the *San Antonio Herald* as to how the state of Texas might rid itself of some of its desperadoes: "As the penitentiary is in a very crowded condition at present, would it not be a good idea for the district judges to give prisoners convicted of horse stealing, and the like, the choice either to go to the penitentiary or to DeWitt county? Some of the prisoners might, in their ignorance, choose the latter alternative, and thus, by degrees, a more law-abiding sentiment would spring up in the locality." This was reprinted in the *Statesman* of July 21, 1874, and was no doubt read by Pidge.

Coggia's comet had also received considerable attention in the press generally, not only in the *Statesman*. It was discovered the night of April 17, 1874, by J. E. Coggia in Marseilles, France. Frequent mentions of its visibility were made in the *Statesman* during July. On July 4 it was reported: "We observed the comet last night very plainly. . . . The tail is not very distinct to the naked eye, but it can, by closely observing the Heavens in the north, be seen dashing its way through space, and evidently reckless of its destination or orbit." In the July 8 issue it was reported: "The comet is yet very dim as observed from Austin. The gas company ought to turn the lights off for a night or two, just to encourage the thing."

26. Unfortunately E. A. Northington remains a mysterious figure. He joined McNelly's command at the same time as Robinson, being listed as one of the original nine men recruited at Austin, serving from July 25, 1874, to December 21, 1875. His name later appeared in the *Statesman* in the issue of May 16, 1875, as follows: "Northington, one of Capt. McNelly's soldiers, is in jail in Corpus for shooting a comrade named Patterson. Northington was drunk, and Patterson though seriously, is not mortally wounded." Presumably the companion was J. W. Patterson, who was also a ranger, serving from April 10 to May 9, 1875. No further details were given; what is remarkable is that Northington was not immediately dismissed for this incident.

27. Northington here errs, as the wounded man was Pvt. John W. Chalk, not Clark. Chalk served from July 25 to October 27, 1874. He later returned to Lampasas County and served as constable of Precinct 6, having been elected on November 5, 1878, and again on November 2, 1880. Chalk was typical of McNelly's Rangers, being very young. The 1870 Washington County census, enumerated on July 20 by B. J. Arndt, shows that Chalk was then fifteen years old, helping his father, Whitfield, on the farm. The Chalk and McNelly families both resided in Precinct 3, post office Brenham.

28. In McNelly's report of August 7 he stated that the attacking Tumlinson party consisted of fifteen men and that two of the rangers' horses had been shot. In his report of August 31 he wrote that the attacking party consisted of twenty-five men and that three horses had been wounded.

29. Captain McNelly's report of this incident, dated August 7, 1874, was as follows:

> I have the honor to report that on yesterday evening the Dist Atty Mr Wood requested me to have a subpoena [*sic*] served and to send a guard with John Taylor to Yorktown and that he could secure the Mendane of the witness[.] I accordingly detailed Sargt Middleton and 3 privates to wit, Irvin, Turner, and Chalk, they reached Yorktown and secured the witness and when eight miles

from here (on their return) they were suddenly met in the road by about fifteen armed men who demanded 'Who are you [?]' the Sargt replied 'Who are you [?]' they immediately reported 'Que dow' (or lookout) here they are boys give em hell' and immediately fired a volley from their rifles [.] Sargt Middleton ordered his men to dismount and cross a fence that borders one side of the road but before his order could be obeyed one of the men (Chalk) was shot through the shoulder and disabled[;] the other three returned the fire and for about ten or fifteen minutes from behind the fence the entire party taking position behind trees [;] they being in the shade and my men behind a fence were placed at quite a disadvantage and only succeeded in putting two holes through their hats and wounding one of their horses [.] during a lull in the firing they pretended to discover that it was my men and at once stopped, offered assistance to the wounded men and loaning my men three horses (two of our horses being shot) the man they were after (the witness) ran off at the first fire but I caught him this morning and have him in camp. The party was commanded by Old Joe Tumlinson.

Middleton's name first appears on McNelly's muster roll as third sergeant, having enlisted on July 25, 1874. He was discharged on February 24, 1875. A later muster roll from reorganization on August 31, 1875, lists his rank as private when discharged. This same roll of August 31 lists one J. R. Wofford as having been "killed in action Aug[ust] 8, 1874," two days after the battle with Tumlinson's forces. Strangely enough, no mention of this—either Wofford specifically or any other ranger being killed—appears in the Pidge writings during this period. No other reference to a Wofford being killed has been discovered in the McNelly papers. It is most likely that someone mistakenly reported Wofford being killed. A James R. Wofford did serve under McNelly from April 6 to August 31, 1875, and he died on March 20, 1912, in San Antonio. Interestingly Jack Hays Day, a Taylor man who wrote his memoirs of the feud some years after the events, in describing the lynching of Jim White, R. P. "Scrap" Taylor, and Alfred "Kute" Tuggle, wrote that one of the guards overpowered by the Sutton mob was a Jim Wofford.

30. "M—n" was Horace G. Mabin. He served first under McNelly from July 25, 1874, to February 1, 1877, and then under McNelly's successor, Capt. J. L. Hall. Later he served under Capt. T. L. Oglesby and Lts. Joseph Shely, Charles B. McKinney, and William Scott. In all he had served about ten years as a ranger.

31. The date of this article's appearance has not been determined as the early Cuero newspaper files are incomplete. This item was quoted by Victor M. Rose in *The Texas Vendetta.* Rose's work was the earliest serious attempt to provide a history of the feud. The quote in question: "First Square Fight.—Last Thursday night a fight occurred between six of Captain McNally's [*sic*] men and some unknown party about six miles from Clinton, on the Yorktown road. One soldier missing, one wounded, and two horses killed." McNelly's report of the incident to General Steele, written on August 7 from Clinton, indicated that the fight took place on the evening of August 6. Adjutant General Papers, Texas State Archives.

32. It is possible that this Frank W. who had recently left Virginia was the same man "W." to whom the Pidge letter of June 7 was ostensibly written.

33. The Whitworth gun, a rifle with a hexagonal barrel, achieved fame in the 1860s. It enjoyed some popularity as a sniping arm during the American Civil War, but by 1866 it was being eclipsed by other weapons.

34. The names of Tuggle, King, and John Taylor appear frequently in the literature of the Sutton-Taylor feud. The Tuggle referred to here is Lodwick Tuggle. The 1870 DeWitt County census shows Thomas J. and Amelia Tuggle with seven children still living at home: John A., Lodwick, Catherine, Nathaniel, Thomas, Elizabeth, and Adeline. John A. was twenty-one in 1870, his occupation given as a constable. Alfred Tuggle's name does not appear, as he was living elsewhere. His name did appear on the 1860 census, where he was listed as being fourteen years of age, born in Alabama in 1846. Alfred, Rufas P. "Scrap" Taylor, James White, James Monroe Bockius, G. W. Parker, J. Elder, and Thomas Bass were delivered to the DeWitt County sheriff, William J. Weisiger, in June, 1874, according to a report of Sgt. J. V. Atkinson, Company A, Frontier Battalion. They were accused of being cattle and horse thieves as well as being members of the John Wesley Hardin band of desperadoes. During the night of June 21–22 Taylor, White, and Tuggle were taken from the DeWitt County jail and lynched not far from Clinton. John Taylor's nephew was of course William Taylor, who, along with James Taylor, was considered a leader of the Taylor forces. On March 11, 1874, William Taylor killed Gabriel Slaughter while Jim Taylor killed William E. Sutton on the deck of the steamship *Clinton* at Indianola. Joe Tumlinson became leader of the Sutton forces after the death of William E. Sutton.

35. The "illustrious namesake" of young Milam was Benjamin Rush Milam (1788–1835), the Texas hero killed during the siege of Bexar. As yet I have found no source for the three-line poetic excerpt.

36. Pidge here misspells the word *teetotum,* a small top, a child's toy. In Roman antiquity the *retiarius* was a gladiator armed with a net and a trident.

37. The term *gotched* referred to floppy ears. Apparently Pidge is trying to describe an ear that somehow was erect or did not have a dropping angle. Charles Morgan was a shipping and railroad magnate (1795–1878). Because of the success of his early ventures in investing in merchant shipping and iron works he aspired to a monopoly of transportation in the large area from New York to Texas. In 1837 he opened the first scheduled steamship line between New Orleans and Galveston. Before and after the Civil War Morgan dominated intra-Gulf trade through providing excellent service and possession of exclusive United States mail contracts. In 1873 the Gulf, Western Texas and Pacific Railroad became a virtual Morgan monopoly because of his purchasing a partner's share of the project. Because of Morgan's bond purchase, construction beyond Victoria was begun in March, 1872, and was pledged to reach Cuero by October 1, 1872. The schedule was not kept, the railroad not reaching Cuero until March, 1873. It was on the Morgan steamship *Clinton* that Jim and Bill Taylor caught up with the leader of

the Sutton forces and killed him as well as his companion Gabriel Slaughter. It was also on a Morgan steamship that Pidge returned to New Orleans, on his way to spend his savings from money earned as a Texas Ranger. See the final chapter of this book for his letter of March 16, 1876, published on March 31—his last letter in the *Gazette.*

38. The term *short horn* is synonymous with "green horn," or dude. In truth, none of McNelly's men were dudes.

39. The "credulous and kind-hearted gentleman of Clinton" refers to either James T. Wofford or John Wofford. McNelly reported obtaining supplies from both these merchants. On the 1870 DeWitt County census, enumerated in June by Willis Fawcett, there is a John T. Wofford listed. Merchant Wofford was twenty-five years of age, white male, born in Texas, whose occupation was identified as "Merch and mge."

40. It is believed that Thompson and "Cigarette Jim" both refer to J. W. Thompson. "Cigarette Jim" was first mentioned in the letter of April 26, being one of the cowboys working with Pidge. Thompson was one of the Austin men who had enlisted at the same time as Pidge. He received a dishonorable discharge on August 16, 1874, for "conduct unbecoming a soldier and a gentleman." "C—k" refers to John W. Chalk. Adams refers to Spencer J. Adams, who served under McNelly from July 25, 1874, to February 1, 1877. He also authored his memoirs, which appeared under the title "Texas Frontier Reminiscences" in the *Railway Carmen's Journal of the United States and Canada* (September–November, 1911). Unfortunately Adams did not discuss the period of his service under McNelly at any length. Of his captain, Adams wrote: "Filling first one peace office and then another, he was forced to kill in hand to hand combat seven men, the details of either one of these fights would make an interesting story" (October, 1911, 557). Adams at that time was a member of the Lone Star Lodge No. 17 of Dallas.

41. Martin King, although reportedly a Taylor sympathizer, was instrumental in the action at Clinton on December 27, 1875, that resulted in the deaths of Jim Taylor, Mason "Mace" Arnold, alias "Winchester Smith," and A. R. Hendricks. Evidence indicates that King may have betrayed the Taylor trio by preventing them reaching their horses. King was later a jailor at Clinton and was killed there in early October, 1876, during a saloon brawl with two men named Davis, resulting from an argument over a game of cards (see *Victoria Advocate,* October 5, 1876). Of additional interest is that L. B. Wright, who would become first lieutenant in McNelly's company after death Robinson's death, wrote to Steele from Oakville, Texas, on October 8, 1876, about King's death: "Martin King of Clinton . . . one of the best citizens of the county, was killed in Clinton on last Sunday night [October 2]: The murderer, a worthless vagabond, was arrested and lodged in jail. King was unarmed, and it is said that the murder was altogether unprovoked." Adjutant General Papers, Texas State Archives.

42. The "pitched battle" Pidge had in mind had occurred on June 7, 1874, and was reported in the *Statesman* of June 28: "There was a regular battle be-

tween the Taylor and Sutton parties of DeWitt County at Cuero, on Sunday, the seventh. The Taylor party number[ed] some thirty persons, and the Sutton party about sixty. The battle ground had six dead horses on Monday morning. The dead men (if any) had been removed. The fight opened about dark, and lasted several hours. The fight was to be renewed next night. This is a lovely picture of society, and it is thought that many valuable citizens will be driven from the county by it. Can't our friend, Governor Coke, do something in the matter [?]"

McNelly discussed the murder of a Mexican in his report of September 2, 1874, as follows: "There was a murder committed near my camp a few days ago and on getting the information I at once mounted a squad of men and caught the murderer and turned him over to the sheriff [. I] arrested another man charged with an assault with intent to murder [.] He is also in jail." Adjutant General Papers, Texas State Archives.

43. The entire French adage is *L' homme propose et Dieu dispose* (Man proposes, God disposes), expressing the idea that the results of our intentions are sometimes changed by God's will.

44. Here again is an excellent example showing Pidge's literary knowledge. The verse opening this letter is a paraphrase of the opening stanza of Samuel Taylor Coleridge's "The Rime of the Ancient Mariner," beginning:

It is an ancient farmer man
And he stoppeth one of three.
"By thy long grey beard and glittering eye,
Now wherefore stopp'st thou me?"

Certainly the paraphrase was original with Pidge. One can only speculate on the vastness of this young man's literary knowledge. In the same September 24 issue of the *Statesman* editor Cardwell entered the following item concerning the contributions of his popular correspondent: "The great 'Pidge' has a communication in today's issue, brim-full of sparkling wit. His communications are attracting the attention of the press; and we shall not be surprised if some enterprising paper like the New York Herald should employ him to go abroad as a regular correspondent." Had some other newspaper made serious efforts to lure Pidge away from the *Statesman?*

45. Another small clue as to a custom of his life while living in Virginia, perhaps.

46. It was the battle of the Bridge of Lodi, as Napoleon himself claimed, that "first kindled the spark of boundless ambition" in his soul, and it proved to be a turning point in his career. The engagement, while pursuing the retreating Austro-Sardinian Army in May of 1796, was of small military importance. But it did gain for Napoleon the hearts of his soldiers and a reputation for great personal bravery. It was later that day that the French soldiers saluted their commander with the affectionate phrase *le petit caporal.*

47. Very likely Pidge had indeed heard of Hardin prior to coming to Texas, as

eastern newspapers frequently printed items dealing with the violence and lawless conditions of the American West. An item in the *San Antonio Daily Express* of December 4, 1877, dealt with Hardin's killing of Charles Webb in Comanche; it had appeared in the *Spectator* of London, England, in July, 1875! Needless to say the English article contained numerous errors. The description of Hardin's dexterity with a pistol may be only a slight exaggeration. When being taken from Austin to Comanche as a prisoner by the Texas Rangers in 1878 he was allowed to demonstrate his ability with empty pistols. The men of Company E under the command of Lt. N. O. Reynolds—no amateurs themselves—were quite impressed with what he could do.

48. Many years later Thomas Stell, who was a teenager during the seventies when the feud was at its worst and was sheriff of DeWitt County during the 1890s, wrote a memoir titled "The Taylor-Sutton Feud." He concluded with this comment on John Wesley Hardin: "Several times in past years I have seen statements in print as to how 'Wes' Hardin was wont to come to Cuero, order the merchants to close their stores, ride into saloons flourishing his six shooters and terrorizing the inhabitants for hours at a time . . . in defiance of the citizens of Cuero. . . . I say emphatically there is no truth in such statements and the only time that 'Wes' Hardin ever displayed any violence in Cuero was when he killed Morgan in 1874."

49. Here Pidge alludes to "Catherine wheels," an expression he used again in the letter of November 12. The term refers to a spiked wheel symbolizing the instrument of torture involved in the martyrdom of Saint Catherine.

50. "P.P.C." is the abbreviation of the French phrase for taking leave unofficially, *pour prendre congé*. Pidge is saying he would prefer to desert the service than to stand up and fight the deadly Hardin.

51. Pidge may have become familiar with the Hoosac Tunnel as there had been an article about it in the *Statesman* of January 15, 1874, announcing its completion on Thanksgiving Day, 1873. The Hoosac Mountain was a part of the Green Mountain range, across the western end of Massachusetts. This tunnel for the railroad had been started in 1850. The Boston and Albany Railroad had started the project, which was described as "one of the most stupendous engineering feats of modern times." This was the first United States tunnel to be driven with the aid of power drills and high explosives.

52. Referring to Hardin as a "divine" was possibly a coincidence, but it was fairly common knowledge that he was the son of a Methodist minister, and therefore referring to him thus was not exceptional. Even the *Spectator* of London used the expression "a noted divine" in its description of him.

53. The Columbiad was an obsolete, heavy, long-chambered muzzle-loading gun, designed for throwing shot and shell at a high degree of elevation.

54. David and Jonathan represent the epitome of loving friends, as "the soul of Jonathan was knit with the soul of David, and Jonathan loved him as his own soul" (Samuel I, 18:1). Jonathan was the son of Saul, and David was Saul's ap-

pointed successor as king of Israel. "Damon and Pythias" refer to a rhymed play by Richard Edwards, first performed in 1564 and printed in 1571. In the original legend Damon and Pythias visit Syracuse, and Damon is arrested on a baseless charge of spying and conspiring against the tyrant Dionysius. He is ordered to be executed. Damon obtains a respite of two months to return home to arrange his affairs, and Pythias offers himself as security. When Damon is delayed, Pythias offers himself. Each eventually tries to save the other by offering himself, which so impresses Dionysius that he pardons Damon and asks to be admitted to their brotherhood.

55. The proverb "heart of a stone," with the element of personification added by Pidge, originated with the American journalist and political satirist Seba Smith (1792–1868) in his work *The Life and Writings of Major Jack Downing, of Downingville,* first published in 1833 in Boston. Downing related his grandfather's experiences in a battle: "Well, we marched forward, but still kept firing, and presently we begun to come on to the inemy's [*sic*] ground; and then, O marcy [*sic*], such a sight I never see before and never want to again: stepping over the dead bodies, and the poor wounded wretches wallowing in their blood, mangled all to pieces, and such screeches and groans, some crying out dont kill me, dont kill me, and other begging us to kill 'em to put 'em out of misery. O, it was enough to melt the very heart of a stone, said my grandfather, wiping the tears from his eyes" (18). This is not to say definitely that Pidge had read this particular work; the expression had by this time become a proverb. It was his originality to capitalize "stone," giving it the personification effect.

56. "Sweet Spirit, Hear My Prayer" was composed by William Vincent Wallace. Pidge drew from these opening lines:

> Oh! Thou, to whom this heart ne'er yet
> Turned in anguish or regret,
> The past forgive, the future spare;
> Sweet spirit, hear my pray'r!

I have not located the article in the *Houston Daily Telegraph* to which Pidge refers. The trial of William Riley Taylor began on Thursday, September 24, 1874, at Indianola, with an armed guard stationed in the courtyard. Adj. Gen. William Steele, being present, explained to his honor Judge Barden that Governor Coke had ordered soldiers there to prevent an attempt to release Taylor by his friends or an attempt to mob him on the part of his enemies. The case involved both William and his cousin James Taylor, but since the latter was absent, not having been captured, District Attorney William H. Crain asked for an *alias capias* to every county in the state. Counsel for William Taylor were Colonel Slater of Victoria County, Colonel Jockey of DeWitt County, and General Woodward of Calhoun County. An application for continuance was made because Taylor believed he had not had the necessary time to prepare for trial and that important testimony was not available due to the absence of witnesses Neill Bowen (father-in-law of John

Wesley Hardin), Emanuel Clements (a cousin of Hardin's), and Thomas Caffall, all residents of Gonzales County. Taylor further claimed that he could prove by their testimony that he was not even present at the time William Sutton and Gabriel Slaughter were killed. William Taylor was remanded to Galveston. He and the guard were on the steamer *Morgan* when it left the wharf of Indianola at 3:00 p.m. on September 25, 1874. The group was escorted to the steamer by the Indianola brass band and a large party of citizens. During the violent storm of September 15–17, 1875, that destroyed the town of Indianola, Taylor was released from jail to prevent his drowning, and he made his escape. Taylor's final fate has not yet been determined. James Taylor was never arrested for his part in the killing of Sutton and Slaughter. He was killed at Clinton on December 27, 1875 (see Parsons, "Bill Sutton Avenged"). Texas newspapers contained frequent articles dealing with the activities of the Taylors. For the trial, see in particular the *Galveston Daily News* of September 28, citing special items of September 23, 24, and 25, 1875.

57. On October 18 Captain McNelly sent a brief report to Adjutant General Steele containing this paragraph, which also reflected a quieter situation in DeWitt County: "Everything seems very quiet at present. I continue to send out 'scouts' in squads of four or five (four or five squads at a time) instructed to ride in a particular course (so that I can communicate with them if necessary) and to approach towns and country stores in as unexpected a manner as possible and I find that it does a great deal of good and disperses congregations of these parties that usually meet at 'grog shops' to have difficulties or concoct devilment, most of them being under indictment in some part of the State. [They] are in constant expectation of the approach of an officer and when they hear of my coming they scatter." McNelly to Steele, October 18, 1984, Adjutant General Papers, Texas State Archives.

58. John Milam Taylor, uncle of William Taylor, resided in Precinct 3 when census taker Willis Fawcett enumerated DeWitt County in August, 1870. He was listed as thirty-three years of age, his occupation "stock raiser & farmer," with real estate listed at $1,530 and personal estate at $2,000. One child resided in the home, Joseph Creed Taylor. John Milam Taylor's wife Josephine L. was Alabama born; he and son Joseph were Texas born. His nephew William was tried again at Texana for the Sutton-Slaughter killing in May, 1878. Bondsmen listed were John Taylor, R. S. Flourney of Jackson County, Eugene Kelly of Lavaca County, and Bolivar Pridgen of DeWitt County. Taylor was acquitted. Living in the same precinct at the same time were two Tumlinson families: those of John and Joseph, the latter being the "Captain Joe" of whom Pidge wrote. "Captain Joe" was then fifty-nine years old and wealthy—$4,000 in real estate and a $5,000 personal estate. His wife Elizabeth was forty-one years of age; only one child was residing at home, Peter, aged fourteen years.

59. That Pidge gave this much space to Pvt. Josiah F. Turner suggests that he did have a great deal of respect for the man, even though Turner may have been

guilty of crimes. He had been mustered in on July 25, 1874, one of forty-seven men making up the Washington County Volunteer Militia Company. The pay roll shows his discharge on October 4 with two months and ten days of service, with a total of $65.33 due him. McNelly, in a letter to General Steele from Clinton dated October 8 wrote: "The Sheriff of Bastrop Co gave me a capias for Turner (of my Co) the other day & I arrested him & turned him over to the sheriff. I had all ready Some two months since sent him word that 'Turner' was a member of my co—& that on receipt of a capias I would arrest & deliver him in Bastrop Co jail. He knew it was not nessary [*sic*] to go to you for an order to have him turned over I only learned after his enlistment that he was indited [*sic*] or I should not have received him." McNelly to Steele, October 8, 1874.

60. Here is another example of quotations or paraphrases from the poetic work of Lord Byron. This originated in *Don Juan,* canto 3, strophe 84, lines 665–72:

He had travell'd 'mongst the Arabs,
Turks, and Franks,
And knew the self-love of the different nations;
And having lived with people of all ranks,
Had something ready upon most occasions—
Which got him a few presents and some thanks.
He varied with some skill his adulations;
To "do at Rome as Romans do," a piece
Of conduct was which he observed in Greece.

61. Sheriff William J. Weisiger was a native of Kentucky but came to Texas in 1852. During the war he had earned the rank of captain, Confederate States of America. The 1870 DeWitt County census, enumerated by Willis Fawcett on June 1, listed Weisiger as a thirty-seven-year-old farmer with real estate valued at $6,000 and personal estate at $2,000. He and his wife Susan M., aged thirty-three years, had six children ranging in age from one to thirteen. Weisiger was a DeWitt County sheriff from 1873 to 1880 and later served as tax collector. He died in 1885.

62. Pidge was old enough to have served in the Confederate Army, but I have found no record that he actually served.

63. I have not determined the source of this paraphrase.

64. It would certainly be valuable to learn more about this Turner who could earn such a high degree of respect from McNelly as well as Pidge. This is perhaps the highest praise given any of his ranger companions.

65. Pidge here shares his love of Byron's romantic poetry. This line is from Byron's 1812 work "And Thou Art Dead, as Young and Fair." Stanza 3 reads:

Yet did I love thee to the last
As fervently as thou,
Who didst not change through all the past,

And canst not alter now.
The love where Death has set his seal,
Nor age can chill, nor rival steal,
Nor falsehood disavow:
And, what were worse, thou canst not see
Or wrong, or fault, or change in me.

66. Here again is an example of the nautical metaphors occasionally found in the Pidge writings. It is of course only a suggestion that he had spent some time at sea.

67. *Old Mortality* was a novel by Sir Walter Scott, published in 1816. The title is taken from the nickname of a certain Robert Paterson, who toward the end of the eighteenth century wandered about Scotland cleaning and repairing the tombs of the Cameronians, a religious group who took up arms for their religious opinions during the reign of Charles II. The story is said to be based on anecdotes told by him and covers a period from religious intolerance to the more peaceful days of William III.

68. I have not determined the source of this paraphrase.

69. Presumably Pidge is here making some reference to an incident taking place on Coleto Creek, which rises in several branches in southwestern DeWitt County, forming portions of the county lines between DeWitt and Goliad and Victoria counties. This stream was known as Coleto Creek at least as early as 1836.

70. This is a paraphrase from Robert Burns's "Farewell":

It was a' for our rightfu' King
We left fair Scotland's strand;
It was a' for our rightfu' King
We e'er saw Irish land,
My dear—
We e'er saw Irish land.

71. Probably Pidge alludes here to John Graham of Claverhouse, Viscount Dundee, who in 1689 defeated Scottish government forces under Hugh Mackay. Dundee, leader of the victorious Jacobite Highlanders, was killed in the battle. William Wordsworth composed the sonnet "In the Pass of Killicranky" based on this battle, a sonnet with which Pidge was no doubt familiar.

72. The phrase "Let us have peace" is from the acceptance speech of Ulysses S. Grant, accepting the nomination of the Republican Party for president on May 29, 1868. Grant's party, by adopting the policy of Reconstruction that treated the South as a conquered province—and in its unsuccessful attempt to impeach President Johnson—was hardly promoting peace. But its candidate ventured to declare for peace.

73. The complete line is from Luke 2:29: "*Nunc dimittis servum tuum Domine*" (Lord, now lettest thou thy servant depart in peace). Not long before

this letter was written Pidge had been raised to the rank of lieutenant, as the *Statesman* later noted in its issue of December 9.

74. This reference to Hardin besieging Tumlinson in his "castle" refers to the action of August 12, 1873. The *Houston Daily Telegraph* of August 20 reported, in an article from the *Gonzales Inquirer,* that Hardin with thirty-five or forty well-armed men had held Tumlinson in a state of siege in his own home for two nights and a day. The Tumlinson party managed to dispatch a courier to Clinton for the sheriff, who, with a posse of some fifty men, arrived at Tumlinson's the following morning, August 14. Peace was declared, and the groups proceeded to Clinton. Hardin's group was in the lead, followed by the sheriff and his posse, who were followed by the Tumlinson group. At Clinton documents were prepared and signed and recorded at the clerk's office.

75. I have not determined the source of these lines. Possibly the courier was named Abraham, called "Ab." for short, but certainly not Abracadabra. This term describes a magical charm or incantation used to ward off calamity. Pidge is revealing his own literary knowledge, not Tumlinson's.

76. It is significant that Pidge should mention George "Tennell," pronounced as Pidge wrote it but correctly spelled Tennille. He has not received much attention in the literature of the feud or by western writers in general, which is curious, for apparently at the time of the feud itself he was considered an important individual. Hardin wrote of Tennille as a trusted friend and dependable companion. Tennille met his death fighting on July 8, 1874, in Gonzales County, surrounded by the sheriff and a posse of some twenty-five men. His death was reported in the *Statesman* of July 14, and in all probability Pidge had read of it: "A report has reached this city that George Tenneille [*sic*] was killed in Gonzales County by Sheriff [Green] DeWitt's posse last Friday. He was one of the leaders of the gang of desperadoes that has been making so much trouble in DeWitt county for some time past." The 1870 DeWitt County census enumerated by Willis Fawcett in September shows Tennille a resident of Precinct 3, with real estate valued at $10,000 and personal estate at $2,000. He was forty-four years old and was described as a "stock raiser & farmer." He was a native Texan. His wife was Amanda J. Tennille; after George's death she would marry James M. Bockius, who narrowly escaped from lynch mobs during the feud. Tennille's first daughter, Ann, thirteen years old in 1870, would in two years be married to Jim Clements, first cousin of John Wesley Hardin. For a brief biographical sketch of Tennille, see Parsons, "Forgotten Feudist."

77. These lines are from a popular French song, beginning:

Le Roi Gaillard qui s'appelle la Guerre,
C'est mon souverain tout debonair;
Au bouche qui rit, au main qui tue,
Au front d'airain, aux yeux de feu!
Comme il est beau ce roi si gai,
Qui fait le diable a quatre au gre,

Qui brule, qui boit, qui foudre, qui fume,
Qui aime le vin, le sang, l'ecume,
Qui jette la torche.

Seemingly Pidge was familiar with the entire poem.

78. There were at least two compromises or treaties of peace between the Sutton and Taylor forces, neither of which brought about a peaceful solution to the problems. Perhaps Pidge is here referring to the treaty that was published in the weekly *Cuero Star* of Friday, January 9, 1874, only the twenty-second issue of that newspaper. Eighty-seven names appear, many of which are well known in the feud literature. The agreement was signed before DeWitt County Justice of the Peace O. K. Tuton on January 3. Several who signed were killed in the turbulence, including Gabriel Webster Slaughter, John Guyns, George Culver Tennille, Alfred Tuggle, James C. Taylor, William Sutton, and Rufus P. Taylor. They would be killed within a year or so of signing the treaty. Some were killed by others who had signed one or both of the treaties. The first treaty was prepared and signed on August 12, 1873. For a more detailed consideration of the two treaties see Parsons, "Treaties of Peace, Acts of War."

79. This is a reference to the New York newspaper the *Ledger*. Under this title Robert Bonner achieved tremendous journalistic success, being editor from 1851 to 1887. Prior to the Civil War its circulation reached the astonishing number of 400,000. However, the quality of much of its content was low. Frank Luther Mott, in his *History of American Magazines*, wrote that the program of the *Ledger* was "innocuous romance, innocuous adventure, innocuous sentiment" (360). Many well-known authors were published in the *Ledger*, such as Edward Everett, Horace Greeley, Henry Ward Beecher, William Cullen Bryant, and Henry W. Longfellow. Dickens and Tennyson were two English authors represented.

80. It is possibly significant that Pidge again employs a nautical metaphor in describing the death of Jack Helm. Actually Hardin and Jim Taylor together killed Helm in Albuquerque, Gonzales County, in June of 1873, in the blacksmith shop in which Helm was working. He had formerly been a captain in the State Police under Governor E. J. Davis, appointed on July 1, 1870, as had McNelly. Helm's work as an officer received considerable negative criticism, in part due to the Kelly killings. On August 26, 1870, he and his posse killed Will and Henry Kelly, prisoners. Women of the Kelly family were witnesses, and the resulting outcry forced Governor Davis to suspend Helm. Although dismissed from the force, he remained a power in the anti-Taylor forces, acting as sheriff of DeWitt County.

The press of the day reported Helm's death very coldly, and the following example from the *San Antonio Daily Express* of July 25, 1873, is representative: "JACK HELM KILLED—In DeWitt County a desperado by the name of Hardin with several others of the same stripe rode up to the blacksmith shop of Jack Helm, while he was engaged at his work and riddled him with bullets."

81. See note 22 to this chapter regarding Morgan's railroad. The reference

to the brothers most likely involved two men named Peace, Christopher and Madison "Matt" Peace, who were early participants in the feud and were "known desperadoes" (Rose, *The Texas Vendetta,* 17). Another possibility is found in the *List of Fugitives from Justice,* compiled from reports of Texas county sheriffs, in which Dave and James Pace are listed as wanted by Lavaca County authorities. Dave Pace was wanted for theft of a gelding and for a murder committed in 1873; brother James Pace was wanted on an 1874 charge of assault to kill (Steele, *List of Fugitives,* 71–72).

82. See note 20 to this chapter in reference to lynchings.

83. The incident on New Year's Day was also noted in Robert J. Clow's diary. The entry for January 1, 1874, reads: "The hostile forces had a 'skirmish' in suburbs of the town. No one hurt. Both parties stopped all night. One at B & Bros [Brown and Brothers] Hotel & other in Lumber Yard." On January 2 Clow wrote: "Last night very quiet. Both warparties still in town. The forces mustering. Hardin has arrived. Expect fight this evening. Very warm. [And later the same day] The hostile forces are still in town. Took possession of Brown's hotel. Thompson & Openheimer's famalies [*sic*] went to Houston [.] Dark. No fighting yet. Things look gloomy. Everybody complaining. Don't know what will be the result" (Clow, "Memo and Account Book"). Of interest is that like the press, Clow described the hostilities as acts of war, using much military terminology.

It is doubtful if there is any truth in Pidge's statement that the peacemakers were so unpopular. The entire treaty that was drawn up and signed before O. K. Tuton was printed in the *Galveston Daily News* of May 19, 1875, in a lengthy article dealing with the feud. Eighty-six signatures were listed. Besides the expected names of the feudists appears the name of O. F. Pridgen, the son of Senator Bolivar J. Pridgen. This O. F. Pridgen later became a McNelly Ranger, serving alongside Pidge from April 1 to August 31, 1875.

84. This is an allusion to what Pidge himself did while employed in the office of the *Statesman.* The "blank spaces" would be easy type to set, due to the frequent profane words.

85. This quotation originated with the German play *Der Sohn der Wildness,* written in 1842 by Friedrich Halm and translated by Maria Lovell.

Zwei Sellen und en Gedanke,
Zwei Herzen und ein Schlag!

Its popularity is underscored by the lines being quoted in a local in the *Lynchburg Virginian* of December 14, 1874: "'MATRIMONIAL.—Two souls with but a single thought, two hearts that beat as one,' passed through Lynchburg yesterday morning, from Amherst county, where the services of a minister or of a magistrate will be in order, and that quickly."

86. McNelly's report to General Steele dated August 31 included the following reference to the railroad incident: "On one occasion one of my noncommissioned officers was compelled to use force in ejecting one of the Sut-

ton party from a car on the Indianola R. R. into which he attempted to force an entrance for the purpose of raising a difficulty with one of the Taylors, who was being guarded to and from the trial of his nephew [William Taylor]." McNelly to Steele, August 31, 1874, Adjutant General Papers, Texas State Archive. It is interesting to note Pidge's first mention of the Mexican bandit chieftain Cortina this early in his writings. It would not be until April 1875 that the Washington County Volunteer Militia Company would enter the border war. The *Statesman* of April 21, 1874, ran a lengthy article dealing with the "depredatory war waged by Mexicans." In this article Cortina received considerable attention. He was described as having "descended from a very respectable Mexican family. He is the 'black sheep' of the flock. A man of much more than ordinary intelligence, of pleasing address, rather good looks, as 'mild a mannered man as ever cut a throat or scuttled a ship.'" For the definitive study of Cortina see Thompson, *Cortina: Defending the Mexican Name in Texas.*

87. The *Galveston Daily News* carried two short articles about the Cuero Volksfest. Presumably Pidge is referring to one or both of the following, which appeared in the issues of October 11 and October 18, 1874.

> From Victoria—Special to the *Galveston News* Austin, October 10, 1874. The Volkfest of Cuero, DeWitt County, came off today. It is presumed they had a pleasant and refreshing time, as it has been a bright and lovely day, and a large number of excursionists from Indianola were joined by others at this place going up to Cuero.
>
> The excursion train was somewhat delayed on account of the regular freight train from Cuero this morning running off the track by striking a beef, throwing the engine and one car off the track. No one hurt.

The second item was in the form of a letter to the editor of the *News,* datelined Cuero, October 14.

> Last Saturday was a grand day for Cuero, the occasion being the first Cuero Volksfest. Over 5,000 people were in the procession, representing almost all trades and avocations of mercantile life. It was a magnificent spectacle, and far surpassed the most sanguine expectations. The people were delighted, and everything went off pleasantly.
>
> The grand display of fireworks at night, conducted by Dr. J. M. Reuse of Indianola was well worth riding a hundred miles to see.
>
> The merchants and people of Cuero have spared neither time, labor or money to make the Volksfest a success and well have their efforts been rewarded.

88. The humorous reference to "Teutons" was quite appropriate. A large proportion of the DeWitt County population was of Germanic heritage, and two of the principal business establishments were operated by native-born Germans: the Seider Hotel, founded by Ernest Seider in 1872, and Otto Buchel's estab-

lishment, founded in the summer of 1873. The mercantilist referred to here was Alexander Hamilton. The complimentary terms are from *Hamlet* (act III, scene i, line 162). Hamlet had cruelly told Ophelia to get herself to a nunnery. Her response, beginning with line 158, is as follows:

> O, what a noble mind is here o'er-thrown!
> The courtier's, soldier's, scholar's, eye, tongue, sword;
> The expectancy and rose of the fair state,
> The glass of fashion and the mould of form,
> The observed of all observers, quite, quite down!

89. Lieutenant Governor Richard Bennett Hubbard (1832–1901) had an extremely successful career in law and politics. He had graduated from Harvard Law School in 1853 and established his first law practice in Tyler, Texas. During the Civil War he commanded the 22nd Texas Regiment of Cavalry and earned the rank of colonel. In 1873 and 1876 he was elected lieutenant governor. In December, 1876, he became governor when Governor Richard Coke became senator. After retiring from public office Hubbard resumed his private law practice. The play on words here can best be appreciated by realizing that Hubbard's physical size was impressive, and the Austin *Statesman* itself was being increased in size. In mid-October a number of articles had appeared in the *Statesman* discussing its enlargement. In the issue of October 8 appeared this brief item: "The large WEEKLY STATESMAN, one of the neatest and best papers in the State, is issued this morning. Parties wishing copies to send off can call at our counting room and be supplied. The WEEKLY STATESMAN has the largest circulation of any journal in the State, outside of Galveston, and it is, therefore, a superior advertising medium." In subsequent items the editors indicated that although there was an increased cost, there were four additional columns per page. Businessmen were asked to support the *Statesman:* "In giving a liberal support to the STATESMAN they really, to that extent, help to increase their business and the value of their property. We shall therefore expect a generous support, and will give an ample equivalent in a good live, wide-awake daily, which will contain the latest news and market reports" (October 14, 1874).

90. This paragraph is one of the few that allude to Pidge's earlier years. The "patent Bogardus kicker" refers to the American inventor James Bogardus (1800–74), who was most noted for his engraving machine.

91. It is not positive that this poem is from Pidge, but most likely it was. It originated from DeWitt County, where he was at the time, and is similar in tone to several poems that are definitely from Pidge.

92. Pidge's last letter of 1874 and the last letter from DeWitt County to appear in the *Statesman* was printed in the issue of December 9. In the same issue the following was inserted, which may have been editor Cardwell's manner of thanking Pidge for his contributions and indicating that they would no longer continue. "'PIDGE' again favors the readers of the STATESMAN with one of his in-

imitable letters. And we are pleased to be able to state that his services have been appreciated, and he has been promoted to a lieutenancy in Captain McNelly's company. He is bound to be a favorite wherever he goes." Given his earlier difficulty finding employment, the promotion must have been an important honor and pay raise. As a sergeant he earned $22.50 monthly; as a lieutenant he received $133.33 monthly.

93. "Of the dead say nothing but good." The *Statesman* had reported the death of Joe Tumlinson in its issue of December 4, 1874: "The Cuero Star announces the death of the renowned Capt. Joe Tumlinson, who has been so well described by our correspondent 'Pidge.' He was a very prominent actor in the stirring scenes of that action. The correspondent of the Star, from Yorktown, on the twenty-fourth instant, writes: 'The ranks of the old Texas veterans and pioneers have again been thinned by the loss of the fearless old Capt. Joe Tumlinson. He had received baptism only a few days previous to his death, and met death with the same calmness with which he had so often faced it in battle with the treacherous Indian and Mexican. He was buried today with Masonic honors; mourned by his family and his many friends, to whom his aged arm was still a strong protection.'"

McNelly, in his letter to General Steele of November 5, also made reference to Tumlinson's religion. US Deputy Marshal E. S. Roberts had asked McNelly to assist him in serving some twenty-seven writs issued by the US Government in Galveston, for Tumlinson and friends. Wrote McNelly: "These writs include all of the leading spirits of the Tomlinson [*sic*] party and I think have been issued just in time for old 'Joe' has just joined church and I think must be meditating the death of some preacher or some kindred amusement. I have been more on the alert than ever."

Tumlinson was born on February 16, 1811, and died on November 23, 1874. His first wife was Johanna Taylor, whom he had married in Gonzales in the 1830s. She was a sister of William Riley Taylor, who married Elizabeth Tumlinson, sister of Joseph. Thus the Tumlinsons and the Taylors were related by marriage yet on opposing sides during the feud. It was the death of William P. "Buck" Taylor—son of William R. and Elizabeth Tumlinson Taylor—at the hands of a posse commanded by William E. Sutton that started the Texas feud anew in the late 1860s.

The 1870 US Census record shows Tumlinson being fifty-nine years of age with occupation as a "stockraiser." The value of his real estate was listed at $4,000 and personal estate at $5,000. His second wife, Elizabeth, was forty-one years of age. In the same household were Peter Tumlinson, fourteen years of age, and two blacks, Ben West, a "domestic servant" and Van Buren, a "stockhand." The census shows Tumlinson as well as all members of the Tumlinson household as being native to Texas.

94. Capt. John York settled in DeWitt County in 1845. He was killed on October 11, 1848, in an engagement with Indians on Escondido Creek. The town of Yorktown, DeWitt County, was named after him. Andrew Lockhart came to

Texas in 1825 with Green DeWitt's early colony. In 1839 his daughter Matilda was stolen by Comanches, being the first white child stolen by Indians in DeWitt County. Ruby Farrar Pridgen, "John York," and Alice Gray Upchurch, "Matilda Lockhart," in Tyler, *New Handbook of Texas*, 4:1124 and 6:256–57.

95. This brother of Captain Joe was John Jackson Tumlinson, who was born on December 19, 1804, in North Carolina, and died on May 20, 1853, in Texas. He and his first wife, Laura Cottle, had arrived in DeWitt County in 1829. After her death he married Delaney Asher on July 27, 1842, in Gonzales, and after Delaneny's death he married Mary Ann Asher on August 5, 1849, in DeWitt County. Daniel Boone Friar was a successful cattleman with substantial acreage west of the Guadalupe River. He died in January, 1858. His daughter Susan married William Weisiger, sheriff of DeWitt County, during the feud.

96. James F. Blair was one of the county commissioners of DeWitt County.

97. I have found no other reference to this poem or any other verses.

98. The original "Five Points" was an area of Lower Manhattan, an area notorious for disorder and debauchery. One area of Austin was also known by this name. In the *Statesman* of June 19, 1874, this item appeared: "The wickedest man in town is said to live in 'five points' of Austin, southwest of the jail. He ought to live in the jail." The area was sometimes called "Mexico" and was described in the *Statesman* on January 31, 1875, as "about the dirtiest, roughest corner of creation laid down on the city map."

99. Pidge's name was becoming familiar to newspapers readers all over Texas. Besides many admirers, he had his critics, and the editor of the *Cuero Star* found fault with something he wrote. Because many of the early issues of the *Star* have been lost we know of this only from the response printed in the *Statesman*. Editor Cardwell commented on the criticism in the *Statesman* of January 17, 1875:

> We understand that 'Pidge' has gotten himself into some little trouble down in DeWitt county in consequence of some typographical errors in his last letter published in the Statesman. The editor of the Cuero Star, therefore, went for him with a most sarcastic pen. We do not know whether it will get up a rebellion or not, but we are in a state of anxiety about 'Pidge,' and hasten to shoulder all responsibilities. He wrote something, in the shape of hen scratches, about 'eighty men,' and the types converted this valuable piece of information into 'eight men.' Things are conducted in no small style down in DeWitt. The people take pride in conducting such a character, and hence the trouble into which our correspondent has drifted. Hands should be shaken all around.

100. On January 5, 1874, owner W. G. Bowen sold the newspaper to Rudolph Kleberg of Cuero.

101. The description of the power that Hardin held over Cuero is of course an exaggeration, but he was "a whale among little fishes" in that he was considered by all to be the most notorious of Texas' many desperadoes. James B. Gillett, who guarded him during his trial in 1877–78, expressed this notion clearly in his

memoirs, *Six Years with the Texas Rangers*. It was not long after this Pidge letter was printed that the Texas Legislature offered a reward of four thousand dollars for Hardin's capture. This was the largest reward ever offered by the state for a single individual up to that time. The killing of a man in Cuero is a reference to Hardin's killing of J. B. Morgan on April 10, 1873. The version Hardin wrote in his autobiography is that an argument began in a Cuero bar when Morgan insisted that Hardin buy him a bottle of champagne. In the ensuing argument guns were drawn and Morgan was killed. He was the only man Hardin killed in Cuero. Victor M. Rose also wrote of the Hardin killing in his history of the feud. He quoted an item from the *Victoria Advocate*, date not provided: "Homicide.—We learn that a fatal affray occurred in Cuero last Friday morning, between a man named Morgan and a notorious desperado named Hardin, which resulted in the killing of the former."

102. The levity of the description of Hardin's killing of Morgan is strongly contrasted with the serious tone of this following paragraph. The Cox and Taylor referred to here were James W. Cox, assassinated in July of 1873, not long after the killing of Jack Helm, and Pitkin B. Taylor. During the summer of 1872 Taylor was lured from his home one night and killed. Of the Cox killing the *Houston Daily Telegraph* of July 27 reported: "The San Antonio Herald learns that two men named Cox and Chrisman [*sic*] were waylaid and murdered near the edge of DeWitt County. Cox was under indictment for murder in Karnes county and friends of his victim are thought to have been the perpetrators of this last outrage." Victor M. Rose quoted another news item: "There was a shocking double murder committed last week between Helena and Yorktown. It appears that two men, Cox and Cresman [*sic*], were journeying between the two towns named, when they were ambushed by unknown parties and killed. Cox was found with nineteen buckshot in his body, and his throat cut from ear to ear. He was with Helm in his Regulator depredations, and no doubt he was killed to avenge some injury inflicted then. The unfortunate Cresman was a stranger in this section, and not a party to the feud. Capt. Tumlinson and Ragland were riding a few yards to the rear when the volley emptied the saddles of their companions, and thus warned, saved themselves by a hasty retreat" (29–30).

Hardin referred to the double killing in his autobiography, darkly hinting that he was a member of the party doing the ambushing: "It was currently reported that I led the fight, but as I have never pleaded to that case, I will at this time have nothing to say" (Hardin, *The Life of John Wesley Hardin*, 82).

The press of the day frequently blamed the lawlessness of DeWitt County on Governor Coke's form of politics and frequently saw a solution to it in the form of reinstating the State Police of Governor E. J. Davis. Pidge makes a statement remarkable for its utter seriousness in condemning the citizenry itself for not ridding the country of the lawless element.

103. Mr. Mantalini was a character in the novel *Nicholas Nickelby* by Charles Dickens, published in 1838–39. Madame Mantalini was a fashionable dress-

maker whose husband was a selfish affected fop who lived on her earnings, leading to her ruin.

104. This is a word play on the city of Victoria and the English queen. John Wolfe was the English military commander who defeated the French at the Battle of Quebec in 1759. He and the French commander Montcalm both gave their lives in the battle of the Plains of Abraham. Wolfe became a national hero, a monument being erected to him in Westminster Abbey. Supposedly his last words were: "What, do they run already? Then I die happy!"

105. Fletcher S. Stockdale (1827–1902) was a native of Kentucky who moved to Texas in 1846, settling first at Indianola. He served as senator from 1857 to 1861, representing the twenty-sixth district. In 1863 he was elected lieutenant governor of Texas. After the departure of Pendleton Murrah in 1865 Stockdale became acting governor. Following the Civil War he moved to Cuero, where he practiced law. With the return of Democratic control after Reconstruction he became prominent in the Democratic Party. In 1872 he was delegate to the Democratic National Convention. Stockdale died at Cuero in 1902 and was buried in his native Kentucky. The town of Stockdale in Wilson County, Texas, is named after him.

The Victoria Fair that Pidge attended was on November 14–21, 1874. Unfortunately he did not give a serious description, but a correspondent named Lee wrote from Victoria, and his long article dated November 16 was published in the *Galveston Weekly News* of November 23. Since Pidge was present and witnessed some of the same events, the following is of interest:

> On the morning of the 12th (Friday) the road to the Fair Grounds was covered with vehicles and pedestrians. All passed at a little sentry box, where they purchased admission tickets before entering the large gate. Inside were stands, awnings and raised platforms, and benches comfortably disposed under the pleasant shade of trees, to the infinite satisfaction of the juveniles and their nurses. During the day races were in progress, refreshments were bought and sold, candy was made, purchased and eaten on the spot. The Victoria brass band delighted our ears, the children romped to their hearts' content, while the elders participated in the 'feast of reason and the flow of soul,' in listening to the chaste and elegant address delivered by Gov. Stockdale.
>
> It was a regular fete champetre, complete in itself, and will long be remembered by those fortunate enough to have been present.
>
> The ball took place at the Casino, and judging from the bright faces, was an appropriate sequel to the day. It was impossible to duly admire the numerous belles from the neighboring cities, mingled as they were with the youth and beauty of this place. But the youth and beauty were not confined to the softer sex; and certainly, the young men assembled to enjoy the festive hour were a credit to themselves, their parents and their friends. The destinies of our Lone Star State are surely in good keeping, and a beautiful future awaits us. Three cheers for Texas! And three times three for Victoria!

106. I have not been able to explain this reference to the Jenkinses.

107. I have not found the source for the "desolate wilderness" quotation.

108. The ruined mission was that of Nuestra Señora del Espíritu Santo de Zúñiga, and the presidio was Nuestra Señora de Loreta. The Mission Valley settlement was located three miles south of the Mission Valley Post Office, twelve miles west from Iberia on the west bank of the Guadalupe River. An advertisement in the *Cuero Star* of February 13, 1874, claimed: "Having resided in this region for more than twenty years, and giving fruit culture our especial attention we claim to know something of the wants of this country in the fruit line. We have exercised the utmost care in making a collection of varieties most suited to our climate, and best answering the requirements of our people." Local agents were listed as C. Q. Ragland of Goliad, R. W. Owens of Victoria, H. Arnecke of Arneckville, J. T. Kilgore of Clinton, R. C. Eckhardt of Yorktown, and G. Onderdonk of Mission Valley, Victoria County.

109. Did Pidge have an edition of Shakespeare along with him, or is this a quote from memory? The line is from *A Midsummer Night's Dream,* act II, scene i, lines 175. Puck is speaking to Oberon: "I'll put a girdle round about the earth in forty minutes."

110. Pidge's view is mirrored in the guarded optimism that Captain McNelly expressed in his report to General Steele dated November 30, 1874:

> To the law-abiding the presence of the state troops has been of incalculable value; the intimidation of the weak by armed bodies of lawless men has ceased and a feeling of security prevails until recently unknown.
>
> Numbers of both factions would willingly witness a renewal of hostilities as peace leaves them out of employment. These have nothing to lose and everything to gain by a return to open warfare and will do all in their power to promote discord. A strict watch is kept upon these characters and they are beginning to learn that they can no longer persist in their lawless course with impunity.
>
> The next session of court commences in December when both parties will be here in full force, and a difficulty between them may be expected, but if prudence and circumspection can prevent it, shall not occur; but if it does take place you may rest assured that I will have my men in such a position as will render the escape of the survivors impossible, and they will be held to answer and account for their offences.

PIDGE AND THE RIO GRANDE FRONTIER

1. Steele, *Report of the Adjutant General of the State of Texas for the Year 1875,* 10.

2. Capt. L. H. McNelly to Adj. Gen. W. Steele, May 14, 1875.

3. Telegrams from Brownsville, in *Galveston Daily News,* June 1 and 5, 1875.

4. *Texas Frontier Troubles,* House Report No. 343, 42.

5. O'Shaughnessy had been a member of the State Police at the same time

as Captain McNelly. His name appears on a muster roll dated March 29, 1873. Other names appearing on the same list provide a group of fascinating individuals: George A. Hall of Burton, who would serve with McNelly as a ranger; John Henry Hopkins Speights of Milam, who would be shot by John Wesley Hardin but survived the encounter; J. W. Millican of Comanche, who would attempt to capture Hardin while serving under Ranger Capt. John R. Waller. Most interesting of all perhaps is the name of Ricardo Flores of Brownsville, who also appears on this same muster roll. Although it is possible that the State Policeman Ricardo Flores and the Cortina raider Ricardo Flores may be two different people, the fact that the latter's residence was listed as Brownsville in 1873 suggests that they were one and the same.

6. The 1870 Washington County census shows the McNelly family; son "Rivel" was then four years old.

7. Texas Ranger Service Records, Texas State Archives, Austin.

8. One cannot help but conjecture on how much of this poem's content was inspired by the poet's own personal experiences. The mystical nature of the poem reminds one of the tone predominating in Coleridge's "Ancient Mariner," and this is not surprising as it is known that Pidge was familiar with this work. Especially significant is the concept of the murderer being hunted; in the "Ancient Mariner" it is the sailor who had killed the albatross who was hunted, as the man-killer is hunted here. If indeed Pidge had earlier killed a man, this may be his way of revealing that he had also experienced feelings of guilt. Note especially that lines 580–90 of "Ancient Mariner" describe the penance earned by wandering from land to land, agonizing until the Mariner could find someone to listen to his tale of sorrow.

9. Ranger "P" may be a reference to R. H. Pitts, who had joined McNelly on June 22, 1875, and was discharged on February 15, 1876.

10. Pidge refers here to the Shakespearean character Falstaff, rendered as Falstalan. No doubt a typesetter misread Pidge's handwriting and was unfamiliar with the name. This character is later mentioned in the poem "Hynes Store—Santa Maria—1863," printed in the *Gazette* of November 21, 1875.

11. Ranger "N" was probably E. A. Northington, who had joined with Robinson but was discharged on December 21, 1875. Other possibilities include S. M. Nichols, mustered on October 31, 1875; or J. H. Norton, mustered on April 1, 1875. These latter two names appear on the "Muster Roll Company A Vol Mil Washington" stationed at Santa Gertrudis, dated April 31, 1875. Nichols was discharged on February 29, 1876; Northington was discharged on December 21, 1875.

12. John Rogers (1500–55) was a Protestant martyr who, after cruel sufferings, died at the stake in 1555, the first Protestant martyr under the reign of Queen Mary. The "Canal Ring" dates to shortly after the Civil War, when a group of corrupt contractors and politicians conspired to defraud the state of New York by overcharging for repairs and improvements to the state's canal system. They defied an investigation in 1868 and were a powerful enough force for many years

to defeat unfriendly candidates for office. The "Indian Ring" scandal was one of many during the term of President Grant: William W. Belknap, secretary of war, participated in Indian Agency frauds. He resigned in March, 1876, during impeachment proceedings based on charges that he had sold licenses to corrupt agents at Indian trading posts. The "Whiskey Ring" refers to charges involving a conspiracy between Internal Revenue officials and whiskey distillers, located chiefly in St. Louis, and accomplices in Washington, to divide certain illegal abatements of whiskey taxes. This money was intended to raise funds for the Republican Party, especially to procure an additional presidential term for Grant. Because it involved Grant's private secretary, and to some extent the president himself, it was a major political scandal. The revelation of the improprieties did have an impact on the ensuing presidential campaign.

13. Former President Andrew Johnson died in Tennessee on July 31, 1875.

14. Henry Ward Beecher, an influential religious leader, was charged with having committed adultery with Elizabeth Tilton. After her confession, a retraction, much publicity, and public denials, Mr. Tilton charged Beecher with gross immorality. In 1874 he filed a complaint against Beecher for adultery and asked for $1,000,000 in damages. The 1875 trial lasted six months and resulted in a hung jury. He was finally cleared by a council of Congregational churches.

15. Pidge drew from Byron's *Childe Harold's Pilgrimage*, canto 3, stanza 25:

> And there was mounting in hot haste: the steed,
> The mustering squadron, and the clattering car,
> Went pouring forward with impetuous speed,
> And swiftly forming in the ranks of war;
> And the deep thunder peal on peal, afar
> And near; the beat of the alarming drum
> Roused up the soldier ere the morning star;
> While throng'd the citizens with terror dumb,
> Or whispering with white lips—"The foe!
> they come! They come!"

16. I have not found the source of the quotation "slowly and sadly we all marched back."

17. Jesus Sandoval had enlisted as a private under McNelly on May 1, 1875, and was discharged on January 20, 1877, having served a total of eighteen months and twenty-five days. William Callicott wrote of Sandoval:

> Old Casuse Sandoval, [was] a Mexican that had a big cattle ranch on this side of the river. Several years before we went out there he and a white man caught 4 Mexican cow thieves on this side of the Rio Grande River and hung all 4 of them to one tree. After that the Mexicans on the other side swore they intended to kill him. He hadn't slept at his house in over 10 years on account of being afraid he would be killed by the Mexican bandits. He came to Captain

McNelly and wanted to join our company so as he would have a chance to kill a few of the Mexican bandits. He knew the country well on this side of the River and all the Mexicans that lived on this side for miles away so the Captain let him join us, paying him the same he did us.

The Callicott memoirs consist of an autobiographical letter and three separate accounts of engagements in which he participated: the Lost Valley fight, the Palo Alto Prairie fight, and an untitled account of McNelly's invasion of Mexico. These recollections were written in 1921 in long hand and typed under the supervision of Walter Prescott Webb. Lengthy excerpts from these papers were first published in Webb's *The Texas Rangers* (1935) and later appeared in *True West* 9, no. 3 (January–February 1962): 6–10, et seq., and again in vol. 30, no. 8 (August, 1983): 68–75.

Of additional interest is that the *List of Fugitives from Justice, 1878,* prepared from reports received in the Adjutant General's Office, shows a Jesus Sandobal and an Antonio Sandobal wanted by Maverick County authorities for murder, having been indicted in March, 1873. It was reported that they had escaped to Mexico. One may be the McNelly Ranger of the same name. In the 1870 US Census of Cameron County there are two men named Jesus Sandoval (Sandoval and Sandobal would be pronounced the same; the difference in spelling means nothing).

18. The Fourth Earl of Chesterfield (1694–1773), an English diplomat and writer, was the embodiment of English gentility in the Augustan age. His *Letters to his Son* are considered a classic of eighteenth-century English literature, extolling the virtues of compromise, discretion, and the wisdom of always presenting a brave and mannerly appearance and of being the consummate civilized man in control of oneself and one's society at all times. By "their name is legion" Pidge refers to the biblical individual who resided among the tombs with an unclean spirit. He habitually mutilated himself and broke any chains that tethered him. When Christ entered into the country of the Gadarenes the man went to him and worshipped him, saying: "What have I to do with thee, Jesus, thou Son of the most high God? I adjure thee by God, that thou torment me not." Christ answered: "Come out of the man, thou unclean spirit." And then asked: "What is thy name?" He answered: "My name is Legion: for we are many" (Mark 5:7–10). Is Pidge comparing the border thieves, who numbered so many, with the evil spirit—Legion?

19. As an English dandy and wit, Beau Brummell (1778–1840) scorned the gaudy foppery of eighteenth-century fashion and influenced men toward simplicity and moderation in dress. Robinson undoubtedly witnessed some of Sandoval's executions. If the McNelly troop saw a suspicious-looking Mexican he would be captured and turned over to Sandoval for questioning. If it was determined that the prisoner was a "bandit spy" he would be hanged after revealing what information he knew of the raiding parties. Prior to the company's arrival on the river Pidge may have heard of Sandoval from reading the *Statesman.* In

the issue of December 31, 1874, appeared a letter signed "Old Texan," written from Brownsville on December 18, describing the tense situation. Wrote Old Texan: "A crisis will soon be inevitable. The Mexicans are killing and robbing us, and our people, irrespective of nationality, are taking and hanging raiders. Yesterday, [the bodies of] two raiders were brought into town. They had been hung for cattle stealing; the animals were in their possession. It created intense excitement among the Mexicans, one of them made oath as to the parties who did the hanging. Last night, warrants were issued for Bill Burke, deputy sheriff, Lino Saldana and Jesus Sandoval; the first two are in jail. I understand they belong to a large band of rancheros, organized to defend themselves and property. The friends of the thieves are using their influence to have them punished for the hanging. It is doubtful where the matter may end."

According to Private Callicott, McNelly "didn't like this kind of killing, but old Casuse did. He said: 'No use to catch them and let them go again. They would take the news to the other bandits that had the cattle and we never would catch them.'" Immediately preceding the Las Cuevas battle several spies had been executed by Sandoval. For a brief study of Sandoval's career see Joyce, "Jesus Sandoval."

20. Cortina had been arrested on July 1, 1875, by Col. Manuel Parrat of the Regular Mexican Cavalry. A special to the *Galveston Daily News* from Brownsville of that date said: "Cortina's Police have been arrested, disarmed, and imprisoned. There is great excitement in Matamoras, and trouble is anticipated. The Government forces are in possession of the Custom house building and are patrolling the streets. They have two pieces of artillery at the Custom house and others in different portions of the city." This complete item was printed in the *New York Times* of July 2, 1875.

Squire Joe Hynes receives attention later in the poem "Hynes Store—Santa Maria—1868," published in the *Gazette* of November 21, 1875. Lawrence J. Hynes lived at the ranch of Santa Maria thirty-five miles from Brownsville, in Cameron County. In an affidavit sworn on April 28, 1875, before J. F. Parker, clerk of US District Court, Eastern Division, he stated that he had lived there six years, four years as justice of the peace for Precinct 3, and had been engaged in selling goods and farming. He described various incidents of lawlessness perpetrated by Mexican "invaders." He lived in "constant danger of being attacked by marauders from Mexico, of being killed and robbed" (*Texas Frontier Troubles,* House Report No. 343,126–27). Squire Hynes also received attention from Robinson in the letter of March 4, 1876, published in the *Gazette* of March 16, 1876.

21. Edinburg is some fifty miles from Brownsville.

22. General Ramon Treviño was named governor of the State of Nuevo Leon, replacing the ousted Lerdo. This was done by President Díaz in hopes of receiving recognition by the United States government.

23. Fort Brown was established in 1846, on the Rio Grande, adjoining Brownsville. On the opposite side of the river about one mile distant was the city of Matamoros. In 1872 Brownsville had a post office and telegraph station but no rail-

roads in the vicinity. River steamers ran between Brazos Santiago and the post and also to Ringgold Barracks, well upstream. There was room at Fort Brown for four companies of infantry, one company of cavalry, and one battery of artillery. It included a fifty-bed hospital. Supplies were brought from New Orleans by steamer to Brazos, then by river. There were no Indians in the vicinity. The countryside was described as low flat prairie, with timber scarce and grass abundant. Ringgold Barracks, established in 1850, was three quarters of a mile from Rio Grande City, 121 miles from Brownsville. Camargo was five miles distant. The countryside was flat, with some hills of moderate altitude in various places in the vicinity of the river. The climate was listed as mild and dry with "northers" happening at irregular periods from November to May (Sheridan, *Outline Descriptions of the Posts*).

24. Sheridan's *Outline Descriptions of the Posts* gave this description of the river that would be the focal point of the violence for McNelly's company: "The Rio Grande rises in June and sometimes overflows its banks for miles on either side, rendering the roads almost impassable for six months in the year. The climate is mild and dry, that is, with rain at very long intervals, but the air is nearly always saturated with moisture on account of the proximity of the sea coast. Prevailing winds are southeasterly and southerly, with sudden and severe changes to the north. During the autumn of some years the locality has been sickly, the diseases being principally fevers—yellow, intermittant [*sic*] and bilious" (83).

25. This is a misquoted line from Shakespeare's *Richard II,* act II, scene iii, lines 57–58. The Earl of Northumberland says to the lords:

> Here comes the Lords of Ross and Willoughby,
> Bloody with spurring, fiery red with haste.

26. This is a further paraphrase from Byron alluding to the superstition that certain people could inflict injury through a glance from the evil eye. In Byron's long ballad "The Giaour" this superstition is referred to several times. Here Pidge is thinking of lines 608–19:

> Who leads them on with foreign brand,
> Far flashing in his red right hand?
> 'Tis he! 'tis he! I know him now;
> I know him by his pallid brow;
> I know him by the evil eye
> That aids his envious treachery;
> I know him by his jet-black bard:
> Though now array'd in Arnaut garb,
> Apostate from his own vile faith,
> It shall not save him from the death:
> 'Tis he! well met in any hour,
> Lost Leila's love, accursed Giaour!

27. There were several rangers who could be the "H" referred to here. On the pay roll list of those mustered in on September 1, 1875, made at the Tio Cano Ranch on November 30, were Sgt. G. A. Hall and Pvts. M. Halyard, C. W. Howery, A. Hagan, and J. Hickey. Among those who could have been "W" were W. T. Welch, M. H. Williams, B. T. Wilks, and Sgts. L. B. and L. L. Wright. Later a ranger identified only as "F" appears, and this was probably Pvt. M. Fleming. This "F" then later becomes "A," of whom there were three in the company: Sgt. John B. Armstrong and Pvts. S. J. Adams and G. H. Allen.

28. This was a fairly recent slang expression meaning to damage one's face, or to defeat someone severely.

29. This could be a veiled reference to Pidge himself. Seemingly he is deliberately drawing the reader's attention to his familiarity with the works of Lord Byron.

30. I have found no source for the "shriek, shriek" quotation.

31. The Convention of 1875 was presided over by Edward B. Pickett. It met on September 6, sat for eleven weeks, and submitted the new constitution to the people on February 15, 1876. The Democrats had eliminated the radical constitution of 1869. The 1876 Constitution provided for short terms of office, low salaries, and limited powers for officials. It generally indicated a lack of faith in the government. Interestingly, the Dallas *Herald* of September 19, 1875, included the following: "Capt. McNelly, the famous commander of the Frontier Rangers, is in Austin, and is receiving much attention from the citizens and members of the Convention."

32. I have found no source for this poem. It may be an original work by Pidge.

33. This letter about the "invasion" was read before the Schleicher committee in Congress, a committee that conducted an intensive investigation of the troubles along the Texas-Mexican border. Besides Gustave Schleicher, who chaired the committee, it included Alpheus S. Williams, a veteran of both the Mexican War and the American Civil War; Nathaniel P. Banks, a Union Army veteran; Stephen A. Hurlbut, another veteran; and Lucius Q. C. Lamar, a Confederate Army veteran who later became secretary of the interior under President Cleveland. In late 1875 citizens along the frontier nominated Captain McNelly, Col. John L. Haynes, and Capt. John Salmon "Rip" Ford as delegates to proceed to Washington to "represent frontier matters to federal authorities." McNelly's testimony as well as much other valuable material is preserved in *Texas Frontier Troubles,* in the *Congressional Record* of the 44th Congress, First Session, House Report No. 343.

Unfortunately McNelly does not list the names of those rangers who participated in the invasion of Mexico. From the Callicott manuscript some are learned: Captain McNelly, Pidge Robinson, Callicott, Jesus Sandoval, John B. Armstrong, George A. Hall, and Roe P. Orrill. Other accounts identify George Durham, Ed Pitts, William L. Rudd, and Tom Sullivan. Of these it is known for certain that the mounted five were Robinson, Sandoval, Hall, Armstrong, and Orrill. Of interest is that Pidge was riding a horse that had previously belonged to Jack Ellis, an American outlaw who had ridden with the raiders. Ellis had been one of the raiders killed in the battle on the Palo Alto Prairie. The horse was then given the name of his former master. Of additional interest, the 1878 *List of Fugitives from Justice* lists one Jack Ellis, wanted in Bastrop County for "Theft of gelding, committed April 23, 1871; indicted July 28, same year." Capt. James F. Randlett, captain of the 8th Cavalry, commanding Company A, provided an excellent official description of the invasion in his report to Col. Joseph H. Potter, commander of the 24th Infantry:

> About noon [of November 18], Captain McNally [*sic*], of Texas State Troops, arrived on the ground, and that evening, at about 8 o'clock, his company (thirty men) arrived. McNally at once declared his intention to cross the river, and called upon Major Clendenin to give his assistance when he should call for it.
>
> At about 1 o'clock on the morning of the 19th, Major Clendenin called me up, and said that McNally would cross against his advice, and directed me to assist him. I sent a sergeant and six men, mounted, down the river four miles, to a place where the cattle had crossed, to make a diversion, while, with ten other men, I took position on the bank and assisted McNally, and was prepared to cover him if attacked. The crossing was in a small dugout, its utmost capacity being to carry six men. With difficulty, he got his men and five horses over in little less than three hours, the attempt to cross horses causing great delay. Just before day McNally moved up toward Las Cuevas, hitting the upper ranch. I heard pretty sharp firing, and in less than half an hour saw the command back on the bank of the river.
>
> McNally came across to this side, leaving his men and Lieutenant Robinson, of his company, on the side of Mexico. He reported the Mexican regulars on his front, the whole force amounting to 250 men.
>
> Major Clendenin then took his departure for Ringgold. At about 7 o'clock I heard firing on the other bank, which proved that McNally's men had been attacked. I immediately stationed Farnsworth's, O'Connor's, and my own men on the bank and opened fire, under which McNally crossed and joined his men. They were soon attacked again. McNally had asked me to come to their assistance while he was crossing to rejoin his men. He now cried out, 'Randlett, for God's sake come over and help us.' I believed his command was in danger of annihilation, and at once crossed with two men in the boat, directing Farnsworth to command on this side, and send over men as fast as possible. He sent me about half his company and half of my own.
>
> During the forenoon the Mexicans made several weak attempts to advance to dislodge us. Their fire was light, and they were easily repulsed. By noon all firing ceased" (*Texas Frontier Troubles,* House Report No. 343, 94).

34. Recall that in the first stanza of the poem "Rio Grande—1875" there was also mention of the heavy dew.

35. The *Galveston Daily News* of July 14, 1875, reported from Brownsville that

the "Cuevas rancho is called 'Robbers' Den,' and is near Camargo. The people there are all raiders. Cattle thieves ply their vocation independent of Cortina." Several of the cattle thieves were named in a communication to the *alcalde* (mayor) of Las Cuevas from Capt. James F. Randlett, dated November 17 and quoted in the *Daily News:*

> Whereas certain persons of the Republic of Mexico Viz Antonio Flores, Unardo [Ricardo?] Flores, Anasapol de Madina, — Carilla, Bisinta Rodriguez, Leon Zamora, Matilda Romaras, Juan Garza, Vanina Chapala, and others have this day stolen and driven across the Rio Grande to Las Cuevas, 250 head of Horned Cattle, the property of citizens of the States of Texas of the United States of America, I, in the name of the Government of the said United States, demand of you the arrest of all the party above named, and the delivery to me, to be given to the civil authorities of the State of Texas for trial by its laws. I further demand the above named cattle be at once returned to me on this side of the Rio Grande.

36. Mr. Micawber was a principal character in Charles Dickens's novel *David Copperfield.* In chapter 11 appears this quotation which Pidge mis-paraphrases: "I have known him [Micawber] come home to supper with a flood of tears, and a declaration that nothing was now left but a jail; and go to bed making a calculation of the expenses of putting bow-windows to the house, 'in case anything turned up,' which was his favorite expression."

37. This was the command of Maj. A. J. Alexander of the 8th Cavalry. In his report to Lt. Helenus Dodt, acting assistant adjutant-general, District of the Rio Grande, Alexander described his movements on both sides of the river relevant to protecting McNelly and his men. Of additional interest is that he alludes to a raider hanged, the "hideous object waving in the night breeze." Alexander wrote: "From the best information I could get, seven of the thieves and their confederates were killed, and a number wounded. One of these men was killed by the Mexican authorities while taking him to the jail at Camargo, and another was hung by Mexican rancheros living on this side" (Alexander's report from Fort Brown, Texas, November 29, 1875, is reproduced in *Texas Frontier Troubles,* House Report No. 343, 90).

38. This is an attempt to write from memory or a paraphrase of stanza 13 of the anonymous fifteenth-century poem "The Nut-Brown Maid." The original is as follows:

> For an outlaw this is the law,
> That men him take and bind:
> Without pitie, hanged to be,
> And waver with the wind.

The raider who was thus executed was mentioned in the *Galveston Daily News* article of December 12, in special correspondence from Brownsville dated

December 3. The raider "was captured by the troops and delivered to some rancheros for safe keeping, who, recognizing him as the murderer of Alexander Movel, (killed near Rio Grande City in April last) suspended him to a tree."

39. In the Texas State Archives concerning McNelly's invasion there are numerous telegrams to General Steele relating specifically to the crossing of the Rio Grande. One dealt with Robinson's arrival on November 19: "I commence crossing at one oclock tonight[.] have thirty one men[.] will try & recover our cattle[.] the U S troops promise to cover my return[.] Lt Robinson has just arrived making a march of fifty miles in six hours."

40. The muster roll shows that the second sergeant was R. P. Orrill.

41. Pidge here borrows a line from Lord Byron's ballad "The Giaour," lines 364–70:

> Thou speakest—sooth: thy skiff unmoor,
> And waft us from the silent shore;
> Nay, leave the sail still furl'd, and ply
> The nearest oar that's scatter'd by,
> And midway to those rocks where sleep
> The channel'd waters dark and deep.

The mention of Noah is one of the rare biblical references in Pidge's writings. Johannes von Dollinger (1799–1890) was a German church historian and theologian, a prolific writer of both general and specialized works on church history, criticizing Protestantism as a break with the historical continuity and development of Christianity. There is also present in this passage the old idea that the Devil entered the ark of Noah by hiding in the shadow of Noah's wife.

42. The "Sinking Fund" contains a double play on words. The obvious is their sinking vessel as it crosses the Rio Grande. But the second reference—not surprisingly—is to a Byron poem. In *Don Juan,* canto 16, strophe 99, appears:

> The poets of Arithmetic are they
> Who, though they prove not two and two to be
> Five, as they might do in a modest way,
> Have plainly made it out that four are three,
> Judging by what they take, and what they pay.
> The Sinking Fund's unfathomable sea,
> That most unliquidating liquid, leaves
> The debt unsunk, yet sinks all it receives.

Byron was referring to the scheme devised by Walpole in 1717–18 to reduce the national debt, which failed miserably. Pidge's use of the term is further evidence that he was very familiar with the poetry of Byron, though there had been various "Sinking Funds" in United States history as well.

43. There were several privates in the company to whom R— could have referred: J. Racy, H. G. Rector, W. O. Reichel, Jose Ramirez, and W. L. Rudd. The

statement of "R" was a mock oath in which "timbers" was a slang term for an individual's legs.

44. There seems to be some confusion about the spelling of this ranch. William Callicott identified it as the "Cachattus." Of the number killed at Las Ancharvas ranch, and the number of Mexicans fighting McNelly, the captain telegraphed the following to Adj. Gen. William Steele on November 20, datelined "Mexico near Las Cuavas":

> I crossed the river on the eighteenth[.] on the nineteenth I marched on foot to ranch Las Cuevas[.] Killed four men before reaching the ranch & five afterwards[.] on my arrival I found about three hundred men after a few shots I retreated to the river as the U S [troops] were ordered not to cross[.] The Mexicans followed me to River and charged me[.] they were repulsed & as they seemed to be in force some forty U S Soldiers came over[.] the Mexicans made several attempts during the evening to dislodge us but failed[.] The United States troops withdrew to the left bank last night[.] I am in temporary earthworks and Have refused to leave until the cattle are returned[.] The Mexicans in my front are about four hundred[.] what shall I do[?]

This was signed "L H McNelly Capt Rangers." The number of men killed in the Las Cuevas battle varies. McNelly here indicates a total of nine; however, in William Steele's *Report of the Adjutant General of the State of Texas for the Year Ending August 31, 1876,* prepared for Governor Richard Coke, there is a different tally: "NOVEMBER, 1875.—On 19th, 20th and 21st, company on Mexican soil, at Las Cuevas, after cattle thieves and a herd of two hundred and fifty head of stolen cattle. Killed five Mexicans and wounded one. One company horse wounded. Received sixty-five head of cattle, turned over by the Mexican authorities" (9).

45. In defeat Shakespeare's Richard III had screamed, "A horse! A horse! My kingdom for a horse!" (act V, scene iv, line 7).

46. As earlier noted, Byron's "The Destruction of Sennacherib" begins: "The Assyrian came down like the wolf on the fold." It cannot be determined who "little M—" was. He could have been any of six privates with appropriate dates of service: E. McGinnis (June 22–December 21, 1875), A. S. McKay (June 22, 1875–February 1, 1877), Horace Mabin (July 25, 1874–February 1, 1877), G. Mathews (June 22, 1875–May 22, 1876), Pedro Mayniel (July 1–December 31, 1875), or Thomas Melvin (July 22, 1875–October 31, 1876).

47. This communication is also mentioned in the *Galveston Daily News* report of December 12, 1875: "About 4 p.m. a flag of truce, borne by Mexican commissioners, appeared, bringing a communication from the commandant of Camargo, addressed to the 'commandante of the forces invading Mexico.' This Captain McNelly refused to receive, as he had not invaded the country, but had crossed to assist the civil authorities in punishing a band of robbers. It was then opened by Capt. Randlett."

48. This is a line from a popular song by Fanny Steers:

The last line is broken
That bound me to thee,
And the words thou hast spokes
Have render'd me free.

49. O'Connor is mentioned several times in the important House Report No. 343 but is identified as Lieutenant O'Connor. Randlett first referred to him in the following: "While at Carabejals ranch, my courier returned from headquarters the Ringgold scouting party, which I now learned consisted of thirty men of M company, Eighth Cavalry, commanded by Lieutenant O'Connor, Eighth Cavalry" (92). Randlett praised the group: "The conduct and able support that I received from Lieutenant Farnsworth, Lieutenant Wilkinson, and Lieutenant O'Connor, and the brave and cheerful deportment of the enlisted men they commanded, detachments of D, H, and M companies, Eighth Cavalry, is worthy of praise and honor. No officer ever had a better command of its size" (95).

50. Pidge was not alone in thinking the rangers might serve as a second Alamo. A report from Brownsville, dated November 20 and published in the *San Antonio Daily Express* of November 24, said in part: "McNelly and his command are in the pasture of the rancho called Cucharras, near Los Cuevas, on Mexican side, surrounded and cut off . . . the whole Mexican population is under arms and hurrying from all quarters, and ere twenty-four hours at least 2000 men will have gathered around the doomed command, and history will probably be furnished with another Alamo."

51. Gen. Benjamin Franklin Butler (1818–93) had earned the undying hatred of the South with his issuance on May 15, 1862, of General Order No. 28, directed at the populace of New Orleans, which held that any woman showing disrespect to the United States flag or the uniform of the United States Army would be treated as a prostitute. He earned the nickname "Beast Butler" for this. He also earned the nickname "Spoons" Butler due to his alleged habit of pilfering the silverware from Southern homes.

52. At this time the muster rolls show George A. Hall as first sergeant. After retiring from the ranger service he returned to his home in Brenham, where he died.

53. I have found no other reference to Celestin.

54. Xerxes, as king of Persia, executed his father's thwarted plan to conquer Greece. He assembled an enormous army and armada, the largest force that the world had ever seen.

55. Col. Beriah Sellers was a character in Mark Twain's novel *The Gilded Age,* published in 1873, produced in 1874 as a play written by Mark Twain and Charles Dudley Warner. Sellers is depicted as a man of endless schemes and unwearied optimism, an "American Micawber." A monument was erected to the memory of Salinas. In the Walter Prescott Webb Collection, Center for American History, Austin, are photographs of it as well as of the Salinas home and others relating to the Las Cuevas raid. The inscription reads:

"Al Cuidadana Juan Flores Salinas
Que Competiendo Murio Per su Patria
El 19 de Noviembre 1875"

(To citizen Juan Flores Salinas, who died fighting for his country, November 19, 1875).

56. Ivan Mazeppa (1644–1709) was a Ukrainian ruler. As a long-time friend of Peter the Great, he aided the czar's campaigns against Turkey and Sweden. Later, because of fear of Russia's increasing power, he joined Swedish troops fighting against Russia. After Russia's victory at the Battle of Poltava (1709) he fled with Charles XII of Sweden to Turkish Bessarabia. As a young man in the Polish court he made advances to a Polish noblewoman. It is said that her irate husband tied him naked to a wild horse, which carried him to the Cossacks of the Ukrainian steppes. This incident was immortalized in Lord Byron's poem "Mazeppa" in 1819. Pidge became aware of the historical personage from reading Byron. The particular reference is found in lines 112–19:

And we have many a league to go,
With every now and then a blow,
And ten to one at least the foe,
Before our steeds may graze at ease,
Beyond the swift Borysthenes:
And, sire, your limbs have need of rest,
And I will be the sentinel
Of this your troop.

And in lines 854–59:

Let none despond, let none despair!
"To-morrow the Borysthenes
May see our coursers graze at ease
Upon his Turkish bank,—and never
Had I such welcome for a river
As I shall yield when safely there."

57. Pidge again uses the French phrase, correctly spelled *dernier ressort,* meaning "without appeal." McNelly's company received a special reward for the return of these stolen cattle. Capt. Richard King forwarded to McNelly five hundred dollars "as a slight testimonial of his appreciation of their services rendered to the State. It is a source of satisfaction to the soldiers to know that the people, whom they serve, have among them such princely characters" (*Galveston Weekly News,* December 13, 1875).

58. It is impossible to determine exactly which version of the Sharp's rifle McNelly's men carried. Whereas some certainly carried Winchesters, others preferred the Sharp's. Christopher Sharp worked at Harper's Ferry in the 1830s, and the gun soon became popular among hunters. It proved a favorite among the

Union and Confederate armies during the Civil War and became *de rigueur* with the buffalo hunters who nearly eliminated the huge herds in the 1870s. The rifle came in a number of styles and weights, the most famous perhaps being the "Big .50"—the cartridge available in length of 2 inches to 3½ inches. N. A. Jennings, who served for a time under McNelly, recalled that Texas "supplied carbines and ammunition, but the men could choose any style of arms they preferred. Winchesters or Sharp's carbines were the favorite guns, and Colt's, or Smith & Wesson's large-calibre six-shooters were used exclusively for small-arms" (Jennings, *A Texas Ranger,* 111).

59. Pidge had not created the name of Ricardo Flores from imagination. The name had appeared in the *Galveston Daily News* of June 15, 1875. In a special of June 14 appeared the following regarding the Palo Alto Prairie fight:

> One raider escaped, named Jose Maria Olguin. He was wounded, and feigned death, crawled into high grass, and was not found. He is in Matamoros, and had a ball extracted late yesterday. The raiders' casualties of the fight sum up twelve killed and one wounded. They lost, besides eleven horses, saddles, etc., all their arms, repeating rifles and pistols.
>
> Capt. McNelly could not go after the raiders under Ricardo Flores, because his horses were broken down. He gets but half rations and forage and has hard work to do. He should have full rations.
>
> Gen. Cortina is incensed at the killing of his cattle thieves. The Mexican papers say the raiders were assassinated while asleep. Capt. McNelly says if they were asleep he don't want to find any of them awake. Cortina swears he will have revenge.
>
> Flores and a party of armed Mexicans had robbed and killed Frenchman Vidal la Haille on March 16, 1874. Flores was arrested and jailed until trial before district court. He escaped and fled to Matamoros.

This item from the *Brownsville Sentinel,* reprinted in the *Statesman* of December 3, 1874, is of interest: "Ricardo Flores, who was accused and arrested for murdering a Frenchman for his money, and escaped from our jail a few months ago, is now in the cattle stealing business. A few days past he made a raid with his party into this county [Cameron], and gathered up a drove, which were crossed about two miles below this city. He was engaged in crossing his drove while the Aguja [Jose Maria Olguin] was doing the same, some miles further down the river."

The Cameron County census in 1870 enumerates one Ricardo Flores, age twenty-eight, farm laborer, living with his wife Santas, age twenty-five, and three children, in Precinct 1. This may be the same Ricardo Flores. In addition Flores's name appears in the *Lynchburg Virginian,* a newspaper with which Robinson was certainly familiar, in the issue of November 17, 1874. A special to the *Galveston Daily News* from Brownsville gave an account of a raid in Los Alamos by raiders from Matamoros. The account noted that "Ricardo Flores is stealing cattle from this side" but gave no additional details. One wonders whether this was sent to the Lynchburg newspaper by Robinson himself; Lynchburg, some seven miles from Rustburg, had the principal local paper, and the Robinson home was between the two towns.

60. Elsewhere in the *Gazette* of Saturday, March 18, editor Elliott presented this brief item in the "Local News."

> The letter of our Rio Grande correspondent will be read with deep interest. Another of the 9th inst. will appear tomorrow, giving further details on the Mexican revolution. Pidge's letter in the GAZETTE, giving an account of McNelly's raid in Mexico, was read before the Schleicher committee in Congress and attracted deep interest with the members.

Farther down in the same column appeared this longer item, which provided tantalizing clues as to the possible identity of the ranger-correspondent:

> On the first page of to-day's GAZETTE will be found a very able letter from our Rio Grande correspondent, "Pidge." Who in the name of thunder is Pidge," the reader may ask, and Brutus like, pause for reply. We answer that. "Pidge" is the nom de plume for one of our gallant rangers, and our special correspondent. Right in the very front and in every hair breadth 'scape from the time of McNelly's guardianship of DeWitt county to raid after cattle thieves in Mexico, and from thence down to the present time, he has been our faithful and humorous chronicler of border events. They are always reliable for they come from the seat of war, really and truly Pope's headquarters in the saddle—though without that gentleman's egotism or lack of accuracy. "Pidge" is not quite so good a humorist as Mark Twain, but he would be with development and is quite as original as "Doesticks" and all the rest of the genius, and mark the prediction and underline it will make his mark sometime. He always eats three or four greasers before breakfast to found his puns on—a good foundation truly—and is capable of greater things. Our advice to our readers is this: Read these letters carefully—and apart from the fun contained in them, there is a pearl of true wisdom—the real and actual history of events as they occur on ours and the Mexican borders.

61. Gen. José de la Cruz Porfirio Díaz (1830–1915) began as a young man in military life, leading a battalion against Santa Anna in 1854 after joining the army in 1847. He adhered to the Juarez party in the War of the Reform. From the early 1860s he fought the French, entering Mexico City in June, 1867. That year he was a candidate for the presidency, but Juarez was elected. Juarez was succeeded by Sebastian Lerdo de Tejada, and finally in 1876, after continued opposition, Díaz drove Lerdo out. Díaz served as provisional president in 1876–77 and became president in May, 1877. He was reelected president in 1884 and served until 1910, resigning in 1911 faced with the revolt of Madero, Zapata, and Villa. He died in exile in Paris. The statement that Díaz supposedly made regarding starting a revolution, quoted in a New York newspaper, has not been located; it

was in not the *New York Times*. Earlier, in January of 1876, Díaz had appeared in Brownsville seeking financial aid from the United States. He was referred to John S. "Rip" Ford, who told him the United States would provide him with financial aid if he gave his word that Cortina would be removed from the frontier. Díaz did make the promise (Hughes, *Rebellious Ranger*, 258–59).

62. The "Kilkenny cats" expression was quite popular at this time. It had appeared in the *Daily Democratic Statesman* of April 18, 1874, in an article concerning Colonel Christo, General Canales, and Cortina, quoted from the *Brownsville Sentinel*. The *Statesman* commented editorially: "It will be a good thing for Mexico and our citizens on the Rio Grande, if they would be like the Kilkenny cats, fight with each other until nothing was left. It matters not who is the victor. Like a pestilence, their exit from the community will be a cause for the most profound congratulations."

63. Sebastian Lerdo de Tejado (1825–1880) became the chief minister of Benito Juárez, serving from 1863 to 1871. On the death of Juárez in 1872 he became president. He was elected to that position and served until November, 1876, when he was driven out of Mexico by the revolutionary army of Porfirio Díaz.

64. Guadalupe Espinosa was identified as one of the thieves killed in the Palo Alto Prairie battle (*Texas Frontier Troubles*, House Report No. 343, 58). The report contained the following:

> On Saturday the 12th day of June, Captain McNally [*sic*] had a fight with a band of cattle-thieves near the old battle-field of Palo Alto, about twelve miles from Brownsville, and about the same distance from the mouth of the Rio Grande, in which he killed eleven of the thieves, wounded three others, and recaptured from them two hundred and fifty-three head of stolen beeves, of various American brands, that the thieves were driving in the direction of the mouth of the Rio Grande; and, from the fact that Pancho Lopez, Guadalupe Espinosa, and Rafael Salinas were killed, and Jose Maria Olguin, alias El Aguja, was wounded in this action, and that they had been recognized with Cortina during the delivery of his contract, which was short the amount of the stolen herd, the evidence is irresistible that the thieves were sent over by Cortina to steal the necessary number of cattle to complete his contract.

Pidge no doubt uses "historic" to describe the battle because of an earlier battle on the same prairie during the Mexican War. It was the first battle of that war, taking place on May 8, 1846. This battle brought victory to the American forces under the command of Gen. Zachary Taylor, who defeated a Mexican force twice the size under the command of Gen. Mariano Arista.

65. D. W. C. Kells, a native of New York, had received his appointment in 1861 and had entered the service as an acting volunteer officer; he was actively engaged throughout the Civil War. Commissioned a lieutenant on December 18, 1868, he received his commission as lieutenant-commander in 1870. He commanded the *Pawnee* 1871–72 and was on special duty in New Orleans in com-

mand of the *Canonicus,* an ironclad, in 1873–74. Kells was interviewed in New Orleans while there to recruit more men for the Rio Grande. The interview appeared in the *Times Picayune* of November 23, 1875: "He reports all things quiet along the Mexican border with the exception of the disturbances caused by the inroads of cattle thieves. The *Rio Bravo* has been stationed at Brownsville, Texas, and acts as a provision ship, aggressive movements being carried on by steam launches. Capt. Kells has come to the city to obtain recruits for service on the above river, and he will find himself surrounded by a perfect storm of applications for enlistment."

66. The *Rio Bravo* was a light draft, side-wheel steamer, purchased by the navy in 1875 for special service on the Rio Grande as requested by Brig. Gen. E. O. C. Ord, commander of the Department of Texas. For five years the *Rio Bravo* would operate out of Brownsville, cooperating with the military commander to protect the Texas frontier against raiders based in Mexico and to inhibit smuggling into the United States from the "free zone" in Tamaulipas. In *Frank Leslie's Illustrated Newspaper* of January 1, 1876, appeared the article "Troubles on the Rio Grande: A War Cloud," which included illustrations showing the *Rio Bravo,* captioned: "The United States Flotilla Steaming Up the Rio Grande." Of interest is that J. L. Haynes, in testimony given on March 4, 1878, produced a document dated Brownsville, November 16, 1875, showing that Kells had attempted in various ways to precipitate a confrontation involving the *Rio Bravo.* Supposedly Kells wanted the *Rio Bravo* to be fired upon so that he could retaliate in kind against the Mexican forces. With this idea rejected by Haynes, Kells suggested that some of McNelly's men could be induced to cross the river and fire upon the *Rio Bravo,* or else some Mexicans could be hired for that purpose. Kells was relieved of his duty shortly afterward. Haynes also testified: "I will do Commander Kells the justice to say that I am fully convinced that he thought he was carrying out the purposes for which he had been sent to the Rio Grande with his gunboat, and that his only fault was an entire want of discretion, and of any perception of the morality, or the right or wrong of the means to be used to accomplish his purposes, and that he seemed to be governed by the idea that the end justified the means." Testimony of J. L. Haynes (document dated Brownsville, November 16, 1875), in *Testimony Taken by the Committee on Military Affairs in Relation to the Texas Border Troubles* (Washington, D.C.: Government Printing Office, 1878). The important details of Kells's plan appear on 281–82.

67. Prior to the ship becoming the *Rio Bravo* it was known as the *Canonices,* hence the pun "Cannon, I cuss."

68. The "Zona Libra" or free zone was a narrow strip along the Rio Grande free of custom duties, which had been established by the State of Tamaulipas in 1858. Two problems this created were that smuggling operations were encouraged as there was no duty to be paid on goods entering the United States, and it diverted the population from Texas to Mexican towns on the lower Rio Grande. Of course the biggest problem for Texans was the stealing of cattle and hides.

When the United States requested the government of Mexico to abolish the zone, as it discriminated against US commerce and interests, the free belt was extended to almost double its former length, that belt being six miles in width and about three hundred miles in length. (See *Texas Frontier Troubles,* House Report No. 343, 172.)

69. I have not learned the identity of this Jenkins.

70. The item from a late *Gazette* was in the issue of February 20, 1876:

> Capt. McNally [*sic*], commander of the Texas frontier forces, has returned from the national capital and will stay a few days at the capital. The captain has earned an undying reputation for his gallant conduct on the Rio Grande and is a worthy successor to those old heroes who fought the enemy in the years that have past. His evidence carried great weight with the congressional committee, for he was direct from the seat of war, and made practical suggestions based upon his own experience, of the greatest value. Col. Schleicher has managed this delicate business very admirably for Adjutant General Steele. McNally and Gen. Ord corroborated each other, and their chain of evidence was so complete that it was impossible to break it.

71. Only two days after the writing of this letter Pena took possession of Camargo. A March 6 special to the *Galveston Daily News,* reprinted in the *New York Times* of March 7, 1876, included the following: "Pena after taking Reynosa and his force being augmented by about four hundred volunteers, received orders from Diaz to advance immediately on Camargo. It is reported that he has reached Las Cuevas, the noted den of cattle thieves and the point at which McNally [*sic*] recently crossed into Mexico, where his force will probably be increased. . . . Pena is sufficiently strong to make an attempt on Matamoras."

72. Matamoros was frequently referred to by this term. Interestingly, a long communication from General Cortina, dated September 8, 1875, was printed in House Report No. 343 and was datelined "Heroic Matamoras." The term originated in 1851 when one Carvajal headed a revolt against the government at Matamoros. He surrounded the public plaza held by General Avalos. Finally Avalos drove out the superior force of Carvajal. Because of this heroic action the Matamoros government decreed that the title "Heroic" should be a part of the name on all legal documents.

73. The expression *quien sabe* received attention in House Report No. 343 also. J. L. Haynes, in his report discussing the "Population Between the Nueces and the Rio Grande." stated: "It is a general and notorious complaint on the part of our officers of justice that our population of Mexican origin are not prompt to give information against raiders and cattle-thieves, and that they are reluctant to testify in the courts against them, and that when questioned on the subject, they too often reply with their expressive shrug of the shoulders and the inevitable quien sabe with which they avoid testimony" (House Report No. 343, 56). Haynes was customs collector of the District of Brazos de Santiago, which included Cameron,

Hidalgo, and Starr counties. He had been named chair of the permanent committee, appointed at a meeting of the citizens of Brownsville on April 17, 1875.

74. The references all involve extended wanderings. Sir John Franklin (1786–1847) was a famed nineteenth-century English explorer, present at the battle of Trafalgar in 1805 and the naval campaign against New Orleans in 1814. His claim to fame was a failed 1845 expedition to find the Northwest Passage; he was never seen again, but the many search parties did contribute a great deal of knowledge of the Arctic. Dr. David Livingstone (1813–73) was a medical missionary who conducted extensive explorations of southern and Central Africa beginning in the 1850s; he is buried in Westminster Abbey. Charley Ross was a four-year-old child when kidnapped from his Philadelphia home on July 1, 1874, the first child kidnapped for ransom in United States history; his fate was never determined. William March "Boss" Tweed (1823–78) and associates plundered taxpayers out of vast sums of money in the late 1860s. Thomas Nast exposed Tweed in *Harper's Weekly* during 1870. Tweed was tried and imprisoned; released in 1875, he was jailed again following a civil suit but escaped and fled to Spain, where he was identified through another Nast cartoon and was returned to a New York City jail. The Wandering Jew is a Christian legend: supposedly the Jew who joined in the mocking of Christ at the Crucifixion, he was doomed to wander the earth until Judgment Day.

75. I have been unable to locate any copies of this newspaper.

76. Possibly Pidge here alludes to an item that appeared in the *Galveston Daily News* of December 10, 1875: "The Verse del Pueblo, of the 7th instant, in conclusion of a long tirade of abuse of Captain McNelly, says of his crossing into Mexico, that the government of Mexico should demand indemnity for the lives lost, and force the American flag at Brownsville to salute the national colors of Mexico. In case of failure it proposes for Mexico to tear up the existing treaties."

77. I have not been able to locate this item that reportedly appeared "in a Brownsville paper."

78. I have not been able to locate the source of this poetic phrase. William Kidd was a notorious pirate of the latter half of the sixteenth century. In April, 1698, most of his crew mutinied, ransacking and destroying the *Adventure Galley,* stealing Kidd's journal and log to destroy evidence against themselves. Kidd was later arrested and imprisoned in Newgate in April, 1700. Charged with having murdered his mutinous gunner William Moore, and with piracy, he was hanged in London in 1701.

79. This was the title and the first line of a six-verse hymn:

> On Jordan's stormy banks I stand,
> And cast a wishful eye,
> To Canaan's fair and happy land,
> Where my possessions lie.

If Pidge had a verse in mind this would undoubtedly have been the one.

80. In a communication to General Steele the day prior to writing this letter, Pidge alluded to Díaz's forces capturing Mier. The company was at Laguna de las Flores, "eighteen or twenty miles north of Santa Maria & ten miles from Arroyo Colorado." He had sent out a scouting party to intercept a group with stolen horses. He suspected the herd had been captured by some of General Díaz's revolutionists. His last statement was: "The Diaz party it is said, has captured Mier, & three fourths of the Republic is stated to be in revolt."

Ironically, on April 2, 1876, only days after Pidge had returned home to settle the old score, Díaz crossed the Rio Grande into Matamoros, Tamaulipas, with a handful of followers. Shortly thereafter he became provisional president, 1876–77. He was elected president 1877–80 and afterward served seven consecutive terms from 1884 to 1911.

81. Elsewhere in this issue of the *Gazette* appeared this item in the "Local News," drawing readers' attention to another letter from Pidge: "On the first page of to-day's GAZETTE will be found an interesting Rio Grande letter from our frontier correspondent—Pidge."

82. These lines, quoted almost exactly, lead one to suspect that Pidge had a copy of the poem before him as he wrote the letter. The lines compose the seventh and last verse of Joaquin Miller's "Pilgrims of the Plains." Possibly Pidge had the *Lynchburg Virginian* of August 26, 1875; it could be loosely termed his hometown newspaper. For some reason Miller altered the poem after the initial publication; readers wanting to locate the entire poem in later editions of his works will not find this verse. The verse as it appeared in the *Virginian* is as follows:

> They learned to read the sign of storms,
> The moon's wide circles, sunset bars.
> And storm provoking blood and flame;
> And like the Chaldean shepherds came
> At night to name the moving stars;
> And in the heavens pictured forms
> Of beast and fishes of the sea;
> And marked the great bear wearily
> Rise up and drag his clinking chain
> Of stars around the starry main.

83. A great deal of controversy centered around President Grant and the possibility of his running for a third term as president. His first term began in 1869 and he served until 1877. As early as 1875 he was literally forced to respond to the pressures as to his seeking a third term. In a long letter of May 29, 1875, he wrote: "Now, for the third term. I do not want it any more than I did the first. . . . I am not, nor have I ever been, a candidate for a renomination. I would not accept a nomination if it were tendered, unless it should come under such circumstances as to make it an imperative duty—circumstances not likely to arise" (McPherson, *A Handbook of Politics*).

84. This was an easy play on words for Pidge as the first sergeant at this time was George A. Hall.

85. Victoria Claflin Woodhull (1838–1927) distinguished herself as a stockbroker in New York in 1870, then ran for president in 1872. She later lectured on free love and, in the eyes of many contemporaries, generally made a public display of herself. She and her sister Tennessee Claflin began a newspaper to present their views, the *Woodhull and Claflin's Weekly.* Theodore Tilton (1835–1907) earned early recognition as a newspaper reporter for the *New York Tribune* and later became managing editor of the *Independent,* a Congregationalist journal of New York City. His publication included such noteworthy authors as Elizabeth Barrett Browning, Whittier, Lowell, and Garrison. He regularly published the sermons of Henry Ward Beecher. His career was totally disrupted when his wife confessed having had intimate relations with Beecher. After formal charges, a lawsuit, and a trial that ended with a hung jury, Tilton was ruined in fortune and reputation.

86. Emma Nevitte Southworth (1829–99) was perhaps the most popular woman novelist of the nineteenth century. One of her earliest novels was *Retribution* (1849). Encouraged to give up her teaching career and turn exclusively to writing, for many years she wrote serials for the *New York Ledger,* with which Pidge was almost certainly familiar. Her greatest novel, *The Hidden Hand,* was published in 1859, its plot being sentimental and melodramatic. Augusta Evans (1835–1909) was a Georgia-born author whose early writings were pedantic and romantic. These characteristics caused Pidge to term her "inexpressible and irrepressible." Her novel *Macaris, or Alters of Sacrifice* was published in Richmond, Virginia, in 1864 and had disastrous effects on the morale of Federal soldiers. This book did become very popular in the North as well as in the South.

87. This is a mocking reference to Bonner's *New York Ledger,* so popular at the time, which Pidge had earlier termed the "Dredger." In 1875 appeared several serials by Sylvanus Cobb Jr., a name that became "Sylvanus Snob" with Pidge. The *Ledger's* masthead read: "Devoted to Choice Literature Romance, the News and Commerce." It frequently carried news items describing action on the Rio Grande border as well as violence that had occurred in DeWitt County, where Pidge had first served. For example, in the issue of May 22, 1875, was this item: "MEXICAN raiders are reported to be ravaging settlements near the Texas border, and it is expected that the Texans will wreck bloody retaliation upon them." The January 1, 1876, issue contained this relevant item: "RECENTLY, at Cuero, Texas, five men entered a saloon and murdered Reuben Brown, the city marshal, riddling his body with bullets. The saloon was full of men, and one of them was killed by two of the shots. It is supposed the crime was committed to avenge the arrest of a murderer named Taylor, by the city marshal." Brown's murder was another act in the Sutton-Taylor feud; evidently the feudists were able to control their hatreds when McNelly and his company were present. With their departure the feud flared up again.

88. Elizabeth Cady Stanton (1815–1902) was an early leader of the movement for women's rights. She advocated removing legal restrictions and discrimination against women, working closely with Susan B. Anthony, and was an important figure in the temperance and antislavery movements. Because of her views on these issues, as well as her demands that women be allowed to control their own property and to obtain divorce on grounds of brutality and drunkenness, she was considered a radical.

89. Lydia Thompson (1836–1908) was an English actress who journeyed to the United States in 1868. She was considered a pioneer of latter-day burlesque and was the first star to bring a fully organized company across the Atlantic. In 1870 she made a tour of leading American cities, returning to England in 1874.

90. James Franklin Randlett was born in 1834 in New Hampshire. In July, 1861, he enlisted as a private in Company F, 3rd Regiment, New Hampshire Volunteers. By late August he was appointed captain, and he was appointed major in 1864. In May, 1864, he was severely wounded at Drewry's Bluff, Virginia. He was mustered out with the rank of lieutenant colonel in July, 1865. Finding civilian life unattractive, he was appointed captain in the US Army in June, 1867, and in December, 1870, he was assigned to the 8th Cavalry. He retired in December, 1896.

Randlett received considerable publicity for his actions on the Rio Grande fighting Cortina's raiders. Besides numerous local newspaper accounts, no less a national publication than *Frank Leslie's Illustrated Newspaper* contained an article with several illustrations purporting to show Randlett leading his 8th Cavalry from Fort Brown "in pursuit of Mexican raiders across the Rio Grande." This appeared in the issue of January 1, 1876.

91. George William Childs (1829–94) was an American publisher and philanthropist. He began working as a clerk in a stationery and book store while still in his teens and for the rest of his life was connected with the publishing industry. His greatest success came with the *Philadelphia Public Ledger*. After he purchased it in 1864 circulation increased tremendously, reaching a daily circulation of ninety thousand by 1876. The *Ledger* maintained a high standard of accuracy and decency. Robinson was certainly familiar with the *Philadelphia Ledger*.

92. John Leslie (1527? –96) was a Scottish priest and a supporter of Mary, Queen of Scots. He was made a judge in the Court of Session and later bishop of Ross in 1866. After Mary fled to England, being accused of murdering her second husband, Leslie wrote a defense on her behalf, which was very influential among Roman Catholics. He was later imprisoned for plotting against Queen Elizabeth. On his release he took refuge in France.

93. McNelly gave the Schleicher committee a description of the difficulties. He testified regarding the character of the country: "It is a strip of country about twenty miles wide on each side of the river . . . is covered with what is called in Mexico 'chaparral.' It is a thicket of tropical or semi-tropical shrubs, which, on account of its density and its immense thorns with which it is thickly covered, is

literally impenetrable except where trails have been cut through it. I hardly know how I can convey to you a definite idea of its character. But you may judge something of the difficulties of campaigning in such a country when I tell you that, although two trails may extend almost parallel with each other and not more than fifty yards apart, still it is often necessary to travel as far as seven or eight miles in order to find a point where it is possible to pass from one to another. It is like a thicket of enormous thistles fifteen feet high, with the thorns hard and woody and as large as your finger." A lengthy interview with McNelly appeared in the *Galveston Daily News* of February 3, 1876.

94. Pidge almost certainly learned of this bill from reading the *Lynchburg Virginian,* as the issue of February 9, 1876, contained a lengthy and humorous article reprinted from the *Evening Journal*—"Rules for Stamping and Collecting the Taxes in Profanity, Intemperance and Tobacco Using." It offered a list of seven rules for "collecting taxes under the proposed bill to license drinking, chewing and 'cussing.'" Following is a representative example of the humor: "The stamps must be as follows[.] For profanity, a bright yellow with the letter D.A.M.C.U.W. printed thereon[.] For intemperance, a bright green with the letters D.R.U.N.C.A.G.I.N. printed thereon." The matter appeared on February 24, 1876, in the *Daily Democratic Statesman,* which Pidge may also have read: "In Virginia they propose to tax each person who uses tobacco on the quo pro 'quid' principle."

95. See the chapter "The Last Gunfight" for discussion of the journey home and promised later correspondence. Although it is possible that at least one additional letter may have been written to the *Gazette,* no more were printed.

THE LAST GUNFIGHT

1. *Democrat and Ranchero* (Brownsville), February 28, 1880.

2. A gauger was one whose duties consisted of inspecting, branding, and stamping all spirits required by law to be inspected. A gauger had to be sworn in and provide bond of not less than $5,000. *Internal Revenue Record,* 50.

3. The *Evening Star* was one of three Lynchburg newspapers at the time. It existed apparently from 1875 to 1877, but only one issue is known to have survived, that of June 28, 1876.

4. *Lynchburg Virginian,* April 4, 1876.

5. *Lynchburg News,* April 4, 1876.

6. Ibid.

7. Campbell County, Register of Deaths, James River District.

8. *Lynchburg News,* April 5, 1876.

9. *Richmond State,* April 4, 1876.

10. *Lynchburg News,* April 7, 1876.

11. Letter reprinted in the Chicago Corral's *Westerners Brand Book,* (see Parsons, "'Pidge' Burial Stone Discovered," 37). Olivia Glass, who became Mrs. Olivia Perrow, was fifteen years old in 1876 when the shooting occurred, and as she was

a neighbor of the Robinsons she may have seen the shooting or heard adults speaking of it. The 1870 Campbell County census shows the Glass family in household number 904, while the Robinson family was number 902. Olivia was the daughter of Jesse C. and Susan Glass. Her siblings included William E., eighteen; James, fifteen; John, thirteen; and Thomas H., six. At the time of the census the older boys were all listed as "works on farm," while Olivia and Thomas H. were simply "at home." US Census, Campbell County, Virginia, enumerated September 2, 1870, by J. M. Wood, 155.

12. *Daily State Gazette,* August 27, 1876.

13. Campbell County, Record of Deeds, Deed Book no. 40, 508–509.

14. This deed was recorded before Notary Public Andrew J. DeWitt, County Clerk, December 26, 1879.

15. *Lynchburg Virginian,* March 10, 1880.

16. Ibid., March 11, 1880.

17. Ibid., March 13, 1880.

18. Campbell County, Marriage Register. The register shows the ages of each: he was thirty-three, she was twenty-seven.

19. US Census, Augusta County, Virginia, enumerated June 10, 1900, by John Sullivan. The 1900 census shows that Booker was born in Virginia in April 1845 and was fifty-five years old; Lizzie was also born in Virginia, in July 1858, and was forty-one.

20. Campbell County, Marriage Register, vol. 2, 69. They were married by James O. Moss.

21. *Rockbridge County News* (Lexington, Virginia), February 8, 1923.

22. *Buena Vista News,* April 8, 1926.

23. US Census, Campbell County, Virginia, enumerated June 12, 1880, by Emmet W. Wright. This was the enumeration of the county jail in Rustburg.

24. Campbell County, Marriage Register. The "Certificate to Obtain a Marriage License" shows Mitchell was white, forty-five years old, and single, his occupation a farmer. Mrs. Mary T. Flynn was thirty-five years old and widowed. Their marriage was performed by Elder E. C. Dodson.

25. *Lynchburg News,* May 17 and 18, 1900.

26. I visited the Robinson cemetery in August, 2008. An early informant had indicated that it was densely overgrown with weeds and virtually abandoned. At the time of my visit the small graveyard was clean and neat. The three stones of the Robinson family were easily found. Pidge's stone has an interesting history in itself. It is uncertain who determined the unusual inscription on the stone marking his final resting place; possibly his friend Whitfield Clark was responsible for it, with the assistance of Pidge's sister Lizzie May. The stone did disappear for some time. In researching Pidge's life and death in the early 1980s I was informed that the stone had been stolen, leaving only the stones of his parents to indicate the approximate place where Pidge himself was buried. However, a subsequent request to the late western history enthusiast Mark Dugan proved

that occasionally, lost items can be recovered. Dugan, a resident of North Carolina, visited the Rustburg area and discovered, after numerous inquiries, that the stone was being "stored" in a certain garage. The stone was indeed located and returned to the cemetery, with "no questions asked." It is believed that someone was fascinated with the unusual inscription and found it irresistible. See Parsons, "'Pidge' Burial Stone Discovered," 38.

In the Robinson-Green Family Cemetery are eleven legible stones: the three Robinsons; six members of the Green family; one Hall; and that of Elizabeth Harlow, the wife of George V. Harlow, who purchased the Robinson farm in 1879. His grave is presumably among those marked only with a fieldstone. The church across the highway is now called the Providence United Methodist Church.

Bibliography

BOOKS, JOURNALS, AND PAMPHLETS

Adams, Spencer J. "Texas Frontier Reminiscences." *Railway Carmen's Journal of the United States and Canada,* September, October, and November, 1911.

Anonymous. *Lest It Be Forgotten: A Scrapbook of Campbell County, Virginia.* Rustburg: Historical Committee of the Bicentennial Committee, Altavista Printing Company, 1976.

———. *Historical Review 1872–1972: Our 100th Year Souvenir Program.* Cuero, Tex.: N.p., 1972.

———. *Campbell County, Virginia Heritage Book, 1781–2003.* N.p., 2003.

Barkley, Mary Star. *History of Travis County and Austin 1839–1899.* Waco: Texian Press, 1963.

Baughman, James T. *Charles Morgan and the Development of Southern Transportation.* Nashville: Vanderbilt University Press, 1968.

Bradner, Chuck. "A Texas Ranger from Campbell County." *Chronicle of the Campbell County Historical Society,* January, 2005.

Caren, Eric C., comp. *Texas Extra: A Newspaper History of the Lone Star State 1835–1935.* Edison, N.J.: Castle Books, 1999, reprint of "A Strange Story," *Democrat and Ranchero* (Brownsville, Tex.), February 28, 1880.

Christian, W. Asbury. *Lynchburg and Its People.* Lynchburg: J. P. Bell Company, Printers, 1900.

Cox, Mike. *The Texas Rangers, 1821–1900: Wearing the Cinco Peso.* New York: Tom Doherty Associates, 2008.

———. *Time of the Rangers: From 1920 to the Present.* New York: Tom Doherty Associates, 2009.

Crouch, Barry, and Donaly E. Brice. "Appendix: Roster of the Texas State Police." In *The Governor's Hounds: The Texas State Police, 1870–1873.* Austin: University of Texas Press, 2011.

Douglas, C. L. *The Gentlemen in the White Hats: Dramatic Episodes in the History of the Texas Rangers.* Dallas: South-West Press, 1934.

Durham, George. *Taming the Nueces Strip: The Story of McNelly's Rangers* (As Told to Clyde Wantland). Austin: University of Texas Press, 1962.

Gillett, James B. *Six Years with the Texas Rangers, 1875–1881.* Chicago: Lakeside Press, 1943.

Ginther, Herman. *Captain Staunton's River.* Richmond, Va.: Dietz Press, 1968.

Gray, S. A. *Mercantile and General City Directories of Austin, Texas, 1872–1873.* Austin: Gray and Moore Printers, 1873.

Hardin, John Wesley. *The Life of John Wesley Hardin.* Seguin, Tex.: Smith and Moore Publishers, 1896.

Hudson, Frederic. *Journalism in the United States from 1690 to 1872*. New York: Haskell House Publishers, 1873.

Hughes, W. J. *Rebellious Ranger: Rip Ford and the Old Southwest*. Norman: University of Oklahoma Press, 1964.

Jennings, N. A. *A Texas Ranger*. 1899; facsimile ed., Ruidoso, N.M.: Frontier Book Company, 1960.

Joyce, Lynn R. S. "Jesus Sandoval: Real Life 'Lone Ranger' On the Rio Grande." *Real West* 26, no. 191 (June 1983).

King, Edward. *The Great South: A Record of Journeys*. Hartford, Conn.: American Publishing Company, 1875.

King, Adj. Gen. Wilburn H. "The Texas Ranger Service and History of the Rangers with Observations on Their Value as a Police Protection." In Dudley G. Wooten, *A Comprehensive History of Texas, 1865–1897*. Dallas: William G. Scarff, 1898.

Lea, Tom. *The King Ranch*. Research by Holland McCombs. Boston: Little Brown, 1957.

Mayfield, G. C. "Capt. W. L. Rudd of Yorktown, Ex-Ranger." *Frontier Times*, September, 1932.

McPherson, Hon. Edward (Ed.) *A Handbook of Politics for 1876*. Washington, D.C.: Solomon and Chapman, 1876.

Mott, Frank Luther. *A History of American Magazines 1850–1865*. Cambridge: Harvard University Press, 1957.

Murphree, Nellie. *History of DeWitt County*. Ed. Robert W. Shook. Victoria: Rose International, 1962.

Nunn, W. C. *Texas under the Carpetbaggers*. Austin: University of Texas Press, 1962.

Parsons, Chuck. "Forgotten Feudist." *Frontier Times* 51, no. 1, n.s. 99 (January 1976): 28–29, 44–45.

———. "Bill Sutton Avenged: The Death of Jim Taylor." *Quarterly of the National Association for Outlaw and Lawman History* 4, no. 3 (March 1979): 3–5.

———. "'Pidge' Burial Stone Discovered." *Westerners Brand Book*, Chicago Corral, vol. 41, no. 2 (Summer 1986): 38.

———. "Treaties of Peace, Acts of War." *Real West* 24, no. 180 (October 1981): 26–28, 54; repr. *Real West Annual*, Fall 1982, 50–52.

Perry, Laurens Ballard. *Juarez and Diaz Machine Politics in Mexico*. DeKalb: Northern Illinois University Press, 1978.

Pierce, Frank C. *A Brief History of the Lower Rio Grande Valley*. Menasho, Wis.: George Banta Publishing Company, 1917.

Raymond, Dora Neill. *Captain Lee Hall of Texas*. 1940; Norman: University of Oklahoma Press, 1982.

Rose, Victor M. *Some Historical Facts in Regard to the Settlement of Victoria, Texas: Its Progress and Present Status*. Laredo: Daily Times Printing, 1883.

———. *The Texas Vendetta: or, The Sutton-Taylor Feud.* New York: J. J. Little and Company, 1880; facsimile ed., Houston: Frontier Press of Texas, 1956.
Sheridan, General P. H. *Outline Descriptions of the Posts on the Military Division of the Missouri.* Chicago: N.p., 1872.
Sonnichsen, C. L. *I'll Die Before I'll Run: The Story of the Great Feuds of Texas.* New York: Harper and Brothers, 1951.
Stambaugh, J. Lee, and Lillian J. Stambaugh. *The Lower Rio Grande Valley of Texas.* San Antonio: Naylor Company, 1954.
Sweet, Alex E., and J. Armory Knox. *On a Mexican Mustang through Texas, from the Gulf to the Rio Grande.* Hartford, Conn.: S. S. Scranton and Company, 1883.
Thompson, Jerry. *Cortina: Defending the Mexican Name in Texas.* College Station: Texas A&M University Press, 2007.
Tyler, Ron, ed. *The New Handbook of Texas.* Austin: Texas State Historical Association, 1996.
Utley, Robert M. *Lone Star Justice: The First Century of the Texas Rangers.* 2 vols. New York: Oxford University Press USA, 2002.
Walsh's Lynchburg City Directory for 1900. Lynchburg: J. P. Bell Company.
Webb, Walter Prescott. *The Texas Rangers: A Century of Frontier Defense.* Boston: Houghton Mifflin, 1935; repr. Austin: University of Texas Press, 1977.
Webb, Walter Prescott, ed. *The Handbook of Texas.* Austin: Texas State Historical Association, 1952.
Wilkins, Frederick. *The Law Comes to Texas: The Texas Rangers 1870–1901.* Austin: State House Press, 1999.
Wilkinson, J. B. *Laredo and the Rio Grande Frontier.* Austin: Jenkins Publishing Company, 1975.
Wooten, Dudley G. *A Comprehensive History of Texas, 1865–1897.* Dallas: William G. Scarff, 1898.

NEWSPAPERS

Kells, D. W. C. Interview. *Times Picayune* (New Orleans), November 23, 1875.
Nast, Thomas. Cartoon. *Supplement, Harper's Weekly,* May 2, 1874.
Spectator (London, England), July 1875.
"Troubles on the Rio Grande: A War Cloud." *Frank Leslie's Illustrated Newspaper,* January 1, 1876.

Texas

Advertiser (Bastrop), August 21, 1873; 1874–76. *Cuero Star,* 1873–75.
Daily Democratic Statesman (Austin), 1873–78; April 22, 1890; August 12, 1931.
Daily Herald (Dallas), September 19, 1875.
Daily Inquirer (Gonzales), 1873–76.

Daily State Gazette (Austin), 1873–78.
Democrat and Ranchero (Brownsville), February 28, 1880.
Galveston Daily News, April 2, 7, 1868; 1874–78.
Galveston Weekly News, November 23, 1874; December 13, 1875.
Houston Daily Telegraph, July 27, 1873.
San Antonio Daily Express, 1873–78.
San Antonio Herald, 1873–78.
Victoria Advocate, October 5, 1876.

Virginia

Buena Vista News, April 8, 1926.
Lexington Gazette, April 7, 1926.
Lynchburg News, 1868–76; May 17, 18, 1900; 1916.
Lynchburg Virginian, 1868–76; 1880.
Richmond State, 1876.
Rockbridge County News (Lexington), 1923, 1926.

GOVERNMENT PUBLICATIONS, UNPUBLISHED MANUSCRIPTS, AND OTHER SOURCES

Bedford County, Virginia. Marriage Records.
Bradner, Charles K. "Campbell County Virginia Family Cemeteries: Robinson-Green Family Cemetery."
Callicott, William. "Reminiscences." Dated July 21, 1921. Original in Walter Prescott Webb Collection, Briscoe Center for American History, Austin.
Campbell County, Virginia. Chancery Order Book, 1879–1885.
———. Common Law Order Book, 1877–1892.
———. Marriage Register.
———. Order Book no. 29.
———. Record of Deeds. Deed Book no. 40.
———. Register of Deaths.
———. Township Map of the County of Campbell. Prepared by Charles A. Pugh, 1870.
Clow, Robert J. "Memo and Account Book." Diary. Briscoe Center for American History, Austin.
Internal Revenue Record. Vol. 8, no. 8: "Duties Established, Act of July 20, 1868."
Rio Bravo Deck Log. Ship commanded by Lt. D.C. Kells. November, 1875.
Steele, William. *A List of Fugitives from Justice, 1878.* Facsimile ed., *Fugitives from Justice: The Notebook of Texas Ranger Sergeant James B. Gillett,* Austin: State House Press, 1997.
———. *Report of the Adjutant General of the State of Texas for the Year 1875.* Austin.
———. *Report of the Adjutant General of the State of Texas for the Year Ending August 31, 1876.* Austin.

Stell, Thomas. "The Taylor-Sutton Feud." Manuscript in C. L. Sonnichsen Collection, El Paso.

Talley, Amelia. "Descendants of James S. Mitchell." Vertical file, Jones Memorial Library, Lynchburg.

———. "Descendants of Thomas Robinson." Vertical file, Jones Memorial Library, Lynchburg.

Texas Frontier Troubles. 44th Congress, 1st Session. House of Representatives Report No. 343.

Texas Rangers. Muster Rolls of the Texas Rangers. Capt. L. H. McNelly, 1874–75. Texas State Archives, Austin.

Texas State Police Roster, March 29, 1873. Texas State Archives, Austin.

U.S. Census, Texas. Cameron, DeWitt, Gonzales, and Washington counties, 1870.

———. Virginia. Augusta, Amherst, Bedford, Campbell, and Rockbridge counties, 1870, 1880, 1900.

———. Virginia. Campbell County Slave Schedule, 1850, 1860.

Index